Instructor's Manual: Preparator's Guide

to accompany

Biology in the Laboratory

Second Edition

DORIS R. HELMS

Clemson University

WORTH PUBLISHERS

Instructor's Manual: Preparator's Guide

by Doris R. Helms

to accompany **Biology in the Laboratory, Second Edition**

ISBN: 0-87901-688-4

Printing: 5 4 3 2 1

Year: 97 96 95 94

Worth Publishers

33 Irving Place

New York, New York 10003

CONTENTS

Appendixes

FOREWORD

The *Instructor's Manual: Preparator's Guide* is written for both the laboratory instructor and the course preparator using *Biology in the Laboratory, Second Edition.* This manual offers teaching techniques and hints for success in the laboratory as well as directions for mixing solutions. Separate guides to investigative activities (page xii) and laboratories that require prior preparation and ordering of live materials (page vii) are included to help you with long-term planning. A course outline (page xvi) suggests exercises that can be used as the core of your course.

Another supplement, the *Instructor's Manual: Answer Guide* presents sample data for all experiments as well as explanations and sample answers for all questions that appear in the laboratory manual.

The *Instructor's Manual: Preparator's Guide* contains the following information for each laboratory topic:

I. FOREWORD A brief overview of all activities in the laboratory.

II. TIME REQUIREMENTS An estimate of the time required for each exercise.

III. STUDENT MATERIALS AND EQUIPMENT This section is designed to help you plan. Only materials used by the students are listed. The numbers or amounts necessary per student, per pair, per group of four students, and per class of 24 are indicated. Pay particular attention to the amounts given for solutions and whether these are needed by each student, each pair, each group, or each class. Items requiring additional preparation instructions are followed by a boldface number in parentheses, which refers you to a note in Section IV, "Preparation of Materials and Solutions."

IV. PREPARATION OF MATERIALS AND SOLUTIONS Specific directions for mixing solutions and preparing materials are presented in this section. Setup directions and cautions are also included. The amounts given are sufficient for a class of 24 students. Materials and equipment needed by preparators are also referenced here. For instance, the "Student Materials" section for Laboratory 12, "Mitosis: Making Duplicates," Exercise C, lists "stained onion root tips" followed by the reference number (**2**). In Section IV, item (**2**) describes the materials, the solutions, and the procedure for preparing stained onion root tips.

V. PREPARATION SUGGESTIONS The shortcuts, pitfalls, and additional details given for each exercise should help you to have a successful laboratory experience.

VI. ORDERING INFORMATION Only materials not usually found in a teaching laboratory are listed here. Carolina Biological Supply Company, Fisher Scientific, and Sigma Chemical Company are the main suppliers cited. However, by referring to the descriptions of specific materials in these catalogs, you will have sufficient information to order comparable materials from other sources, if you prefer.

To prepare your order for the academic year, select the exercises you plan to use, then check Sections III and IV to identify the necessary materials and equipment. For those materials not already on hand, see Section VI for specific ordering information.

I would like to thank to Beverly George, Director of Laboratories at Clemson University, and Brent Walling, a talented student and friend, for their able assistance in developing the *Instructor's Manual: Preparator's Guide*.

I hope that *Biology in the Laboratory* provides you and your students with many exciting and enjoyable experiences. Please let me know if you have any suggestions or encounter any difficulties. I will be happy to discuss and to assist.

Clemson University
Biology Program
330 Long Hall
Clemson, SC 29634
(803-656-2418)
<BIOL110@clemson.clemson.edu>

Dr. Doris R. Helms
June, 1994

LABORATORIES REQUIRING PRIOR PLANNING OR LIVE MATERIALS

Laboratory 3   Water

Exercise C and
  Let's Investigate

Students should collect water samples from local environments and bring them to the laboratory.

Laboratory 4   pH

Exercise C

Students should bring samples of cleaning solutions, beverages, or soils from local areas to the laboratory.

Laboratory 5   Organic Molecules

Let's Investigate

Students should bring food or beverage samples to the laboratory to test for carbohydrate, fat, and protein content.

Laboratory 6   Cells I

Exercise C

Live *Elodea* and *Paramecium*; collect pond water sample prior to laboratory.

Exercise D

Students should bring in a selection of small objects—insects, flowers, etc., for study using the dissecting microscope.

Laboratory 7   Cells II

Exercise B (Part 2)   Live *Oscillatoria, Nostoc, Cylindrospermum.*
Exercise B (Part 3)   Live *Elodea.*
Let's Investigate   Live *Elodea.*
Exercise C   Live *Stentor* and *Volvox.*

Laboratory 8   Osmosis and Diffusion

Exercise D (Part 3)   Live *Chara, Elodea, Spirogyra.*

Laboratory 9   Enzymes

Let's Investigate

Have students bring selections of fruit juice to test for "juice release" properties.

Exercise B

Have students bring spices for cheesemaking—announce this during the prior laboratory period.

Laboratory 10   Energetics, Fermentation, and Respiration

Exercise A (Part 1)   Prepare yeast solution 12 hours before laboratory.
Exercise A (Part 4)   Prepare yeast solution 24 hours before laboratory.

Laboratory 11   Photosynthesis

Exercise A, Part 1   Order fresh *Elodea.*
Let's Investigate   Plant 2 flats of wheat seedlings 4-5 days before the laboratory.
Exercise C   Place a variegated *Coleus* plant in the dark for 2 days prior to laboratory. Alternatively, cover parts of leaves of a green *Coleus* one week prior to the laboratory.
Let's Investigate   Purchase several large geranium plants.

Laboratory 12   Mitosis: Making Duplicates

Exercise C   Start onions for root tips 3-4 days prior to the laboratory to allow ample time for fixing and staining.
Exercise E   Order *Drosophila mojavensis* at least 2 weeks in advance. Third instar larvae are obtained approximately 8 days after eggs are laid.

Laboratory 13   Meiosis: Independent Assortment and Segregation

Exercise C (optional)   Order wild type and mutant tan *Sordaria fimicola* cross. Order 3 weeks in advance.

Laboratory 15   DNA Isolation and Protein Synthesis

Exercise B   DNA kits need to be made from posterboard patterns. Allow sufficient time to prepare.

Laboratory 16   Molecular Genetics: Recombinant DNA

Exercise B   Order kits ahead to ensure availability. If a kit is not used, order live *E. coli* cells ahead so that streak plates can be made at least 3 days prior to the laboratory. Cells must also be ordered 3-5 days ahead if the instructor plans to prepare competent cells rather than using a rapid-colony transformation technique.

Laboratory 18   Behavior

Exercise A   Collect or order live isopods (pill bugs).

Exercise B (Parts 1, 2, 3)   Order live crickets—must be isolated 2-3 days in advance of laboratory. Crickets have a 2 week life span.

Exercise C   Order live mealworms.

Let's Investigate   Collect or order live termites.

Laboratory 19   Diversity—Kingdoms Monera and Protista

Exercise A   During the previous week's laboratory, distribute nutrient agar plates for students' bacteria experiments.

Exercise B, Part 1   Order live *E. coli* and *S. aureus*. Prepare antibiotic sensitivity plates 24-48 hours prior to laboratory.

Let's Investigate   Order live *E. coli* and *S. aureus*. Have students bring in cleaning solutions from home.

Exercise B, Part 2   Inoculate soybean plants with *Rhizobium* 8 weeks prior to laboratory.

Exercise C   Order live *Nostoc, Cylindrospermum, Oscillatoria, Anabaena,* and *Gloeocapsa*.

Exercise D   Order live *Paramecium*..

Exercise E   Order live *Physarum*. Start *Physarum* slime mold cultures 2 days prior to the laboratory.

Exercise F   Order live *Euglena, Ectocarpus, Polysiphonia,* and *Corallopsis*.

Exercise G   Order live *Chlamydomonas, Spirogyra, Gonium, Volvox, Zygnema, Stigeoclonium, Ulva,* and *Ulothrix*.

Let's Investigate   During the previous week's laboratory, assign a student to bring in a plankton sample.

Laboratory 20   Diversity—Fungi and the Nonvascular Plants

Exercise A   Distribute bread (in plastic bags) to students during the previous week's laboratory.

Exercise B   Start water mold cultures at least 4-5 days prior to the laboratory

Exercise C   Order live *Sordaria*. Start *Sordaria* cultures 7-8 days prior to the laboratory.

Exercise D   Collect basidiomycetes for demonstration.

Let's Investigate   Students should be told during the previous week's laboratory to collect basidiomycetes just before coming to laboratory (material must be fresh).

Exercises F, G   Assign fungus and lichen collection during the previous week's laboratory.

| Exercise H | Collect or order live *Marchantia* and hornworts. If ordering *Marchantia* archegonia and antheridia from a biological supply company, order at least 4 weeks prior to the laboratory. |

Laboratory 21   Diversity—Vascular Land Plants

Exercise A	Order live *Psilotum, Lycopodium, Selaginella, Equisetum,* and fern leaves, or obtain from a greenhouse.
Exercise B	Order live male and female cycads or obtain from a greenhouse.
Exercise C	Make arrangements for a variety of fresh flowers for dissection.

Laboratory 22   Diversity—Porifera, Cnidaria, and Wormlike Invertebrates

Exercise B	Order live *Hydra.*
Let's Investigate	Order live *Hydra.*
Exercise C, Part 1	Order live planaria.
Let's Investigate	Order live planaria, *Dugesia.*
Exercise C, Part 3	Order live *Tubatrix.*
Exercise D, Part 4	Order live *Lumbricus.*

Laboratory 23   Diversity—Mollusks, Arthropods, and Echinoderms

Let's Investigate	Order live freshwater mussels or clams.
Exercise A (Part 3)	Order live pulmonate snails.
Exercise B (Part 5)	Order live *Oncopeltus* (milkweed bugs), *Tenebrio* (mealworms), *Manduca* (tobacco hornworms), and *Vanessa* (painted lady butterflies).
Let's Investigate	Students should bring soil samples to the laboratory for isolation of nematodes.

Laboratory 25   Animal Tissues

Exercise A	Order live frogs.
Exercise B	Order live frogs (optional). Demineralize chicken bones 2 weeks prior to laboratory.

Laboratory 26   The Basics of Animal Form—Skin, Bones, and Muscles

Exercise C	Demineralize chicken bones 2 weeks prior to laboratory.

Laboratory 27   The Physiology of Circulation

Exercise D	Order or obtain live goldfish.
Exercise G	Order *Daphnia magna.*

Laboratory 28   The Physiology of Respiration and Immunity

Exercise A (Part 1)	Obtain fresh or frozen fish heads from local market.
Exercise A (Part 2)	Make arrangements to obtain fresh sheep pluck from local abattoir.
Exercise B	Make arrangements to obtain fresh cow's blood from a local abattoir.

Laboratory 29   The Digestive, Excretory, and Reproductive Systems

Exercise B	Expose and develop a role of black and white film.
Exercise C (Part 1)	Make arrangements to obtain a fresh kidney from a local abattoir.

Laboratory 31   Animal Development

Exercise C (option)	Order live sea urchins.
Exercises C - F	Order live frogs (if desired as a substitute for preserved embryos.

Exercise H	Incubate chicken eggs 96 hours prior to the laboratory. Incubate another group of chicken eggs 5 to 6 days prior to the laboratory. Incubate chicken eggs 72 hours prior to the laboratory (optional).

Laboratory 32 Plant Anatomy—Roots, Stems, and Leaves

Exercise B	Ask students to bring in a collection of herbaceous plants (weeds or house plants).

Laboratory 33 Angiosperm Development—Fruits, Seeds, Meristems, and Secondary Growth

Exercise A	Check with local grocery store one week prior to laboratory to ensure a variety of fruits for dissection.
Exercise B	Order live *Phaseolus* (lima bean) and *Zea* (corn) seeds. Soak lima bean and corn seeds overnight.
Exercise D	Order live *Phaseolus* (lima bean, *Zea* (corn, and Little Marvel pea seeds. Germinate lima bean, corn, and pea seeds 6 days prior to the laboratory. You will also need older plants—plant seeds 8 to 12 days prior to the laboratory.
Exercise E	Obtain live *Coleus*. Order live radish seeds. Germinate radish seeds 2 days prior to the laboratory.

Laboratory 34 Water Movement and Mineral Nutrition in Plants

Exercise A	Obtain a live *Zebrina* plant.
Exercise B	Check on availability of plants to be used for transpiration experiment.
Exercise C	Plant barley seeds one week prior to use in the laboratory.
Exercise D	Order or obtain live carnations.
Exercise E	If the mineral nutrition experiment is to be done as a demonstration, prepare, in appropriate solutions, one set of sunflower seeds 9 weeks prior to the laboratory and one set 6 weeks prior to the laboratory. In both cases, and to provide plants for student experiments, plant sunflower seeds 3 weeks prior to placing them in nutrient solutions.
Let's Investigate	Order live lettuce, kale, spinach, and tomato seeds.

Laboratory 35 Plant Responses to Stimuli

Exercise A (Part 1)	Plant sunflower seeds 4 weeks prior to the laboratory (5 weeks if the experiment is started during the previous laboratory).
Exercise A (Part 2)	Obtain *Coleus* plants. Start cuttings 4-6 months prior to the laboratory to produce necessary number of plants.
Exercise A (Part 3)	Plant dwarf peas 12 days prior to the laboratory (19 days if the experiment is started during the previous laboratory).
Exercise B (Part 1)	Treat gizzard plants 2 to 3 days prior to the laboratory.
Exercise B (Part 2)	Order live corn seeds.
Exercise B (Part 3)	Germinate bush beans 48 hours prior to the laboratory.
Exercise B (Part 4)	Plant wheat seeds 1 week prior to the laboratory. Plant tomato seeds 2 weeks prior to laboratory or obtain tomato plants from a local greenhouse.
Exercises C and D	Order lettuce seeds.
Let's Investigate	Order lettuce seeds.
Exercise E	Start petunia and morning glory, spinach, radishes, and kidney beans 6-8 weeks prior to the laboratory.

Laboratory 36   Communities and Ecosystems

Exercise A   Order and set up live *Paramecium caudatum* and *Paramecium aurelia* cultures one, two, and three weeks prior to the laboratory.

Exercise B   Students should collect leaf litter before coming to the laboratory. Alternatively, collect leaf litter one week prior to the laboratory and separate organisms for observation in the laboratory.

GUIDE TO "LET'S INVESTIGATE" ACTIVITIES

Let's Investigate activities range from simple observations and experiments to complex and open investigations. Each one emphasizes hypothesis formation, development of experimental procedures, critical thinking, and writing skills.

Laboratory 1   Science—A Process

Experimenting with Bean Seeds This investigation introduces the scientific method, the major focus of Laboratory 1. Students set up this experiment during the laboratory, take it home to make observations, collect data over the course of 3 to 4 weeks, and complete their work by writing a laboratory report. Each student should carry out an individual investigation, but some collaboration is possible.

Laboratory 2   Measuring What You Observe

Variation in Measuring This in-lab investigation allows students to form hypotheses and set up experiments to determine the accuracy of measuring devices such as beakers, flasks, and graduated cylinders. Approximately 20-30 minutes will be needed to complete this investigation.

Laboratory 3   Water

Is All Water Equal? Students test water samples from local areas and should be encouraged to compare results. This investigation, an extension of Exercise B (which can also substitute for Exercise B), requires approximately 30 minutes to set up once Exercise B has been completed. If productivity is to be measured, a 24-hour incubation will be required. Students will have the opportunity to make hypotheses about water quality and should be allowed to pursue additional sample tests. A written laboratory report could accompany this investigation. Students should be encouraged to gather articles from the news dealing with pollution and water quality. These could be summarized as part of the literature background for the laboratory report. This investigation is an excellent opportunity for developing a collaborative project and for teaching students to use journals.

Laboratory 5   Organic Molecules

Food Molecules This investigation can be used as an extension of Exercises A, B, and C. Students can bring food items to the laboratory to test for carbohydrates, fat, and protein content and can form hypotheses regarding the organic molecules they contain. Qualitative data is collected and can be presented in a laboratory report.

Laboratory 7   Cells II

Cell Size and Surface Area Students hypothesize about the relationship between cell surface and volume. This investigation can be completed in the laboratory in 30 minutes or could be done at home.

Chloroplast Movement Students observe cyclosis in *Elodea* and hypothesize about and experiment with factors affecting cyclosis, including light, heat, and cold. Students make observations, record data, and improve their microscopy skills.

Laboratory 8   Osmosis and Diffusion

Does Temperature Affect the Rate of Diffusion? Students form hypotheses and null hypotheses about the effects of temperature on diffusion. This can be completed in the laboratory in approximately 25 minutes or students can design an experiment to do at home. There is opportunity for graphing data and a laboratory report can be assigned.

Laboratory 9   Enzymes

Making Juices Juicier Working individually or collaboratively, students use the enzyme pectinase to test for the "juice release" properties of a selection of fruit juices. This investigation improves data-collection and graphing skills, can result in a laboratory report, and makes a good extra credit project to be carried out after the laboratory period.

Laboratory 10   Energetics, Fermentation, and Respiration

Overcoming Competitive Inhibition   Students explore competitive enzyme inhibition in a laboratory setting. Data can be presented in tabular and graphic form. This investigation improves skill with the Spectronic 20 and makes an excellent extra credit or extension project.

Laboratory 11   Photosynthesis

Without Light, Would Plants Be Green?   Students observe wheat seedlings grown in the light and in the dark to investigate whether plants need light to be green. Hypothesis formation is emphasized. Materials may already be available (grown ahead by the instructor) or students may be given Styrofoam pots and wheat seeds to design their own do-at-home experiments. In the latter case, observational data can be collected and a laboratory report can be developed.

Do All Plants Store Starch?   Students can conduct this investigation in the laboratory as an extension to Exercise B. Encourage students to work in collaboration. Some may wish to test other types of potatoes, such as a sweet potatoes, that store sucrose. Hypotheses can be tested and observational results presented in a short laboratory report.

Can a Plant Write Your Name?   This investigation can be done on the window sill in the laboratory using several large geranium plants. Setup requires only 15 minutes, but students will need to decide how to pretreat the plant and how many days to leave it in the sun. They must then wait at least 2 or 3 days or for results. Several attempts may be required to achieve written letters appearing on a leaf. The investigation can be accompanied by a written laboratory report, but the best evidence of a successful experiment is the leaf with the student's initials.

Laboratory 15   DNA Isolation and Protein Synthesis

Point Mutations in DNA   This investigation builds on Exercise B. Students make a base substitution in DNA and then determine the consequences to the protein that would be synthesized. The investigation can be completed at home.

Laboratory 18   Behavior

Termites Trails   Termites react to the pheromone analogs found in some types of ink. Students can form hypotheses to test which factors are involved in trial-following behavior. This is a short observational investigation which may result in multiple hypotheses and experimental designs.

Laboratory 19   Diversity—Kingdoms Monera and Protista

How Effective is Your Soap?   Students practice aseptic technique and develop their ability to design experiments. The investigation should be carried out in the laboratory as an extension to Exercise B (Part 1). Qualitative observational data can be included in a laboratory report.

Symbiosis in the Termite   During this guided investigation of the flagellates that live in the termite gut, students form a hypothesis about the relationship between the termites and their symbionts.

Laboratory 20   Diversity—Fungi and Nonvascular Plants

Conditions for Fungal Growth   Students can experiment with the conditions necessary for fungal growth at home. Each student should carry out an investigation individually. Sharing of results and class discussion could be followed by a laboratory report.

Gill Patterns in Basidiomycetes   This simple investigation compares gill patterns and sporulation in a diversity of Basidiomycetes. Observations should be carried out in the laboratory because spore prints cannot be easily moved. Setup time is minimal.

Laboratory 21   Diversity—Vascular Land Plants

How Do Ferns Disseminate Their Spores?   Students investigate the mechanisms by which ferns release spores and the conditions necessary for spores to germinate. The experiment can be set up in the laboratory and be taken home. Students learn responsibility for daily maintenance and observation of an on-going experiment. Journal-keeping will help students identify which experimental data is most important.

Laboratory 22   Diversity—Porifera, Cnidaria, and Wormlike Invertebrates

Feeding Behavior in **Hydra**   Students investigate how *Hydra* feed. Hypotheses can be formed to study the affects of heat or light on feeding behavior and to determine whether the type or condition of food (for example, dead or alive) affects feeding behavior. The investigation needs to be completed in the laboratory, but can be done after the laboratory period on the student's own time. Students often adopt their hydras as pets!

The Eyespots of Planaria   Students use all steps of the scientific method in a short experiment that usually yields surprising results. Most students develop hypotheses that are not supported by results and must form alternative hypotheses—a good experience in the way science works. The experiment needs to be completed in the laboratory, but can be carried out after class. A laboratory report can be assigned.

Nematode Populations in the Soil   In this collaborative investigation, students test local soils for nematode populations and design a number of different experiments to compare populations in different soil types. Students improve their microscopy skills and practice using keys to identify organisms. Quantitative and qualitative data can be included in a written report. The experiment must be set up in a location where it can run overnight. After specimens are collected, students can study them at any time and the apparatus can be used by the next group of students.

Laboratory 23   Diversity—Mollusks, Arthropods, and Echinoderms

Filter Feeders   Students observe live clams or mussels to study the function of the gills in a mollusk. Hypothesis formation is part of the investigation and results are qualitative.

Laboratory 26   The Basics of Animal Form: Skin, Bones, and Muscles

Amazing Discoveries in a Colonel Sanders™ Bucket   Using chicken wings from the grocery store, students investigate the relationship between muscles, bones, and tendons and compare the structure of the human arm to that of the chicken wing. This investigation could be done at home, but chicken wings are fairly messy and students should take time to look at skeletons on demonstration in the laboratory. Observations can serve as the basis for an excellent independent study that can be completed at several levels of detail. Homologies of skeletal muscle structures in different organisms can be discussed and students can gain experience in comparing specific muscles to their functions. Most students approach this investigation as a puzzle to be solved.

Laboratory 27   The Physiology of Respiration and Immunity

How Does Smoking Affect Lung Capacity?   If no smokers are present, students can perform this investigation around campus or at home—all they need is a balloon and ruler. Students should collect enough data to make observations relating age, sex, years smoking, etc., and should learn the value of repeated trials as they test their hypotheses. Data can be presented in a variety of ways and can form the basis for a written laboratory report or debate among students. Students can also investigate smoking-related diseases such as emphysema and cancer.

Laboratory 29   The Digestive, Respiratory, and Excretory Systems

Where Is It Digested? Enzymes and pH   Students determine how pH affects digestive enzymes. Experiments can be designed to test multiple hypotheses and qualitative results can be collected and reported.

Laboratory 30   The Nervous System

Does It Taste the Same to Everyone?   In this investigation, students use taste papers—PTC, thiourea, and sodium benzoate—to explore differences in sensations of taste experienced by a different individuals. An at-home survey of foods that are liked or disliked by family members can be used to investigate correlations between reactions to the taste papers and food preferences. Students can make hypotheses and inferences based on genetic relationships.

Does It Smell Like What It Tastes Like? Students investigate the relationship between taste and smell. Using Life Savers, students make hypotheses and design short experiments to determine how these two senses affect one another. Results can be reported qualitatively, or, if enough students participate, quantitative data can be obtained. The investigation can be conducted at home or in the dormitory with a large sample of students.

Laboratory 32 Plant Anatomy—Roots, Stems, and Leaves

Celery Strings This investigation is an extension of Exercise A, which introduces students to the plant body. Students hypothesize about the function of the strings in celery and design experiments to test their function. Qualitative data are collected. A laboratory report relating this investigation to the structure of plant organs gets students thinking about how plants carry out the physiological tasks of water movement and the distribution of food and minerals.

What Kind of Weed Is This? Students form hypotheses about how plants can be classified as monocots or dicots. They test their assumptions about plant characteristics by making hand-microtome sections from a diversity of samples and collecting data as a series of observations, drawings, or even pictures taken by a camera attached to a microscope. This investigation can be a long-term project undertaken by individuals or by groups, followed by a laboratory report.

Laboratory 34 Water Movement and Mineral Nutrition in Plants

Experiments With Hydroponics Hydroponics makes possible many excellent experiments on plant growth conditions. Students can add or subtract specific minerals and experiment with fertilizers, pH, oxygen content of the water, light conditions, and more. This open investigation requires students to be innovative and perhaps do some research in the library. Data collected over a period of several weeks to several months can be presented in tables and graphs, a laboratory report or a more extensive term paper. After completing the **Let's Investigate** adventures throughout *Biology in the Laboratory*, students should be well prepared for an independent investigation of this type.

SUGGESTED LABORATORY OUTLINE FOR GENERAL BIOLOGY

First Semester

LABORATORY 1   Science—A Process

I. FOREWORD

This laboratory is designed to introduce students to the scientific method. It is important that students understand science as a process—a way of "doing" and not just as a body of facts to be learned. Instructors should help students to see that the scientific method is used daily by all of us as we ask questions and seek answers about problems in our daily lives or our world. The exercises in this laboratory will introduce students to the art of making observations and understanding inferences. Students will learn how to formulate and test hypotheses as well as how to predict outcomes—a valuable step in designing experiments. Techniques for presenting and graphing data are also introduced. Exercises A through F should be done in sequence.

This laboratory is an important "first step" and is conducted as an on-going investigation that will allow students to apply what they are studying to an independent investigation. Unlike other laboratories in which exercises can be treated separately, Exercises A-F in this laboratory all deal with parts of the same investigation and should be completed by the students during their course of study. The investigation will take approximately three weeks to complete. It uses a minimum of supplies and can be carried out at home or in a dormitory room. This laboratory sets the stage for other investigations. Throughout the laboratory manual, additional "take-home" experiments identified as "Let's Investigate" exercises will provide students with opportunities to reinforce their investigative skills.

This first laboratory will give students a chance to examine their environment in the dormitory or at home and to develop a pattern of behavior conducive to successful experimentation.

During Laboratory 1, students will also be asked to construct a Laboratory Report. This can be accomplished by referring to Appendix I, Writing Laboratory Reports.

II. TIME REQUIREMENTS

Exercise A—30 minutes (may be completed prior to laboratory)
Let's Investigate—30 minutes (set up)
Exercise B—20 minutes
Exercise C—30 minutes

III. STUDENT MATERIALS AND EQUIPMENT

	Per Student	Per Pair (2)	Per Group (4)	Per Class (24)
Exercise A				
laboratory manual written exercise				
Let's Investigate				
bean seeds (several types) (1)	6			144
Styrofoam cups	3			72

	Per Student	Per Pair (2)	Per Group (4)	Per Class (24)
Let's Investigate—continued				
potting soil (cups)	3			72
Petri dishes	3			72
scalpel			1	6

Exercises B-F

laboratory manual written exercises

IV. PREPARATION OF MATERIALS AND SOLUTIONS

(1) Select several varieties of bean seeds, including pinto beans, lima beans, kidney beans, and northern beans. You may purchase these from the grocery store or you may wish to purchase seeds from a supply house (see ordering information). Seeds can be kept in the hydrator of your refrigerator for 1-2 years, although viability will decrease over time. Soak the seeds overnight so they can be cut open by students if desired. To speed up the experiment, you may wish to have some germinated seeds available. After soaking overnight, wrap seeds loosely in wet paper towels. Place the wrapped seeds in a plastic bag, but do not seal the bag (or the seeds will rot). Place the packages in a warm, dark place for 24 hours. I have great luck using an electric blanket on a low setting (2 or 3).

V. PREPARATION SUGGESTIONS

Exercise A

You may want to have a class discussion about how various students identified the stages of scientific inquiry used in the skiing scenario. Although it seems simple, you will find that students have difficulty identifying the processes involved. It is important that students become aware that science is something they do everyday and not just something for the laboratory.

Let's Investigate

This exercise begins after completing Exercise A and is the foundation for the remaining exercises. Students are asked to make a hypothesis and predict what might happen if an experiment is conducted. Expect these first hypotheses to be "rough." The remaining exercises, B-F, are designed to return to these first approximations of experimental design and to refine them step by step.

Students may make hypotheses about the size of the seed and the size of the plant it will produce; the results of planting seeds in different orientations; the effects of moisture levels, light, and temperature; the effects of different types of soil; whether roots or shoots will develop first; the speed of germination relative to seed size, etc. It would be helpful to have on hand some diagrams of longitudinal sections through seeds and some information regarding germination—the fate of the cotyledons, epicotyl, and hypocotyl. You may wish to assign the pages from your text that deal with this topic.

When the students plant their seeds, make sure that they are only 1/2 to 1 inch below the soil surface. If they are placed too deep, they will not germinate. If you are using Styrofoam drinking cups, make several holes in the bottom of the cup. This can be easily done by heating a glass pipette in a Bunsen burner and using the pipette to burn a hole in the Styrofoam. If you do this, you can use Petri dishes (used ones are fine) under the cups to collect excess moisture.

You may wish to vary the experiment and use many different types of seeds—corn, peas, sunflowers, etc. Although the experiment could be done more quickly with fast germinating seeds such as lettuce or radishes, part of the reason for doing this first experiment is to manage an investigation at home (how to explain things to parents or roommates) and how to be responsible for an ongoing investigation that will require daily attention—watering, measuring, and recording observations. These techniques will be necessary throughout the school year if other Let's Investigate exercises are pursued.

Wisconsin Fast Plants could also be used for this experiment if your laboratory is set up for growing *Brassica rapa*. You might also wish to do a completely different experiment starting with observations on density of objects or a simple enzyme digestion. Exercises A-F can be used to walk through any experiment.

Exercise B-D

Although Exercises B-D can be carried out at home, you may find that allowing students some time to work on each exercise and then discussing their work in the laboratory will help those who struggle with asking appropriate questions and designing experiments. Students usually have difficulty with identifying variables and with formulating null hypotheses. Often working with partners or in small groups is helpful if all participants get involved—watch out for the student who sits back and simply listens to others doing the thinking. Since there are no "right" answers to single solutions to what is asked, a lively discussion should take place.

Exercise E-F

Although it may appear that Exercise E does not have to be completed until the end of the experiment, it is wise to have students complete this exercise before recording data. If students do not understand what information is needed in order to report data accurately, they may miss recording necessary information or may record it inappropriately. Students must understand that data need to be recorded the same way each time—there must be a method for obtaining data. Students must decide when to record and what to record and this must remain constant throughout the investigation. If students wait to complete Exercise E until late in their experiment, they may find serious errors in their experimental design. Exercise F can be completed at the end of the investigation.

Let's Investigate—continued

At the end of their investigations, students are asked to write a laboratory report. Remind students that the purpose of a report on any experiment is to allow someone who knows nothing about the experimental material or the experimental design to repeat the investigation. Students must be specific about materials, experimental conditions, and methods, including methods for making observations and recording data. Refer to Appendix I on Writing Laboratory Reports for assistance.

VI.   ORDERING INFORMATION

broad beans—Carolina Biological, # 15-8302
castor beans—Carolina Biological, # 15-8322
lima beans—Carolina Biological, # 15-8330
navy beans—Carolina Biological, # 15-8380
pinto beans—Carolina Biological, # 15-8400
kidney beans—Carolina Biological, # 15-8420
Styrofoam cups—local grocery store
potting soil—local hardware or lawn and garden store
Petri dishes—Carolina Biological, # 74-1348; Fisher, # 08-757-12

LABORATORY 2   Measuring What You Observe

I. FOREWORD

This laboratory is designed to introduce students to the metric system and to give them experience using the metric system while collecting quantitative data. Students should review Appendix II, Using Scientific Notation, to learn how to report metric data in scientific notation.

II. TIME REQUIREMENTS

Exercise A—25 minutes (can be completed prior to laboratory)
Exercise B—30 minutes
Exercise C (Part 1)—20 minutes
Let's Investigate—20 minutes
Exercise C (Part 2)—20 minutes
Exercise D—20 minutes

III. STUDENT MATERIALS AND EQUIPMENT

	Per Student	Per Pair (2)	Per Group (4)	Per Class (24)
Exercise A				
written laboratory materials				
Exercise B				
millimeter ruler	1			24
objects to be measured (**1**)		10	60	
Exercise C (Part 1)				
100 mL glass graduated cylinder		1		12
100 mL Nalgene graduated cylinder		1		12
colored liquid, bottle (200 mL) (**2**)		1		12
Let's Investigate				
100 mL graduated cylinder		1		12
100 mL volumetric flask		1		12
150 mL beaker		1		12
100 mL Erlenmeyer flask		1		12
colored liquid, bottle (200 mL)		1		12
Exercise C (Part 2)				
1 mL pipette	1			24
10 mL pipette	1			24
10 mL graduated cylinder	1			24
red liquid, bottle (50 mL) (**3**)		1		12

	Per Student	Per Pair (2)	Per Group (4)	Per Class (24)
Exercise C (Part 2)—continued				
Propipette	1			24
Exercise D				
balance (± 0.1 g)			1	6
weighing paper or boat			3	18
objects for weighing—prunes (**4**)			3	18

IV. PREPARATION OF MATERIALS AND SOLUTIONS

(**1**) objects to be measured—
   A bag of 10 leaves (do not pick poison ivy!) gives students an excellent set of objects to be measured. Students will have to decide on some rules to employ while collecting data; for example, whether or not to include the petiole. Other objects such as nails, screws, or lengths of yarn could also be used.

(**2**) colored liquid—
   Although students can use plain water, a drop or two of food coloring to give some color to the water helps students to identify the surface of the meniscus and to make necessary measurements.

(**3**) red liquid—
   Add a few drops of red food coloring to tap water to make practice solutions for pipetting exercises.

(**4**) objects for weighing—
   Prunes provide a ready source of objects to weigh rather than using reagents. Small blocks of wood, small stones or pebbles, fishing weights, or a number of other objects can also be used.

V. PREPARATION SUGGESTIONS

Exercise A

Students usually experience difficulty with scientific notation and the metric system. Assign the problems in Appendix II and the written section of Exercise A to be completed before students come to the laboratory. You may wish to give a short quiz at the beginning of the laboratory to identify those students who are still having difficulty (these could be graded by the students themselves if given a sheet of answers). If quiz papers are placed on the laboratory bench so that the instructor can look at the results, each student could be given extra help during the laboratory period.

Exercise B

Objects used for measuring should all be of a size that conversion to different units is possible (this gives students extra practice). You should use objects that are large enough for students to measure in centimeters and then convert to millimeters or meters. Be sure to review the material on constructing histograms before students attempt to organize and present their data. Most problems are encountered when students attempt to group data that has been recorded without rounding to whole numbers.

Exercise C (Part 1)

Use a Nalgene cylinder if possible. Some plastic cylinders distort the meniscus, turning the sides downward. Test your cylinders before using them in the laboratory.

Let's Investigate

Although this seems like a simple exercise, this investigation provides students with a simple experiment for which they must formulate a hypothesis. It also gives the instructor an excellent opportunity to check what students have learned about the scientific method as presented in Laboratory 1. You might ask students to form a null hypothesis as well as a hypothesis. This simple exercise will also provide you with an opportunity to assist students who have difficulty with experimental design. Students should start with one measuring device and assess the accuracy of all other glassware relative to the first instrument. Many students will try to test their hypothesis by dispensing liquid from one measuring device to the next but this will lead them in circles and will not provide satisfactory data. Students may wish to use the balance to determine whether a graduated cylinder or volumetric flask is more accurate and then use the more accurate device as the instrument to test the accuracy of the other measuring devices.

If you are running multiple laboratory sections, you may wish to have two sets of volumetric flasks so that one can be dried in a drying oven while the other set is being used.

Exercise C (Part 2)

Pipettes to be placed on demonstration should be taped onto pieces of cardboard in sets to show a "to deliver" or blow out pipette and a standard delivery pipette. You might also include an example of at least one volumetric pipette. If you do not tape the pipettes together on some cardboard, the students will pick them up and scatter them. Consequently, students will have a difficult time identifying the types of pipettes they are supposed to study.

Be sure to announce that, in the laboratory, there will be NO mouth pipetting. Demonstrate the Propipette or Pi-Pump prior to this exercise. Tell students to keep the pipette pointed downward after filling it using the Pi-Pump. If students turn it upward, the Pi-Pump will fill with fluid. Warn students to never leave a pipette with a Pi-Pump attached in a bottle or container of liquid—this makes the solution very easy to spill and often the weight of the Pi-Pump will tip the container over.

Also, be sure to watch students as they learn to use the pipette. The most common mistake is that they try to examine the markings on the tip by holding it—sometimes even after it is filled! Warn them about what this might do to their fingers if the material they are using is acid OR what a well-fingered pipette might do to a solution which should be kept sterile.

Students will find that it is difficult to get water out of the 10 mL graduated cylinders used to check their pipetting technique. If you are running multiple laboratory sections, have students place the cylinders upside down in a test tube rack that has a paper towel covering the mesh at the bottom of the rack.

Exercise D

It is important to use objects which will show significant changes in mass when added one at a time to the balance pan. Be sure to warn students that the balance pan should always be protected by a sheet of weighing paper or by a weighing boat. If you use the terms "mass" and "weight" interchangeably, you may wish to discuss this usage with your students.

VI. ORDERING INFORMATION

clear plastic millimeter ruler—Carolina Biological, # 70-2604
10 mL pipette (blow out)—Fisher, # 13-675M
5 mL pipette (to deliver)—Fisher, # 13-665K
1 mL pipette (blow out)—Fisher, # 13-674-32H
150 mL beaker—Fisher, # 20-140; Carolina Biological, # 72-1208A
125 mL Erlenmeyer flask—Fisher # 4980-125; Carolina Biological, # 72-6686A
weighing boats—Fisher # 02-202C; Carolina Biological, # 70-2332
weighing paper—Fisher # 09-898-12B; Carolina Biological, # 70-2332
100 µL volumetric pipette—Fisher, # 13-157-5S
Propipette (safety pipette filler)—Fisher, # 13-681-50 or Carolina Biological, # 73-6868
Pi-Pump (Pipette Pump)—Fisher, 13-683C or Carolina Biological, # 73-6875
100 mL volumetric flask—Fisher, # 10-199D

LABORATORY 3   Water

I.   FOREWORD

In this laboratory, students will learn about some of the physical properties of water, including adhesive and cohesive properties and density. Students will investigate the ability of oxygen to dissolve in water and will learn how this is important to organisms that live in water or respire on land. Students will also learn about the importance of water as a solvent and will practice making percent and molar solutions.

II.   TIME REQUIREMENTS

Exercise A—20 minutes
Exercise B—60 minutes
Let's Investigate—30 minutes
Exercise C (Part 1)—20 minutes
Exercise C (Part 2)—20 minutes

III.   STUDENT MATERIALS AND EQUIPMENT

	Per Student	Per Pair (2)	Per Group (4)	Per Class (24)
Exercise A				
drinking glass		1		12
pennies		50		600
needle		1		12
glass slides		3		36
cooking oil (dropping bottle)				1
liquid detergent (dropping bottle) (**1**)				1
water (dropping bottle)		1		12
Exercise B				
water (40° C), 1000 mL (**2**)		1		12
water (10° C), 1000 mL (**2**)		1		12
LeMotte Dissolved Oxygen test kit		1		12
Let's Investigate				
water sample (**3**)	1			24
LeMotte Dissolved Oxygen test kit				4
Exercise C				
written laboratory exercise				
balance (± 0.1 g) (optional)			1	6
weighing boat (optional)		3		36

	Per Student	Per Pair (2)	Per Group (4)	Per Class (24)

Exercise C—continued

NaCl, bottle (optional)			1	6
glucose ($C_6H_{12}O_6$), bottle (optional)			1	6
NaOH, bottle (optional)			1	6
spatulas (optional)			3	36

IV. PREPARATION OF MATERIALS AND SOLUTIONS

(1) liquid detergent—
Use a clear liquid detergent if possible. Dilute the detergent 1:1 with water before use. Place in a dropping bottle to dispense for students

(2) water at 40° and 10° C—
Collect water in advance. Let stand overnight, if possible, in a water bath incubator or refrigerator. If you take water directly from the tap, you will have additional air in the water and the results from each student group will vary greatly. Although you do not need 1000 mL for the sample, this amount in a 1000 or 2000 mL beaker will allow you to fill the LeMotte sample bottles easily.

(3) water sample—
For the Let's Investigate experiment, students should be encouraged to use water from locations around school or home. A comparison of water from fast running streams, stagnant ponds, water traps on golf courses, farm ponds, etc. should prove interesting. Combine this with some observations using the microscope (Laboratory 6) for students to determine what types of organisms are living in the water they sampled. During Laboratory 6, encourage students to bring in samples from the same source as used for the present laboratory.

If you elect to use salt water, a 3.5% solution of NaCl should be made available to students. This approximates the salinity of the open ocean.

V. PREPARATION SUGGESTIONS

Exercise A

Be sure to use a drinking glass for this exercise. A beaker will not work because of the pouring spout.

When coating slides with cooking oil or soap, use only a thin film. Allow the soap film to dry before wetting the slide. You can use other substances such as Vaseline or silicon in a tube (often used for caulking).

Exercise B

Although you can measure dissolved oxygen using reagents that have been prepared in the laboratory, the LeMotte Dissolved Oxygen Kit is simple and requires smaller water samples. For under $30, you can perform 50 dissolved oxygen tests. A $15 refill kit allows for 200 additional tests. The kit comes in a plastic carrying case and can be used in the field for other experiments or coursework. Additional collection bottles and microburet titrators can be ordered from LaMotte so that several groups of students can work simultaneously from a single kit. Directions for using the kit are also found in the lid of the carrying case for fast reference. Students find this easy to use and follow the steps without problems.

Make sure that students submerge their sample bottle completely when filling it—otherwise, excess oxygen will bubble into the bottle. If you wish to use a siphon to fill sample bottles from a single source, make sure that the source is above the level of the collecting bottles to be filled. Overfill the bottles to exclude air. Place bottles in a bucket to avoid puddles on the floor!

Let's Investigate

If you use salt water for a simple investigation, let it sit overnight as in Exercise B. If students use their own samples, make sure to explain that they must submerge the collection bottle when sampling their water source.

Dissolved oxygen experiments can be extended to look at productivity. Each student would need three bottles; one to fix immediately as the Initial Bottle, one to leave in the light (Light Bottle) so that both photosynthesis and respiration can occur (if appropriate organisms are present in the water sample), and one to leave in the dark (Dark Bottle, covering the sample bottle with aluminum foil) so that only respiration can occur. The Light and Dark Bottles should be kept at the same temperature for 24 hours and then should be fixed. All three samples, Initial, Light, and Dark, should be analyzed for oxygen content.

Net productivity = Light – Initial (positive number represents increase)

Respiration = Initial – Dark (negative number represents decrease)

Gross Productivity = Light – Dark

Using this simple approach, students can conduct a class project to compare water in different ecosystems.

Exercise C

This exercise is designed to be completed on paper. It is simple to ask students to actually prepare the solutions if this is not already being done in their chemistry course.

If students will be using NaOH, remember that it is very caustic. Make sure that the balance pans and tops of balances are well protected. Have students wear safety glasses.

You will find it helpful if beakers and spatulas are labeled and present at designated balances. You may wish to attach spatulas to the proper bottle by using a glass vial taped to the bottle. Place the spatula in the vial. Make sure the spatula is labeled. Weighing boats can be reused if labeled with a water proof pen. Have students rinse all spatulas, weighing boats, and beakers after completing the exercise.

You will also find it helpful if reagents for preparing solutions are located in a separate area of the laboratory. You will need several magnetic stirring plates, magnetic stirring bars, and a retriever. Students should have ready access to running water for mixing solutions. Provide plenty of paper towels and some absorbent toweling for drying rinsed glassware.

VI. ORDERING INFORMATION

LaMotte Dissolved Oxygen test kit—LaMotte[*] , Model EDO AG-30, Code # 7414; Ward's, # 21 W 0054

refill for dissolved oxygen test kit—LaMotte, Code # R-7414; Ward's, # 21 W 0050

bottle for dissolved oxygen test kit—LaMotte, Code # 0688-DO

microburets for dissolved oxygen test kit—LaMotte, Code # 0377

sodium chloride (NaCl)—Fisher, # S271-500; Carolina Biological, # 88-8880

D glucose ($C_6H_{12}O_6$)—Fisher, # D16-500 (500 g); Carolina Biological, # 850-7440 (500 g)

sodium hydroxide (NaOH)—Fisher, # S320-500; Carolina Biological, # 88-9460

weighing pans—Fisher, # 02-202B; Carolina Biological, # 70-2332

spatulas—Fisher, # 14-375-20; Carolina Biological, # 70-2700

microscope slides (75 X 25 mm)—Fisher, # 12-544-1; Carolina Biological, # 63-2000

dropping bottles (Barnes)—Fisher, # 02-980; Carolina Biological, # 71-6525

---

[*] LaMotte Chemical, PO Box 329, Chestertown, MD 21620. 800-344-3100 or 301-778-3100 (in Maryland)

LABORATORY 4   pH

I. FOREWORD

This laboratory is designed to introduce students to the concepts of ionization, acid and base relationships, and pH. If pH meters are available, students may wish to test the accuracy of their work using these instruments. Appendix III explains the use of the pH meter. The instructor should choose appropriate exercises from those presented. Since the combination of all exercises cannot be completed within the laboratory period, Exercise A should be completed before coming to the laboratory. (An understanding of scientific notation—Laboratory 2—is necessary to complete Exercise A.) Students may choose from several options in Exercise C.

Throughout this laboratory, students should be working in pairs or groups to save both time and reagents.

II. TIME REQUIREMENTS

Exercise A—60 minutes (may be completed prior to laboratory)
Exercise B (Part 1)—30 minutes
Exercise B (Part 2)—15 minutes
Exercise B (Part 3)—15 minutes
Exercise C (Part 1)—20 minutes
Exercise C (Part 2)—20 minutes
Exercise C (Part 3)—20 minutes
Exercise C (Part 4)—20 minutes
    student pairs may choose to do one or more parts of Exercise C

III. STUDENT MATERIALS AND EQUIPMENT

	Per Student	Per Pair (2)	Per Group (4)	Per Class (24)
Exercise A				
laboratory manual written exercise				
Exercise B (Part 1)				
red cabbage indicator, bottle (25 mL) (1)		1		12
test tubes		9		108
test tube rack		1		12
buffers, pH 1, 2, 4, 6, 7, 8, 10, 12, 14, bottles (300 mL) (2)			1	6
5 mL pipettes (1 per buffer)			7	42
Parafilm (small squares)		7		84
Exercise B (Part 2)				
test tubes	2			48
solution A (10 mL) (3)			1	6

13

	Per Student	Per Pair (2)	Per Group (4)	Per Class (24)

Exercise B (Part 2)—continued

	Per Student	Per Pair (2)	Per Group (4)	Per Class (24)
solution B (10 mL) (**4**)			1	6
red cabbage indicator, bottle (25 mL) (**1**)		1		12

Exercise B (Part 3)

	Per Student	Per Pair (2)	Per Group (4)	Per Class (24)
test tubes	4			96
solution A (50 mL) (**3**)			1	6
solution B (50 mL) (**4**)			1	6
solution C (50 mL) (**5**)			1	6
solution D (50 mL) (**5**)			1	6
bottle plus stirring rod for each solution (A–D)				
alkacid test paper, 2 inch piece	4			96
forceps	1			24

Exercise C (Part 1)

	Per Student	Per Pair (2)	Per Group (4)	Per Class (24)
test tubes	4			96
test tube rack	1			24
apple juice (10 mL) (**6**)			1	6
coffee (10 mL) (**6**)			1	6
7-Up (10 mL) (**6**)			1	6
white wine (10 mL) (**6**)			1	6
red cabbage indicator, bottle (25 mL) (**1**)			1	6
alkacid test paper, 2 inch piece	2			48

Exercise C (Part 2)—Optional

	Per Student	Per Pair (2)	Per Group (4)	Per Class (24)
test tubes	4			96
test tube rack	1			24
aspirin solution (10 mL) (**7**)			1	6
Milk of Magnesia (10 mL) (**8**)			1	6
sodium bicarbonate solution (10 mL) (**9**)			1	6
Maalox (10 mL) (**10**)			1	6
red cabbage indicator, bottle (25 mL) (**1**)			1	6

Exercise C (Part 3)—Optional

	Per Student	Per Pair (2)	Per Group (4)	Per Class (24)
test tubes	4			96
test tube rack	1			24
Drano solution (10 mL) (**11**)			1	6
Ivory Liquid solution (10 mL) (**12**)			1	6
Cascade solution (10 mL) (**13**)			1	6
Tide solution (10 mL) (**14**)			1	6

	Per Student	Per Pair (2)	Per Group (4)	Per Class (24)

Exercise C (Part 4)—Optional

	Per Student	Per Pair (2)	Per Group (4)	Per Class (24)
potting soil, beaker, and stirring rod (15)			1	6
clay, beaker, and stirring rod (16)			1	6
sand, beaker, and stirring rod (17)			1	6
lime, beaker, and stirring rod (18)			1	6
peat moss, beaker, and stirring rod (19)			1	6

IV. PREPARATION OF MATERIALS AND SOLUTIONS

(1) red cabbage indicator (cabbage extract)—
Shave thin slices from a head of red cabbage. Fill a 250 mL beaker half full with the cabbage and add 150 mL of water. Boil until the water turns a medium purple-red in color. If the solution is too light, add more cabbage. Each group of students (or pair) should prepare its own extract. However, to save time, it is possible to make the extract before the laboratory and distribute it in bottles. Simply increase the amounts (fill a 1000 mL beaker half to three-quarters full with shaved cabbage and add 500 mL of water).

(2) buffers (2000 mL each)—
Buffers can be prepared from chemicals normally found in the chemistry stockroom as given below. Alternatively, buffer concentrates can be ordered in liquid form, as capsules, or dried salts from Fisher or Carolina Biological Supply Company (see ordering information).

pH 1
Use 2000 mL of 1 N HCl (order from Fisher prepared)

pH 2
Part 1. Dissolve 14.91 g KCl in 400 mL of distilled water and dilute up to 500 mL with distilled water
Part 2. Mix the 500 mL of potassium chloride solution prepared in Part 1 with 260 mL of 0.1 N HCl and add distilled water to make 2000 mL.

pH 4
Part 1. Dissolve 20.42 g of potassium hydrogen phthalate in 700 mL of distilled water and dilute up to 1000 mL with distilled water.
Part 2. Mix the 1000 mL of potassium hydrogen phthalate solution (Part 1) with 998 mL of distilled water and 2 mL of 0.1 N HCl to make 2000 mL.

pH 6
Part 1. Dissolve 13.61 g of potassium phosphate (monobasic) in 700 mL of distilled water and dilute up to 1000 mL with distilled water.
Part 2. Mix the 1000 mL of potassium phosphate (monobasic) solution (Part 1) with 888 mL of distilled water and 112 mL of 0.1 N NaOH to make 2000 mL.
Note: You may wish to double the amount of pH 6 buffer in order to prepare pH 7 buffer if you are teaching large sections.

pH 7
Mix pH 6 solution and pH 8 solution together until you obtain a solution of pH 7.

pH 8

    Part 1. Dissolve 13.61 g of potassium phosphate (monobasic) in 700 mL of distilled water and dilute up to 1000 mL with distilled water.

    Part 2. Mix the 1000 mL of potassium phosphate (monobasic) solution (Part 1), 922 mL of 0.1 N NaOH, and 78 mL of distilled water to make 2000 mL.

    Note: You may wish to double the amount of pH 8 buffer in order to prepare pH 7 buffer if you are teaching large sections.

pH 10

    Part 1. Dissolve 7.46 g of potassium chloride and 6.18 g of boric acid in 700 mL of distilled water and dilute to 1000 mL with distilled water (heat to dissolve the boric acid).

    Part 2. Mix the 1000 mL of potassium chloride and boric acid solution (Part 1), 874 mL of 0.1 N NaOH, and 126 mL of distilled water to make 2000 mL.

pH 12

    Part 1. Dissolve 7.1 g of sodium phosphate (dibasic) in 700 mL of distilled water and dilute to 1000 mL with distilled water.

    Part 2. Mix the 1000 mL of sodium phosphate (dibasic) solution, 538 mL of 0.1 N NaOH, and 462 mL of distilled water to make 2000 mL.

pH 14

    Use 2000 mL of 2 N NaOH

(3) solution A—

    Mix 100 mL of 0.1 N HCl and 900 mL of distilled water. Adjust to pH 2 if necessary.

(4) solution B—

    Mix 0.01 mL of 0.1 N HCl and 999.9 mL of distilled water. Adjust to pH 6 if necessary.

(5) solutions C and D—

    Choose any two colored solutions or add several drops of different food colorings to samples of solutions A and B.

(6) apple juice, coffee, 7-Up, white wine—

    Use as bottled

(7) aspirin—

    Dissolve one aspirin in each 100 mL of tap water.

(8) Milk of Magnesia—

    Use as purchased.

(9) sodium bicarbonate solution—

    Dissolve 0.5 g of $NaHCO_3$ in each 100 mL of distilled water.

(10) Maalox—

    Use as purchased.

(11) Drano—

    Dissolve 6 g of Drano into each 100 mL of tap water.

(12) Ivory Liquid—

    Use as purchased.

(13) Cascade—

    Dissolve 6 g of Cascade into each 100 mL of tap water.

(14) Tide—

    Dissolve 6 g of Tide into each 100 mL of tap water.

(15) potting soil mix—

    Fill a 150 mL beaker with potting soil up to the 40 mL mark and add tap water to the 120 mL mark. The pH should be 6 or 7.

(16) clay—

    Fill a 150 mL beaker with clay up to the 40 mL mark and add tap water to the 120 mL mark. The pH should be 8.

(17) sand—

    Fill a 150 mL beaker with sand up to the 40 mL mark and add tap water to the 120 mL mark. The pH should be 7.

(18) lime—

    Fill a 150 mL beaker with lime up to the 40 mL mark and add tap water to the 120 mL mark. The pH should be 9.

(19) peat moss—

    Fill a 150 mL beaker with peat moss up to the 40 mL mark and add tap water to the 120 mL mark. The pH should be 4.

V.   PREPARATION SUGGESTIONS

Exercise A

Students should complete this exercise before coming to laboratory. You may find that an additional "help" session is necessary during the week because students generally find the mathematical manipulations associated with determining hydrogen ion concentration or pH difficult. You may need to review methods for using the log and antilog functions on the calculator if these are to be used.

Exercise B (Parts 1 and 2)

Students find this exercise to be fun as well as instructive. To save time, you may wish to boil cabbage ahead of time. Make sure that the extract is dark purple, otherwise the colors of the different buffer solutions will be too light. To save on glassware, you may wish to use a repipette for each buffer solution (set the dispenser to 5 mL). Place the repipettes on the demonstration bench and tell the students to carry their labeled test tubes (in a test tube rack) to the demonstration bench to fill each with the appropriate buffer. If students do not prepare their own cabbage extract, you may also want to use a repipette for the cabbage extract (set to 3 mL).

Exercise B (Part 3)

Provide alkacid test paper in small pieces in a Petri dish. Students can use forceps to place the alkacid test paper into the solution.

Exercise C (Parts 1, 2 and 3)

To save time, split the class into groups and have one group measure the pH of beverages, another group measure the pH of medicine, a third group measure the pH of common cleaning solutions and a fourth group measure the pH of soils. Record class data on the board. You might also want to assign students to bring in a sample of a particular substance along with a "guestimate" of its pH. Examples could include shampoo, a favorite soft drink, Alka-Seltzer, Tums, iced tea, etc.

Exercise C (Part 4)

Students should use a glass stirring rod to transfer a small amount of soil sample to the alkacid test paper. You might want to assign students to bring in a soil sample from somewhere on campus or at home, noting the types of plants living in the area from which the soil was taken. Class data should be placed on the board and pH values compared for plants from similar areas.

VI.   ORDERING INFORMATION

1 N hydrochloric acid—Fisher, # SA48-4
0.1 N (N/10) hydrochloric acid   Fisher, # SA54 4
potassium chloride—Fisher, # P217-500
potassium hydrogen phthalate—Fisher, # P243-500
potassium phosphate (monobasic) (KH_2PO_4)—Fisher, # P285-500
0.1 N (N/10) sodium hydroxide—Fisher, # SS276-4
boric acid—Fisher, # A73-500
sodium phosphate (monobasic) (NaH_2PO_4)—Fisher, # S374-500
2 N sodium hydroxide—Fisher, # SS264-1
sodium chloride—Fisher, # S271-500
potassium phosphate dibasic (K_2HPO_4)—Fisher, # P288-500
Hydrion buffers in Capsules—Fisher, # 13-640-303 A-J
Fisher certified buffer concentrate—Fisher, # SB99-5XX (see catalog; numbers vary with pH)
buffer, Chemvelope—Carolina Biological, # 84-9XXX (see catalog; numbers vary with pH)
test tubes—Fisher, # 14-958F
5 mL pipettes—Fisher, # 13-665K
Parafilm—Carolina Biological, # 21-5600; Fisher, # 13-374-10
alkacid test paper—Fisher, # A980

LABORATORY 5   Organic Molecules

I.   FOREWORD

This laboratory is designed to introduce students to some of the structures and terminology used in discussing biochemical macromolecules. Tests are not extensive enough to allow all types of macromolecules to be distinguished but major types are represented. Testing for unknowns is done with commercial products rather than specific purified molecules in order to make the laboratory a more familiar experience rather than a "chemistry" laboratory. Students will also test for the presence of vitamin C (ascorbic acid) in familiar food items.

II.   TIME REQUIREMENTS

Exercise A—45 minutes
Exercise B—30 minutes
Exercise C (Part 1)—20 minutes
Exercise C (Part 2)—15 minutes
Exercise D—45 minutes
Let's Investigate—variable

III.   STUDENT MATERIALS AND EQUIPMENT

	Per Student	Per Pair (2)	Per Group (4)	Per Class (24)
Exercise A				
test tube	16			384
test tube rack	1			24
wax pencil	1			16
distilled water, bottle			1	6
2% potato starch, bottle (1)			1	6
6% glucose, bottle (2)			1	6
6% maltose, bottle (3)			1	6
6% sucrose, bottle (4)			1	6
onion juice, bottle (5)			1	6
milk, whole, bottle			1	6
potato				1
pipette (5 mL)			7	42
Pi-Pump or Propipette	1			24
Benedict's reagent, dropping bottle (6)		1		12
hot plate or Bunsen burner		1		12
boiling chips, jar				1
500 mL beaker		1		12
test tube holder	1			24
Lugol's solution, dropping bottle (7)		1		12

19

	Per Student	Per Pair (2)	Per Group (4)	Per Class (24)

Exercise B

	Per Student	Per Pair (2)	Per Group (4)	Per Class (24)
3 inch square brown wrapping paper, unglazed	1	1		24
distilled water, dropping bottle			1	6
vegetable oil, dropping bottle			1	6
onion juice, dropping bottle (5)			1	6
hamburger juice, dropping bottle (8)			1	6
cola (or Sprite), dropping bottle			1	6
Sudan IV, dropping bottle (9)			1	6
test tube	5			120
test tube rack (same as Exercise A)				
wax pencil (same as Exercise A)				

Exercise C

	Per Student	Per Pair (2)	Per Group (4)	Per Class (24)
distilled water, dropping bottle (same as Exercise A)				
6% egg albumin, bottle (10)			1	6
2% potato starch, bottle (1)			1	6
6% glucose, bottle (2)			1	6
amino acid solution, bottle (11)			1	6
test tubes	5			120
test tube rack (same as Exercise A)				
wax pencil (same as exercise A)				
Biuret reagent, dropping bottle (12)			1	6
filter paper (Whatman #1, 15 cm)	1			24
solution A—proline, dropping bottle (13)			1	6
solution B—distilled water, dropping bottle (13)			1	6
solution C—methionine, dropping bottle (13)			1	6
solution D—alanine, dropping bottle (13)			1	6
ninhydrin, dropping bottle (14)			1	6
hot plate or Bunsen burner (same as Exercise A)				

Exercise D

	Per Student	Per Pair (2)	Per Group (4)	Per Class (24)
vitamin C capsules (25 mg) (15)		1		12
1% starch, dropping bottle (16)		1		12
25 mL graduated cylinder		1		12
250 mL beaker		1		12
distilled water (25 mL)		1		12
burette		1		12
burette clamp		1		12
ring stand		1		12
iodine solution (25 mL) (17)		1		12

Let's Investigate

	Per Student	Per Pair (2)	Per Group (4)	Per Class (24)
10 unknown solutions (18) (each solution)				1

IV. PREPARATION OF MATERIALS AND SOLUTIONS

(1) 2% potato starch—
Bring 900 mL of distilled water to boil. Mix 20 g of potato starch in 100 mL of distilled water and slowly pour this mixture into the 900 mL of boiling water. Heat the entire solution to boiling, mix and remove from heat—allow it to cool (cover with aluminum foil while cooling). Some starch will settle out of solution.

(2) 6% glucose—
Weigh 60 g glucose (dextrose). Add distilled water to 1000 mL.

(3) 6% maltose—
Weigh 60 g maltose. Add distilled water to 1000 mL.

(4) 6% sucrose—
Weigh 60 g sucrose. Add distilled water to 1000 mL.

(5) onion juice—
Place a peeled, diced onion into a blender. Cover it with distilled water (100-200 mL, depending on the size of the onion) and blend. Strain through cheesecloth.

(6) Benedict's reagent—
Order prepared solution (powdered or liquid form can be ordered.

(7) Lugol's solution (I_2KI)—
Order prepared solution OR
Dissolve 10 g of potassium iodide in 100 mL of distilled water and add 5 g of iodine. Store in a dark bottle. Prepare 200 mL per class of 24 students.

(8) hamburger juice—
Boil hamburger (1/4 of a 250 mL beaker full) with 150 mL water for 5 minutes. Allow hamburger to settle to the bottom of the beaker and use the liquid.

(9) Sudan IV—
Weigh 0.2 g Sudan IV. Make up to 100 mL with 95% ethanol..

(10) 6% egg albumin—
Weigh 60 g egg albumin. Add distilled water to make 1000 mL.

(11) amino acid solution—
Weigh 0.8 g of amino acid (choose any on hand). Add distilled water to 100 mL. If amino acid does not go into solution, adjust pH with 0.1 N NaOH and heat slightly.

(12) Biuret reagent—
Order prepared solution. Approximately 500 mL per class of 24.

(13) amino acid solutions (A, B, C, and D)—
Weigh 0.8 g proline (or other amino acid). Add distilled water to 100 mL. Suggestion: Bottle A—proline; Bottle B—distilled water; Bottle C—methionine; and Bottle D—alanine. If amino acid does not go into solution easily, adjust pH with 0.1 N NaOH and heat slightly.

(14) ninhydrin—
Weigh 0.2 g ninhydrin. Dissolve in 100 mL of 95% ethanol. AVOID BREATHING POISONOUS FUMES! Prepare in a vented hood.

(15) vitamin C—

Vitamin C capsules (25 mg each) can be purchased at a local drugstore. Students prepare their own solution by adding the contents of one capsule to 25 mL of water. Alternatively, mix 0.5 g ascorbic acid with distilled water to make 500 mL of solution. Dispense 25 mL of this solution to each pair of students.

(16) 1% starch—

Obtain 1 g of soluble starch and make a thin paste using warm water. Stir the paste into 100 mL boiling distilled water. Allow to cool and dispense into dropping bottles. Increase amount as needed for larger classes.

(17) iodine solution—

Using a 1 L graduated cylinder, prepare 250 mL of a 0.01 M potassium iodate solution (0.54 g potassium iodate, KIO_3; add distilled water to 250 mL). Dissolve 10.0 g potassium iodide (KI) in the 250 mL of potassium iodate solution. Add 60 mL of 3 M sulfuric acid (25 mL concentrated sulfuric acid plus 75 mL distilled water). Add distilled water to 1 L.

(18) unknowns—

Use the following materials as unknowns: 1) onion (blend with water and filter); 2) potato (blend with water and filter); 3) 7-UP (regular); 4) 7-UP (diet); 5) salad dressing (regular); 6) salad dressing (diet); 7) egg yolk (blend lightly with water); 8) egg white (blend lightly with water); 9) hamburger (boil—use supernatant); 10) salami (boil—use supernatant).

V. PREPARATION SUGGESTIONS

Exercise A

It is most convenient to prepare solutions for groups of 4-8 students (depending on the seating arrangement in your laboratory). Materials are suggested for groups of 4, but larger groups are possible. Use 500 mL or liter bottles. Tape a test tube to the side of the bottle (use two pieces of tape—top and bottom of tube). Place a 5 mL pipette into the tube. Label the pipette to match the label on the bottle. Use a Pi-Pump or Propipette to dispense the solution from the bottle. Each student should have a Pi-Pump or Propipette for his or her own use. This helps to prevent mixing of pipettes and solutions and cuts down on the amount of dirty glassware generated by the laboratory.

As an alternative, solutions can be placed in dropping bottles and students can use a dropper full of solution to approximate the 2 mL of liquid required.

A bottle of boiling chips should be available in the laboratory. The 500 mL beaker is to be used as a boiling water bath—add 5-6 boiling chips. A bucket of soapy water and test tube brush should be provided for washing dirty test tubes. Also provide some paper towels to use for removing wax pencil marks. This will help with clean up.

Exercise B

Sudan IV is fairly messy and will get into everything in the laboratory if students fail to wash out test tubes in hot soapy water. When several drops of Sudan IV are added to the test tubes, a red droplet will appear if fat is present. Otherwise the red disperses throughout the solution. This can be done as a demonstration and tubes placed in a test tube rack on the demonstration table if necessary. Sudan IV can be purchased in powder or liquid form.

Exercise C (Parts 1 and 2)

Do not use spray cans of ninhydrin for Part 2 of this exercise because FUMES ARE POISONOUS. Store ninhydrin solutions in dark bottles. Cover dropper bottles with aluminum foil if you do not have amber glass dropper bottles. Everything (including clothes and skin!) will react and stain with ninhydrin, so warn students to be careful.

Exercise D

You may wish to demonstrate the proper technique for titration. One drop of iodine solution should change the solution to a permanent blue color at the end of the titration. You will find that the actual endpoint color will vary if colored liquids are tested. Try to use a selection of liquids that are all the same color (i.e., orange juice, orange soda, orange Gatorade, etc.). You will find that pineapple juice and orange juice contain the highest amounts of vitamin C. Grape juice (white) and High-C, are also moderately high in vitamin C content. Apple juice, Tang, and most sodas are fairly low in vitamin C content. Milk also rates fairly low. You will find that the conversion factor will be approximately 0.75 mL/mg vitamin C.

Let's Investigate

Unknowns can be from commercial sources or unknowns can be the same materials as those used during the class period (i.e., vegetable oil, glucose, starch, albumin, amino acid solution, distilled water, and proline solution). Using unknowns from commercial sources is more fun for the students.

Ten or fewer unknowns can be made available. Students can try as many as they can or you can tell them how many to use depending on the length of the class period.

One set of unknowns in 500 mL bottles prepared as in Exercise A (with labeled pipettes in test tubes attached to the bottles) will be sufficient for the entire class. A Pi-Pump should be provided with each bottle if individual students have not been given one to use in earlier exercises.

VI.   ORDERING INFORMATION

soluble potato starch—Carolina Biological, # 89-2530 (125 g)

maltose (certified)—Fisher, # M75-100 (100 g); Carolina Biological, # 87-3750 (100 g)

D-glucose (dextrose) (certified)—Fisher, # D16-500 (500 g); Carolina Biological, # 85-7440 (500 g)

sucrose (certified)—Fisher, # S5-500 (500 g); Carolina Biological, # 89-2870 (500 g)

Benedict's reagent—Carolina Biological, # 84-7091 (powder, sufficient for 1000 mL); # 84-7111 (solution, 500 mL)

Lugol's solution—Carolina Biological, # 87-2793 (100 mL) or # 87-2795 (500 mL)

Biuret reagent—Carolina Biological, # 84-8211 (120 mL)

ninhydrin (powder)—Carolina Biological, # 87-7460 (5 g)

amino acids:

    L-alanine—Eastman Organic Chemicals, # 3125 (25 g) or Carolina Biological, # 84-2170 (25 g)

    L-proline—Eastman Organic Chemicals, # 2488 (25 g)

L-methionine—Eastman Organic Chemicals, # 5279 (25 g); Carolina Biological, # 87-5030 (200 g)
Pi-Pump—Fisher, # 13-683C (up to 10 mL)
Sudan IV—Carolina Biological, # 89-2980 (powder, 25 g); # 89-2993 (liquid, 120 mL)
Whatman filter paper, #1 (15 cm)—Fisher, # 09-805G; Carolina Biological (#201), # 71-2712
ascorbic acid—Carolina Biological, # 85-5534; Fisher, # A61-25
buret—Fisher, # 03-700-20B
buret clamp—Carolina Biological, # 70-7360; Fisher, # 05-799
potassium iodate—Carolina Biological, # 88-3700; Fisher, # P253-100
potassium iodide—Carolina Biological, # 88-3808; Fisher, # P410-100
sulfuric acid—Carolina Biological, # 88-3300; Fisher, # A300-500
dropping bottles (amber)—Fisher, # 02-983B

LABORATORY 6   Cells I

I.   FOREWORD

This lab is designed to introduce students to the proper use of both the dissecting and compound microscopes. The ability to use these microscopes will provide the foundation for Laboratory 7, Cells II, and for many other investigations throughout the laboratory course. The preparation of wet-mount slides will provide students with additional techniques to study many fascinating microbes as well as the structure of both single cell and multicellular organisms. Students should work individually on all exercises in this laboratory.

II.   TIME REQUIREMENTS

Exercise A—25 minutes
Exercise B—20 minutes
Exercise C—45 minutes
Exercise D—20 minutes

III.   STUDENT MATERIALS AND EQUIPMENT

	Per Student	Per Pair (2)	Per Group (4)	Per Class (24)
Exercise A				
lens paper packet		1		12
Exercise B				
compound microscope	1			24
letter "e" (prepared slide)	1			24
Oscillatoria (prepared slide)	1			24
Exercise C				
compound microscope	1			24
tap water (dropping bottle)			1	12
Elodea (live piece)				2
forceps (with *Elodea*)				1
microscope slides (75 X 25 mm)	3			72
coverslips (22 X 22 mm)	3			72
Protoslo (dropping bottle)			1	12
Paramecium culture (live)				2
toothpicks	1			24
Exercise D				
dissecting microscope	1			24
three-dimensional specimen (**1**)	1			24

IV. PREPARATION OF MATERIALS AND SOLUTIONS

(1) three-dimensional specimen—

Preserved insects (dried), mounted on small Styrofoam blocks by straight pins, are excellent three-dimensional specimens. Pine needles or cones are also useful specimens.

V. PREPARATION SUGGESTIONS

Exercise A

Save on lens paper by cutting small squares from the booklet and placing them in a Petri dish for use by students

Exercise C

One box of glass microscope slides and a box of coverslips per laboratory will suffice. A dirty slide container (such as a cut-off plastic milk bottle) will help in collecting used slides (have students discard used coverslips).

You may wish to extend this exercise by asking students to hypothesize about what might happen to cyclosis in *Elodea* if you heat up or cool down the slide or whether light is necessary for cyclosis. Students might ask if pH affects cyclosis. Similarly, how might temperature, light, and pH affect organisms in the pond water they study?

If you do not have a good source for pond water, you may wish to start your own microecosystem. This can be kept in your laboratory for several years under normal light conditions. You will find various algae and other protistans, including ciliates and flagellates, in the microecosystem and it will provide a ready source of material for study at all times.

Mix 1 L of each of the following stock solutions (Taub, F. G. and A. M. Dollar. 1964. *Chlorella Daphnia* food chain study; the design of a compatible chemically-defined medium. Limnol. Oceanogr. 9: 61-74):

Solution A:	24.65 g $MgSO_4 \cdot 7H_2O$
Solution B:	13.8 g KH_2PO_4, 2.8 g NaOH
Solution C:	11.7 g $CaCl_2$
Solution D:	26.1 g EDTA, 10.7 g NaOH, 24.9 g $FeSO_4 \cdot 7H_2O$
Solution E:	1.85 g H_3BO_3, 0.28 g $ZnSO_4 \cdot 7H_2O$, 1.98 g $MnCl_2 \cdot 4H_2O$, 0.242 g $NaMoO_4 \cdot 2H_2O$, 0.049 g $CuSO_4 \cdot 5H_2O$, 0.291 g $Co(NO_3)_2 \cdot 6H_2O$
Solution F:	5.84 g NaCl

To prepare 1 liter of microecosystem growth medium:

Mix 1 mL A + 1 mL B + 10 mL C + 0.062 mL D + 0.5 mL E + 15 mL F.

If you desire only autotrophic succession, simply add a selection of algae from an aquarium or nearby lake or pond. If you desire heterotrophic succession in addition to a good culture of autotrophs, add 0.5 g/L proteose peptone to the microecosystem culture medium. Add amoebae, paramecia, or other ciliates as desired.

A hay infusion can also be prepared. Boil 50 g hay for 15 minutes in 750 mL distilled water. Filter through cheese cloth. Increase volume to 1 L with distilled water. This is your stock solution. Use 100 mL stock per 900 mL distilled water as microecosystem growth medium. Inoculate with fresh hay (approximately 4 one-inch lengths of boiled hay/50 mL) or material from a pond (add amoebae and ciliates if available). Add 2 grains of boiled wheat per 50 mL.

If the culture begins to wane, subculture and add new medium.

Exercise D

Suggest to students that they bring a selection of small objects—perhaps live insects, tadpoles, flowers, etc.—to class for study during this laboratory period.

VI.   ORDERING INFORMATION

letter "e" (prepared slide)—Carolina Biological, # BM1

Oscillatoria (prepared slide—Carolina Biological, # B10

Elodea (live)—Carolina Biological, # 16-2100

Protoslo—Carolina Biological, # 88-5141

Paramecium caudatum culture (live)—Carolina Biological, # L2A

magnesium sulfate ($MgSO_4 \cdot 7H_2O$)—Fisher, # M67-3

potassium phosphate (KH_2PO_4)—Fisher, # P285-500

sodium hydroxide (NaOH)—Fisher, # S318-100

calcium chloride ($CaCl_2$)—Fisher, # C614-500

ethylenediamine tetracetic acid (EDTA)—Fisher, # BP118

iron sulfate ($FeSO_4 \cdot 7H_2O$)—Fisher, # I149-3

boric acid (H_3BO_3)—Fisher, # A73-500

zinc sulfate ($ZnSO_4 \cdot 7H_2O$)—Fisher, # Z76-3

manganous chloride ($MnCL_2 \cdot 4H_2O$)—Fisher # M87-100

sodium molybdate dihydrate ($NaMoO_4 \cdot 2H_2O$)—Fisher, # S336-500

copper sulfate ($CuSO_4 \cdot 5H_2O$)—Fisher, # C43-500

cobalt nitrate ($Co(NO_3)_2$)—Fisher, # C378-500

sodium chloride (NaCl)—Fisher, # C378-500

proteose peptone—Carolina Biological, # 79-4301

microscope slides (75 X 25 mm)—Carolina Biological, # 63-2000; Fisher, # 12-544-1

coverslips (22 X 22 mm)—Carolina Biological, # 63-3015; Fisher, # 12-542B

LABORATORY 7   Cells II

I.   FOREWORD

This laboratory is designed as an introduction to cell structure. A study of protobionts facilitates a comparison of simple coacervate structures with living cells. Students then compare prokaryotes with eukaryotes and animal cells with plant cells. The use of the microscope for studying cellular structure, including ultrastructure, is emphasized. All exercises are short and can be grouped together to provide several laboratory approaches.

II.   TIME REQUIREMENTS

Exercise A—45 minutes
Let's Investigate—30 minutes (may be completed prior to laboratory)
Exercise B (Part 1)—10 minutes
Exercise B (Part 2)—20 minutes
Exercise B (Part 3)—30 minutes
Let's Investigate—45 minutes
Exercise B (Part 4)—30 minutes
Exercise C—20 minutes
Exercise D (Part 1)—20 minutes
Exercise D (Part 2)—20 minutes
Exercise E—15 minutes (may be completed prior to laboratory)

III.   STUDENT MATERIALS AND EQUIPMENT

	Per Student	Per Pair (2)	Per Group (4)	Per Class (24)
Exercise A				
1% gelatin (**1**)			1	6
3% gum arabic (**2**)			1	6
5 mL pipette			2	12
Parafilm (pieces)	3			72
test tubes	1			24
glass stirring rod	1			24
pH paper			1	6
microscope slides, box (75 X 25 mm)			1	6
coverslips, box (22 X 22 mm)			1	6
Pasteur pipette	2			48
rubber bulb	1			24
1% HCl, dropping bottle (**3**)			1	6
stain (choice), dropping bottle (**4**)			1	6
5% NaCl, dropping bottle (**5**)			1	6
compound microscope	1			24

	Per Student	Per Pair (2)	Per Group (4)	Per Class (24)

Let's Investigate

wooden blocks (1") (6)				50

Exercise B (Part 1)

Escherichia coli (prepared slide)				1
Staphylococcus aureus (prepared slide)				1
bacterial flagella (prepared slide)				1
compound microscope				3

Exercise B (Part 2)

Oscillatoria (live, class of 30)				1
Nostoc (live, class of 30)				1
Cylindrospermum (live, class of 30)				1
microscope slides, box (75 X 25 mm)			1	6
coverslips, box (22 X 22 mm)			1	6
compound microscope	1			24

Exercise B (Part 3)

Elodea (live sprig)				4
onion				1
Lugol's solution (7)			1	6
potato				1
banana				1
carrot				1
single edge razor blade		1		12
microscope slides, box (75 X 25 mm)			1	6
coverslips, box (22 X 22 mm)			1	6
compound microscope	1			24

Let's Investigate

Elodea (live sprig)			1	6
water, dropping bottle			1	6
microscope slides, box (75 X 25 mm)			1	6
coverslips, box (22 X 22 mm)			1	6
compound microscope	1			24

Exercise B (Part 4)

microscope slides, box (75 X 25 mm)			1	6
coverslips, box (22 X 22 mm)			1	6
compound microscope	1			24
flat toothpicks, box			1	6
methylene blue stain, dropping bottle (8)			1	6
distilled water, squirt bottle			1	6

	Per Student	Per Pair (2)	Per Group (4)	Per Class (24)

Exercise C

neuron, cow (prepared slide)		1		12
Stentor (live, class of 30)				1
Acetabularia (preserved)				1
spermatozoa, human (prepared slide)		1		12
Volvox (live, class of 30)				1
starfish development (prepared slide)		1		12
microscope slides, box (75 X 25 mm)			1	6
coverslips, box (22 X 22 mm)			1	6
compound microscope	1			24

Exercise D (Part 1)

nutrient broth culture tubes (**9**)	1			24
nutrient agar slants (**9**)	1			24
marking pencil	1			24
inoculating loop	1			24
Bunsen burner	1			24
Escherichia coli, nutrient agar slant (**10**)	1			24
Serratia marcescens, nutrient agar slant (**10**)	1			24
E. coli, 24 hour broth culture (**11**)	1			24
S. marcescens, 24 hour broth culture (**11**)	1			24

Exercise D (Part 2)

E. coli, nutrient agar slant (**10**)	1			24
Micrococcus luteus, nutrient agar slant (**12**)	1			24
E. coli/S. marcescens, mixed broth culture (**13**)	1			24
E. coli/M. luteus, mixed broth culture (**14**)	1			24
nutrient agar plate (**15**)	2			48
glass spreading rod	1			24
inoculating loop	1			24
95% ethanol (beaker)	1			24
Bunsen burner	1			24
plaque study plates set (optional) (**16**)				1

Exercise E

student's collection of electron micrographs (**17**)				1

IV. PREPARATION OF MATERIALS AND SOLUTIONS

(**1**) 1% gelatin—
  Dissolve 10 g gelatin powder in enough distilled water to make 1 liter of solution. Adjust amounts for smaller volumes. Adjust pH to 7 using 0.1 N NaOH or 0.1N HCl.

(2) 3% gum arabic—

Dissolve 30 g of gum arabic powder in enough distilled water to make 1 liter of solution. Adjust amounts for smaller volumes. Adjust pH to 7 using 0.1 N NaOH or 0.1N HCl.

(3) 1% HCl—

Add 1 mL concentrated HCl to 99 mL of distilled water. Wear safety glasses. Remember to always add acid to water.

(4) stain for coacervates—

Methylene blue, neutral red, or congo red may be used to stain coacervates:

methylene blue—0.01 g methylene blue stain per 100 mL absolute alcohol

neutral red—0.03 g neutral red stain per 100 mL absolute alcohol

congo red—0.1 g congo red stain per 100 mL absolute alcohol

(5) 5% NaCl—

Dissolve 5 g NaCl in enough distilled water to make 100 mL solution. Mix and dispense into dropping bottles.

(6) wooden blocks—

Use a 1" X 1" strip of soft wood. Saw into 1" blocks. You can also use children's blocks of different shapes—square, rectangular, etc.

(7) Lugol's solution—

Order prepared or mix 10 g potassium iodide in 100 mL of distilled water and add 5 g of iodine.

(8) methylene blue—

Order prepared or mix 0.01 g of methylene blue with absolute (100%) alcohol to make 100 mL (see also **(4)**).

(9) nutrient broth culture tubes and nutrient agar slants—

Prepare nutrient broth (see Ordering Information) **as follows:**

Suspend 0.8 g of dehydrated nutrient broth in 100 mL of distilled water in a 250 mL flask. Prepare a total of 4 flasks. Add 1.5 g of (Bacto) agar to 2 of the 4 flasks and mix well. Cover the flasks with aluminum foil and autoclave at 15 lbs pressure and 121° C for 15 minutes.

Aseptically dispense 5 mL of the nutrient agar into sterile culture tubes and slant immediately to make approximately 40 agar slant tubes.

Aseptically dispense 5 mL of the nutrient broth into sterile culture tubes to make approximately 40 broth tubes.

Alternatively, you may purchase materials already prepared from Carolina Biological Supply Company. Tubes of nutrient agar (# 82-6100) can be melted and slanted. Nutrient broth (# 82-6120) is available in bottles at a reduced cost but must be dispensed into sterile culture tubes. (See Ordering Information.)

If costs are to be kept at a minimum, nutrient broth and agar can be made as follows:

a. nutrient broth

Add 5.0 g peptone and 3.0 g beef extract to 1000 mL distilled water and adjust to pH 7. Autoclave at 15 lbs pressure for 15 minutes.

b. nutrient agar

Prepare nutrient broth as above, but add 15 g Bacto-agar to the flask and mix before autoclaving.

(10) *Escherichia coli*, nutrient agar slant, or *Serratia marcescens*, nutrient agar slant—

These can be purchased as agar slant cultures from Carolina Biological Supply Company (# 15-5065 and # 15-5452, respectively). To prepare additional slants for students, inoculate fresh slants prepared as in **(9)** and incubate for 24 hours at 37° C.

(11) *Escherichia coli* or *Serratia marcescens*, 24 hour broth cultures—

Aseptically inoculate 100 mL of nutrient broth, prepared as in **(9)**, with a generous loop full of the appropriate bacterium. Incubate for 24 hours at 37° C in an incubator or shaking water bath. *Micrococcus luteus* cultures—see **(12)** below—must be started a day ahead of either *E. coli*. or *S. marcescens* cultures.

(12) *Micrococcus luteus*, nutrient agar slant—

This can be purchased as a nutrient agar slant culture from Carolina Biological Supply Company (# 15-5155). To prepare additional slants for students, inoculate fresh slants prepared as in **(9)** and incubate for 48 hours at 37° C. (Note: *M. luteus* slants and broth cultures require an additional 24 hours of incubation and must be started one day ahead of *E. coli* or *S. marcescens* cultures.)

(13) *Escherichia coli/Serratia marcescens* mixed broth culture—

Prepare a single 24 hour broth culture of *E. coli* and *S. marcescens* as in **(11)**. Aseptically mix 2.0 mL of *E. coli* with 1.0 mL of *S. marcescens* to prepare tubes for use by students.

(14) *Escherichia coli/Micrococcus luteus* mixed broth culture—

Prepare a 24 hour broth culture of *E. coli* as in **(11)**. Prepare a 24 hour broth culture of *M. luteus* by inoculating 100 mL of nutrient broth with a generous loop full of the bacterium from the agar slant. (This is the same as the preparation of broth cultures of *E. coli* and *S. marcescens* in **(11)**. The *M. luteus* culture must, however, be started a day ahead of other cultures; i.e., 2 days before the laboratory period.)

Prepare the mixed culture by aseptically mixing 2.0 mL of *M. luteus* with 1.0 mL of *E. coli* in tubes for student use.

(15) nutrient agar plates—

Dissolve 23 g of dehydrated nutrient agar medium in 1000 mL of distilled water in a 2 liter flask. Cover with foil or a cloth stopper and autoclave at 15 lbs pressure for 15 minutes. Cool to 50° C and pour into sterile Petri dishes (yields 40 plates). Plates should be poured at least 2 days ahead to allow moisture to evaporate. Store the plates upside down (inverted) so that condensation on the lid will not drip onto the agar surface.

(16) agar plate demonstration of viral plaques—

Carolina Biological Supply Company offers a plaque study plates set (# 12-1180) with 4 plates demonstrating T even bacteriophages and 2 demonstrating θX174. (See Ordering Information.)

Alternatively, plates can be prepared as follows:

1. Prepare a 24 hour nutrient broth culture of *E. coli* B and a 24 hour broth culture of T_2 bacteriophage (*coli* phage).

    tryptone broth:

tryptone	10.0 g
calcium chloride ($CaCl_2$)	0.02 g
sodium chloride (NaCl)	5.0 g

    Add distilled water to make 1000 mL.

Prepare tubes of tryptone soft agar as follows:

tryptone	10.0 g
potassium chloride (KCl)	5.0 g
agar	9.0 g

Add distilled water to make 1000 mL

2. Prepare Petri plates of tryptone hard agar as follows

tryptone	10.0 g
calcium chloride ($CaCl_2$)	0.2 g
sodium chloride (NaCl)	5.0 g
agar	11.0 g

Add distilled water to make 1000 mL.

3. Prepare 10 tubes, each containing 9 mL of tryptone broth. Starting with 10 mL of the 24 hour T_2 bacteriophage culture, make serial dilutions: remove 1 mL from the 10 mL culture and place it in the 9 mL of tryptone broth (10^{-1} dilution) and mix; remove 1 mL of this mixture (the 10^{-1} dilution) and transfer it to the next tube of 9 mL (10^{-2} dilution); and so on, until dilutions of 10^{-5}, 10^{-6}, 10^{-7}, 10^{-8}, and 10^{-9} have been made.

4. Melt the soft tryptone agar in tubes by placing them in boiling water and cool them to 45° C. To each of 5 tubes, aseptically add 3 drops of the 24 hour *E. coli* B culture and 1 mL of one of the bacteriophage dilutions so that you will have tubes containing 10^{-5}, 10^{-6}, 10^{-7}, 10^{-8}, and 10^{-9} dilutions.

5. Mix and pour each over plates of tryptone agar to form two-layered plates. Incubate plates in an inverted position for 24 hours at 37° C.

(17) student collection of micrographs—

A collection of these can be obtained from electron microscopy laboratories at nearby universities or can be assembled from out-of-date textbooks. The pictures can be mounted on 5 X 8 cards. Alternatively, locate a good cell biology or ultrastructure text. Purchase the text and photograph the relevant plates. Print 4 X 6 copies in several sets. Be sure to acknowledge the source and do not use them for anything but your own classroom use in order to satisfy copyright laws. Carolina Biological Supply Company offers a series of charts (# 57-9950) of cells and their organelles. This can be substituted for individual picture packets.

V. PREPARATION SUGGESTIONS

Exercise A

The most important aspect of successful coacervate production is a careful adjustment of pH. Students must add only 1 drop of HCl at a time. Be sure to shake the tubes—often the cloudiness disappears. You should try this before your class gets started. Often the pH of the water you start with can exceed the acid requirements. For this reason, adjusting the gum arabic and gelatin solutions to pH 7 is suggested. Adjusting the light for proper viewing with the microscope is also important. Students who have never learned to properly focus the microscope may experience difficulty and will be looking at air bubbles or dirt on the coverslip.

Although the coacervates can be seen without staining, methylene blue, congo red, and neutral red can be used. If you prepare all three stains, different students can compare the results from different stains. These three stains are all "vital" stains and can also be used to stain living material such as protozoans. Apply a drop of stain to a clean glass slide and let the stain dry. Store the slides in a box and when you want to stain live materials, simply add a drop of your culture (i.e. pond water) to the slide. The stain will dissolve slowly and color the organisms. You may wish to try the same technique with coacervates if students experience difficulty with diluting the material by adding stain.

Let's Investigate

The idea of surface to volume ratio, although seemingly simple, often eludes students. This very simple exercise takes only a short period of time and really drives home the point. If students use 8 blocks, have different students arrange them in different ways and compare total surface areas. Have students do some research on the size of most human cells. Approximately how many cells are in the human body (approximately 10^{14})? How much surface area does this represent?

Exercise B (Parts 1, 2, 3, and 4)

This exercise is designed to introduce students to the structure of prokaryotic and eukaryotic cells. Living organisms should be used where possible
   In Part 3, stress to students that slices of potato and carrot should be very thin and the smear of banana tissue should also be spread out very thinly. The chromoplasts of the carrot are easy to see if sections are made just below the epidermis (removing all of the epidermis makes this easier).

Let's Investigate

If students did not experiment with *Elodea* during Laboratory 6, you may wish to have them observe cyclosis as a cellular phenomenon. Students should test whether light, heat, or pH affects the rate of cyclosis. At the end of viewing, students should add a drop of 5-10% NaCl to the *Elodea* and watch the protoplast pull away from the cell wall as water leaves the vacuole of the plant cell.

Exercise C

The human sperm slides will be used a second time (Laboratory 31, Animal Development). The starfish development slide is also needed in Laboratory 31. Rather than using a separate slide of starfish eggs, this slide will suffice. Many developmental stages will be included, but students are intrigued by these and often ask some very interesting questions.

Exercise D (Parts 1 and 2)

Be sure to order agar slants of bacteria far enough ahead to prepare broth cultures. You may decide to have students simply do a transfer between slants and not do broth cultures if students cannot come back to the laboratory in one to two days to observe cultures.
   It is important for students to learn how to make a streak plate. This technique will be used again in Laboratory 16.
   Have available a spray bottle of 10% Clorox and have all students spray the surface of the laboratory bench before and after their work with bacteria.

When students have finished with the Petri dishes, spray their surfaces with bleach. Tape plates and disposable tubes together and autoclave in a brown paper bag before disposal. To dispose of cultures in glass tubes, autoclave and then discard. Wash all glassware with 10% Clorox if not disinfected using the autoclave.

Exercise E

Individually labeled micrographs from a packet of electron micrographs (see Preparation Instructions and Ordering Information) can be placed on the bulletin board in the laboratory. If students cannot identify a particular structure in the micrographs included in the laboratory manual, do not name the structures for them. Rather, send them to the bulletin board to locate the structure by comparison with other micrographs. Students will learn about other structures in addition to the one they are seeking. Those in the laboratory manual include: 1) Golgi body, 2) centrioles, 3) a centriole in cross section, 4) nucleus, 5) mitochondrion, 6) plasmodesmata, and 7) chloroplast.

VI.   ORDERING INFORMATION

gelatin—Carolina Biological, # 86-4670
gum arabic—Carolina Biological, # 86-6108
Parafilm—Carolina Biological, # 21-5600; Fisher, # 13-374-10
pH paper (range 4.5-10)—Carolina Biological, # 89-3942
Pasteur pipettes—Carolina Biological, # 73-6060; Fisher, # 13-678-20C
rubber bulbs—Fisher, # 14-065B
microscope slides (75 X 25)—Carolina Biological, # 63-2000; Fisher, #12-544-1
coverslips (22 X 22 mm)—Carolina Biological, # 63-3015; Fisher, # 12-542B
sodium chloride (NaCl)—Carolina Biological, # 88-8880; Fisher, # S271-500
hydrochloric acid (HCl)—Carolina Biological, # 86-7790; Fisher, # A144-500
methylene blue stain—Carolina Biological, # 87-5684 (powder) or # 87-5913 (solution)
neutral red stain—Carolina Biological, # 87-6830; Fisher, # N129-25
congo red stain—Carolina Biological, # 85-5348; Fisher, # C580-25
dropping bottles—Carolina Biological, # 71-6525; Fisher, # 02-980
Escherichia coli (prepared slide)—Carolina Biological, # Ba048
Staphylococcus aureus (prepared slide)—Carolina Biological, # Ba039
bacterial flagella (prepared slide)—Carolina Biological, # Ba017
Oscillatoria (live)—Carolina Biological, # 15-1865
Nostoc (live)—Carolina Biological, # 15-1847
Cylindrospermum (live)—Carolina Biological, # 15-1755
Elodea—Carolina Biological, #16-2100
Lugol's solution—Carolina Biological, # 87-2793
neuron, cow (prepared slide)—Carolina Biological, # H1660
Stentor (live)—Carolina Biological, # L5
Acetabularia (preserved)—Carolina Biological, # PB45
spermatozoa, human (prepared slide)—Carolina Biological, # H4259
Volvox (live)—Carolina Biological, # 15-2635
starfish development (prepared slide)—Carolina Biological, # E582

nutrient agar (powder form)—Fisher, # B11-472; Carolina Biological, # 78-5300
nutrient broth (powder form)—Fisher, # B11-479; Carolina Biological, # 78-5360
(Bacto) agar* —Fisher, # DF0140; Carolina Biological, # 21-6720 or 21-6721
nutrient agar (tubes)—Carolina Biological, # 82-6100 (125 mL bottle)
nutrient broth (tubes)—Carolina Biological, # 82-6120 (125 mL bottle)
peptone—Carolina Biological, # 79-4260
beef extract—Carolina Biological, # 79-4720
Escherichia coli, nutrient agar slant—Carolina Biological, # 15-5065
Serratia marcescens, nutrient agar slant—Carolina Biological, # 15-5452
Micrococcus luteus, nutrient agar slant—Carolina Biological, # 15-5155
student's collection of electron micrographs—Carolina Biological, # 50-1005

---

* Bacto is a designation used on Difco Laboratories products available through Fisher Scientific, Inc. and Carolina Biological Supply Company.

LABORATORY 8   Osmosis and Diffusion

I.   FOREWORD

This laboratory is designed to introduce students to the principles of both diffusion and osmosis and to the concept of water potential. It consists of several separate exercises to be done individually or in pairs.

II.   TIME REQUIREMENTS

Exercise A—15 minutes
Exercise B (Part 1)—15 minutes
Exercise B (Part 2)—15 minutes
Let's Investigate—25 minutes
Exercise B (Part 3)—15 minutes
Exercise C—45 minutes
Exercise D (Part 1)—75 minutes (waiting period 60 minutes)
Exercise D (Part 2)—demonstration
Exercise D (Part 3)—20 minutes

III.   STUDENT MATERIALS AND EQUIPMENT

	Per Student	Per Pair (2)	Per Group (4)	Per Class (24)
Exercise A				
carmine suspension, dropping bottle (**1**)			1	6
microscope slides, box (75 X 25 mm)	1			24
coverslips, box (22 X 22 mm)	1			24
compound microscope	1			24
Exercise B (Part 1)				
filter paper strips	1			24
phenolphthalein, dropping bottle (**2**)			1	6
ammonium hydroxide (500 mL)				1
500 mL Erlenmeyer flask OR				
250 mL graduated cylinder	1			24
brass cup hooks	1			24
corks (# 16 or 18)	1			24
Exercise B (Part 2)				
250 mL graduated cylinder	1			24
India ink or food coloring, dropping bottle	1			24
Petri dish lid (100 mm)	1			24

	Per Student	Per Pair (2)	Per Group (4)	Per Class (24)

Let's Investigate

same materials as used for Exercise B (Part 2)

Exercise B (Part 3)

	Per Student	Per Pair (2)	Per Group (4)	Per Class (24)
absorbent cotton, roll				1
cheesecloth, package				1
ammonium hydroxide (500 mL)				1
hydrochloric acid, conc. (500 mL)				1
ring stand				1
utility clamp				1
glass tubing (90 cm long X 41 mm diameter)				1

Exercise C

	Per Student	Per Pair (2)	Per Group (4)	Per Class (24)
dialysis tubing, 1 X 12 inch strip (7)	1			12
Pasteur pipette	4			48
Pi-Pump or Propipette	2			24
15% glucose, bottle (3)	1			12
1% starch (4)	1			12
250 mL beaker	1			12
Lugol's reagent (5)	1			12
rubber bands	1			12
Benedict's solution (6)	1			12

Exercise D (Part 1)

	Per Student	Per Pair (2)	Per Group (4)	Per Class (24)
dialysis tubing, 1 X 12 inch strip (7)			6	26
0.2 M sucrose, bottle (8)			1	6
0.4 M sucrose, bottle (8)			1	6
0.6 M sucrose, bottle (8)			1	6
0.8 M sucrose, bottle (8)			1	6
1.0 M sucrose, bottle (8)			1	6
plastic cups			6	36
balance (± 0.1 g)			1	6

Exercise D (Part 2)

	Per Student	Per Pair (2)	Per Group (4)	Per Class (24)
40% sucrose with red food coloring, bottle (200 mL) (9)				1
small glass tubing (68 cm long X 3 mm ID)				1
dialysis tubing (large)				1
one-hole rubber stopper, # 7				1
1000 mL beaker				1
ring stand				1
utility clamp				2

	Per Student	Per Pair (2)	Per Group (4)	Per Class (24)

Exercise D (Part 3)

0.5% NaCl, large specimen bowl (**10**)				1
tap water, large specimen bowl				1
Chara (live, class of 12)				1
Elodea (live, class of 12)				1
Spirogyra (live, class of 30)				1
tap water, dropping bottle			1	6
10% NaCl, dropping bottle (**11**)			1	6
microscope slides, box (75 X 25 mm)	1			24
coverslips, box (22 X 22 mm)	1			24

IV.   PREPARATION OF MATERIALS AND SOLUTIONS

(**1**) carmine suspension—
Add 0.05 g of carmine powder to 100 mL of distilled water.

(**2**) phenolphthalein solution—
Order prepared solution OR weigh 0.5 g phenolphthalein and add 95% ethanol to make 100 mL.

(**3**) 15% glucose—
Weigh 75 g of glucose. Add distilled water to 500 mL.

(**4**) 1% starch—
Weigh 5 g of potato starch. Add distilled water to 500 mL. Heat on low heat while stirring and increase heat until starch solution becomes clear.

(**5**) Lugol's solution (I_2KI)—
Order prepared solution.

(**6**) Benedict's solution—
Order prepared solution.

(**7**) dialysis tubing—
Soak dialysis tubing for at least one hour in distilled water before use. If teaching multiple laboratory sections, you may cut the necessary number of 12 inch pieces in advance and place them in a beaker to soak—be sure to store the beaker overnight in the refrigerator so mold does not grow. Bags can be formed by twisting the ends and tying double knots in each end of the pieces of tubing (string may also be used). Make sure students fill the dialysis bags only half to two-thirds full. If you use a smaller diameter dialysis tubing, adjust the sucrose volume within the tubing (the 15 mL suggested is not a critical amount).

(**8**) sucrose solutions—
Approximately 200 mL will be needed by each group to carry out both parts of the exercise. A liter will provide enough for 5 groups (or 1 group at a certain location for 5 laboratory periods).
1.0 M
Dissolve 342.3 g of sucrose in 1000 mL of distilled water.

0.8 M

Dissolve 274.2 g of sucrose in 1000 mL of distilled water.

0.6 M

Dissolve 205.4 g of sucrose in 1000 mL of distilled water.

0.4 M

Dissolve 136.9 g of sucrose in 1000 mL of distilled water

0.2 M

Dissolve 68.4 g of sucrose in 1000 mL of distilled water.

Alternatively, prepare 3 liters of 1.0 M sucrose and dilute as follows (retain 1000 mL of 1.0 M sucrose):

0.8 M

800 mL of 1.0 M sucrose plus 200 mL of distilled water.

0.6 M

600 mL of 1.0 M sucrose plus 400 mL of distilled water.

0.4 M

400 mL of 1.0 M sucrose plus 600 mL of distilled water.

0.2 M

200 mL of 1.0 M sucrose plus 800 mL of distilled water.

(9) 40% sucrose with red food coloring—

Weigh 40 g of sucrose and add distilled water to 100 mL. Mix well. Add red food coloring until solution is dark red.

(10) 0.5% NaCl—

Weight 2.5 g NaCl and add distilled water to 500 mL. Use to fill dropping bottles.

(11) 10% NaCl—

Mix 10 g NaCl in enough water to make 100 mL. Pour into dropping bottles.

V. PREPARATION SUGGESTIONS

Exercise A

Students who are not adept at using the microscope will experience difficulty observing Brownian motion of carmine particles. You may wish to show this using a microscope attached to a video camera if available. Make sure students are focusing on the solution and not dirt on the coverslip which seems to be the most common source of error.

Exercise B (Part 1)

Use small brass cup hooks screwed into the bottom of the appropriate size cork (to fit either a 500 mL Erlenmeyer flask (# 16) or a 250 mL graduated cylinder (# 18). If hooks are not available, a paper clip can be pulled apart and cut with wire cutters. Both of the U-shaped pieces can then be inserted into the corks. A plastic push-pin tack can also be used if hooks are not available.

Exercise B (Part 2)

Make sure that students place the drop of India ink or food coloring onto the water surface very gently. The amount used should not be very large—a small drop will do.

Let's Investigate

This activity gives students a fast and easy way to check on their skills for making hypotheses and designing experiments. Be sure to ask students to form a null hypothesis as well as a hypothesis that can be supported with data. Students should graph their results. This will give the instructor an opportunity to check graphing skills. The process of diffusion should proceed more quickly in the warmer water. Students may wish to try several temperatures, including water that has been heated to boiling. Make sure containers are made of Pyrex or Kimax if very hot temperatures are used.

Exercise C

Tape a test tube to the side of the bottle containing the 15% glucose and 1% starch solutions. Place a Pasteur pipette into the tube. Make sure that the pipette is provided with a label corresponding to the contents of the bottle.

Soak all dialysis tubing for at least 3 hours or overnight in distilled water prior to use in the laboratory. Strips should be cut 6-8 inches long.

Exercise D (Part 1)

Use plastic cups rather than beakers to avoid glassware cleaning. Dialysis bags containing sucrose solutions should be allowed to sit for at least 60 minutes and up to 3 hours in water. Do not leave overnight unless there is a great deal of excess room in the dialysis bags (at least 3-4 times the volume of the contents). Without this space, the bags containing higher molarities of sucrose will take on enough water to become turgid. Osmotic pressure will then stop the NET flow of water into the bags.

You may wish to have students work in pairs or in groups. You might also want to assign certain molarities to different groups to carry this out as a class experiment and reduce solution preparation time or expense. It is recommended, however, that at least two groups have the same molarities so data will be duplicated.

Tie bags by twisting the ends and placing two knots at each end (string may also be used). Dialysis bag clips are the easiest to use but are an unnecessary expense

To answer question (f) on page 8-13, the Y axis of the graph must be extended below zero. In this case, water would flow out of the bag when placed in sucrose solutions of greater than 0.4 M.

Exercise D (Part 2)

Make a groove around the bottom of a # 7 one-hole rubber stopper approximately 1 cm from the bottom surface. Stretch a piece of soaked large dialysis tubing over the bottom of the cork and secure it by tying a piece of string around the cork so that the string fits into the groove. Fill the bag with red sucrose solution through the hole in the stopper until the bag is completely filled and turgid. Use petroleum jelly to grease the end of a piece of glass tubing that has been calibrated (marked) in cm. The tubing should be 65-68 cm long with an ID of 3 mm. Insert the tube in the hole. From a ring stand, suspend the osmometer by the cork in a 1000 mL beaker of distilled water so that the entire bag is below the surface of the water. Use a clamp to hold the cork onto the ring stand and use a second clamp to keep the glass tubing straight. Set a timer for 15 minute intervals during the laboratory period. One student should check the level of fluid in the osmometer at each 15 minute interval, record the value on the blackboard, and reset the timer.

Exercise D (Part 3)

Any of several live materials can be used to demonstrate plasmolysis and loss of turgor in procedure direction (1). Lettuce and celery are easily obtained. The green alga *Chara* is ideal. Students can take it from tap water and place it in a 0.5% NaCl solution and watch it wilt, and then place it back into water and watch it "pop" back into shape almost immediately.

VI.   ORDERING INFORMATION

Lugol's solution (I$_2$KI)—Carolina Biological, # 87-2795

Benedict's reagent—Fisher, # LC-11650-1; Carolina Biological, # 84-7111 (500 mL)

ammonium hydroxide—Fisher, # A-669-500 (500 mL); Carolina Biological, # 84-4010 (500 mL)

dialysis tubing, 32 mm—Fisher, #08-667D; Carolina Biological, # 68-4212 (10 ft)

phenolphthalein—Carolina Biological, # 87-9963 (120 mL); # 87-9940 (powder)

Elodea (live)—Carolina Biological, # 16-2100 (per 12 students)

Chara (live)—Carolina Biological, # 15-1240 (per 12 students, available May until mid-October)

Spirogyra (live)—Carolina Biological, # 15-2525 (per 12)

glass tubing—Fisher, # 11-365CC; Carolina Biological, # 71-1174

utility clamp—Fisher, # 05-768-10, or Carolina Biological, # 70-7376 or 70-7312

Pasteur disposable pipettes—Fisher, # 13-678-20C, or Carolina Biological, # 73-6060

cork borer—Fisher, # 07-845B

TesTape—Carolina Biological, # 89-3840

LABORATORY 9   Enzymes

I.   FOREWORD

The activities in this laboratory are divided into two major exercises. The first exercise examines the effects of temperature, pH, substrate, and enzyme concentration on enzyme activity. Data can be recorded from qualitative observations. It is also possible to record data quantitatively using the Spectronic 20. During this laboratory, students work in groups of four (see suggestions). The team approach should allow plenty of time for cheese making in the second exercise.

II.   TIME REQUIREMENTS

Exercise A (Parts 1, 2, 3, and 4)—90 minutes
Let's Investigate—30 minutes
Exercise B—60 minutes

III.   STUDENT MATERIALS AND EQUIPMENT

	Per Student	Per Pair (2)	Per Group (4)	Per Class (24)
Exercise A (materials common to Parts 1-4)				
test tube rack	1			24
wax pencil	1			24
masking tape			1	6
catecholase potato extract, dropping bottle (**1**)			2	12
0.1% catechol, dropping bottle (**2**)			1	6
pH 7 phosphate buffer, bottle (250 mL) (**3**)			1	6
5 mL pipette (with buffer)			1	6
small squares of Parafilm or wax paper (container with 100 pieces)			1	6
5 mL pipette (with buffer)			1	6
Pi-Pump			4	24
Spectronic 20			1	6
Spectronic 20 cuvettes or test tubes			18	108
Exercise A (Part 1—individual A)				
test tube			3	18
150 mL beaker			2	12
hot plate			1	6
thermometer			1	6
ice bucket with shaved ice			1	6

	Per Student	Per Pair (2)	Per Group (4)	Per Class (24)

Exercise A (Part 2—individual B)

	Per Student	Per Pair (2)	Per Group (4)	Per Class (24)
test tube			5	30
0.1 M phosphate buffer, pH 4, bottle (**4**)			1	6
0.1 M phosphate buffer, pH 6, bottle (**5**)			1	6
0.1 M phosphate buffer, pH 8, bottle (**6**)			1	6
0.1 M borax-NaOH buffer, pH 10, bottle (**7**)			1	6
5 mL pipettes (with buffers)			4	24

Exercise A (Part 3—individual C)

	Per Student	Per Pair (2)	Per Group (4)	Per Class (24)
test tube			4	24

Exercise A (Part 4)

	Per Student	Per Pair (2)	Per Group (4)	Per Class (24)
test tube			6	36

Let's Investigate

	Per Student	Per Pair (2)	Per Group (4)	Per Class (24)
apple sauce (25 mL)			1	6
distilled water, bottle			1	6
pectinase, bottle (**8**)			1	6
spatula			2	12
cheesecloth (4 thicknesses)			2	12
250 mL beaker			2	12
100 mL graduated cylinder			2	12

Exercise B

	Per Student	Per Pair (2)	Per Group (4)	Per Class (24)
250 mL graduated cylinder (sterile)				1
preripened milk (250 mL) (**9**)		1		24
rennilase, bottle (sterile) (**10**)				1
1 mL syringe		1		12
sterile glass rod		1		12
cheesecloth (4 thicknesses, sterile)		1		12
water bath				2
sterile Petri dish (100 mm)		1		12
1000 mL beaker (sterile)		1		12
1000 mL beaker (nonsterile)		1		12
thermometer (clean)		1		12

IV.   PREPARATION OF MATERIALS AND SOLUTIONS

(**1**)   catecholase (potato extract)—
Put 75 g of diced potato into a blender, add 500 mL of distilled water and blend for 2 minutes at high speed. After blending, strain the solution through four thicknesses of cheesecloth. Immediately dispense the solution into dropping bottles and stopper them

tightly since the presence of oxygen will allow the enzyme to work and will lead to darkening of the solution. Prepare this in class immediately prior to use.

(2) 0.1% catechol—

Weigh 0.2 g catechol. Add distilled water to 200 mL. Dispense into dropping bottles.

(3) - (7) buffers—

pH 4—0.1 M potassium phthalate-NaOH buffer

Part A—Dissolve 10.21 g of potassium hydrogen phthalate in 300 mL of distilled water. Bring the solution up to 500 mL with distilled water.

Part B—Mix 500 mL of potassium hydrogen phthalate solution, Part A, with 499 mL of distilled water and 1 mL of 0.1 N HCl to make one liter of buffer.

pH 6, 7, and 8—stock solutions (0.1 M sodium phosphate buffer)

A—0.1 M solution of sodium phosphate (monobasic), $NaH_2PO_4 \cdot H_2O$. Weigh 13.8 g $NaH_2PO_4 \cdot H_2O$. Make up to 1000 mL with distilled water.

B—0.1 M solution of sodium phosphate (dibasic), $Na_2HPO_4 \cdot 7H_2O$. Weigh 26.825 g $Na_2HPO_4 \cdot 7H_2O$ or 35.85 g $Na_2HPO_4 \cdot 12H_2O$. Make up to 1000 mL with distilled water.

for pH 6, mix 877 mL (**A**) and 123 mL (**B**)

for pH 7, mix 390 mL (**A**) and 610 mL (**B**)

for pH 8, mix 53 mL (**A**) and 947 mL (**B**)

pH 10—0.1 M borax-NaOH buffer

Part A—Dissolve 3.73 g KCl and 3.09 g boric acid into 300 mL of distilled water. Then bring the solution up to 500 mL with distilled water. Heat the solution to dissolve boric acid.

Part B—Mix 500 mL of KCl and boric acid solution (Part A) with 437 mL of 0.1 N NaOH and 63 mL of distilled water to make 1 liter.

(8) pectinase—

Order in liquid form. Available from Carolina Biological Supply Company (see Ordering Information),

(9) preripened milk—

Twelve to fifteen hours before laboratory, mix 10 mL of buttermilk into each 1000 mL of whole milk. Prepare 3 liters total. Into each of 12 sterile 1000 mL beakers, put 250 mL of milk to ripen. Cover each beaker with cheesecloth and leave at room temperature. Do not cover the beakers with an air-tight seal—cheesecloth should remain loose.

(10) rennilase—

Mix 1 mL of rennin emporase into 19 mL of cold tap water.

V. PREPARATION SUGGESTIONS

Exercise A (Parts 1, 2, 3, and 4)

The catecholase solution from potatoes needs to be prepared for each class immediately before use. As soon as it is made, it should be stoppered quickly.

For this exercise, groups of four students work as a team. One student examines the effects of temperature, a second studies pH, a third works with substrate concentration, and a fourth student investigates the effects of enzyme concentration. The tests result in a series of colored solutions. These should be saved and shared during discussion of the experimental results among the group members. Each student should explain the procedure used, demonstrate the results, and explain his or her conclusions.

Exercise A can be completed quantitatively by using the Spectronic 20 if available. Directions for using the Spectronic 20 are found in Appendix IV. Students will need to be familiar with this instrument for Laboratory 11. If using the Spectronic 20, it is important to make sure that students realize that their blanks must be made up before they add catechol to their experimental tubes and the timed reactions start. Otherwise, the experimental reactions will be too far along to read results accurately in comparison to their blanks.

If using the Spectronic 20:

For Exercise A, Part 1, use a tube containing 3 mL of pH 7 phosphate buffer, 10 drops of potato juice, and 10 drops of water as a blank. At 2 minute intervals, determine the absorbance for the three samples at 10°, 24°, and 50°.

For Exercise A, Part 2, prepare blanks for pH values of 4, 6, 7, 8, and 10. Fill each tube with 3 mL buffer, 10 drops of potato juice, and 10 drops of water. Use 10 drops of catechol instead of water for the experimental tubes at each pH. At the end of 5 minutes, read the absorbance for each of the experimental tubes using appropriate blanks.

For Exercise A, Part 3, prepare blanks for tubes A-D as follows: Tube A, pH 7 phosphate buffer; Tube B—3 mL plus 25 drops buffer, add 5 drops potato juice; Tube C—3 mL plus 20 drops buffer, add 10 drops potato juice; Tube D—3 mL plus 10 drops buffer, add 20 drops potato juice. Read tubes (using appropriate blanks) at 2 minute intervals. Shake tubes between readings.

For Exercise A, Part 4, use a tube containing 5 mL of pH 7 phosphate buffer, 24 drops of distilled water, and 30 drops of potato extract as a blank. Read absorbance of the 6 tubes at 2 minute intervals.

Note that blanks use potato juice because the floculence of the potato juice solution tends to scatter light which must be corrected for in the procedure. You should encourage some discussion on the use of blanks and how to decide what components of the experimental tubes should be included in the blanks.

It is best to use a wide range bulb in the spectrophotometer. Recall that tubes are to be read at 420 nm. Note that most reactions can be carried out in regular test tubes and the contents can be transferred to Spectronic cuvettes. However, this is messy and students often end up confused with solutions in the wrong tubes. Since the accuracy of matched cuvettes is not necessary for proper interpretation of results from these experiments, it is easier to use Pyrex or Kimax tubes (13 X 100 mm) which are relatively inexpensive and fit into the Spectronic 20. Throughout this laboratory manual, we will refer to these tubes as Spectronic 20 tubes. (Always remember to wipe tubes off before inserting them into the machine!) See ordering information.

If only Exercise A is to done during the laboratory period, then several stations may be set up for each of the four parts and each student can do all four. Alternatively, students can work in pairs.

Class discussion of results is helpful at the end of the laboratory period.

Let's Investigate

This investigation demonstrates the "juice release" action of the enzyme pectinase. Students will have an opportunity to apply what was learned in Exercise A to a product used on a daily basis and prepared by using enzymes. Students should be encouraged to bring their favorite juice to class or to perhaps compare two brands of the same juice. This investigation can be carried out during the laboratory period or it makes an excellent after-class, extra-credit collaborative project that lends itself to using all aspects of the scientific process as well as preparing data in the form of graphs for laboratory reports. All materials for this experiment can also be purchased as part of a Fruit Juice Release Biokit from Carolina Biological Supply Company (# 20-2314)

Exercise B

This exercise is fun for the students and also teaches some practical applications for enzymes. During the preceding week, tell students to bring seasoning (garlic, seasoned salt, pepper, salt, caraway or sesame seeds, etc.) to class. Bring soda and crackers as well.

Make sure that all cheese glassware is either sterile or extremely clean since contamination is a possibility. We keep special glassware just for this laboratory, sterilizing it both after the laboratory is completed and before we do it again the following semester.

By wrapping the cheese in cheesecloth and pressing it into a Petri dish, the consistency is very much like that of a soft, spreadable cheese. You can put a rubber band around the Petri dish and refrigerate it until the following week, but this enhances the possibility of contamination and is not recommended.

To make the activity more meaningful, instructors should be prepared to discuss other examples of enzyme activity which students may be aware of— yogurt making, action of meat tenderizer, enzyme detergents, junket making, cottage cheese production, etc.

VI.   ORDERING INFORMATION

rennin emporase—Dairyland Food Lab, Waukesha, WI 53187
catechol—Fisher, # P370-500; Carolina Biological # 88—3540 (100 g)
potassium hydrogen phthalate—Fisher, # P243-100; Carolina Biological, # 88-3470 (500 g)
sodium borate, tetra (Borax)—Fisher, # S248-500; Carolina Biological, # 84-8570
sodium phosphate (monobasic)—Fisher, # S369-500; Carolina Biological, # 89-1350 (125 g)
sodium phosphate (dibasic)—Fisher, # S373-500; Carolina Biological, # 89-1370
0.1 N NaOH—Fisher, # SS276-1; Carolina Biological, # 88-9551 (500 mL)
pectinase—Carolina Biological, # 20-2380 (100 mL)
Juice Release Biokit—Carolina Biological, # 20-2315
Spectronic 20—Fisher # 07-143-1
wide range phototube and filter—Fisher, # 07-144-12
Spectronic 20 tubes:
    Pyrex (100 X 13 mm)—Fisher, # 14-957C; Carolina Biological, # 73-1408
    Kimax (100 X 13 mm)—Fisher, # 14-923D; Carolina Biological, # 73-1408

LABORATORY 10   Energetics, Fermentation, and Respiration

I.   FOREWORD

This laboratory introduces students to both fermentation and cellular respiration using two major experiments which could be done on separate days if desired. Students will have the opportunity to investigate the reactions of glycolysis and the Kreb's cycle as well as the effects of noncompetitive and competitive inhibition of enzyme activity.

II.   TIME REQUIREMENTS

Exercise A (Parts 1, 2, 3, and 4)—60 minutes
Exercise B—60 minutes
Let's Investigate—45 minutes
Exercise C—10 minutes
Exercise D—20 minutes

III.   STUDENT MATERIALS AND EQUIPMENT

	Per Student	Per Pair (2)	Per Group (4)	Per Class (24)
Exercise A (Part 1)				
stock yeast solution, Erlenmeyer flask (250 mL) (1)				4
microscope slides, box (22 X 25 mm)			1	6
coverslips, box (22 X 22 mm)			1	6
compound microscope	1			24
neutral red, dropping bottle (2)			1	6
incubator, 37° C				1
Exercise A (Part 2)				
sugar and yeast suspension, flask (500 mL) (3)				1
10% sucrose, flask (500 mL) (4)				1
bromothymol blue, flask or cylinder (500 mL) (5)				2
one-hole rubber stopper (# 6 1/2)				4
bent glass tubing ("U")				2
Exercise A (Part 3)				
fermentation apparatus (6)			1	12
wax pencil			1	12
yeast suspension, tube (10 mL) (7)			1	12
boiled yeast suspension, tube (10 mL) (8)			1	12
5% glucose, bottle (25 mL) (9)			1	12
5% sucrose, bottle (25 mL) (10)			1	12

48

	Per Student	Per Pair (2)	Per Group (4)	Per Class (24)

Exercise A (Part 4)

	Per Student	Per Pair (2)	Per Group (4)	Per Class (24)
test tubes	1			24
24 hr yeast culture (11)				1
10 mL pipette (to deliver, with Pi-Pump)				1
10% sodium hydroxide (NaOH) (12)			1	6
Lugol's reagent (13)			1	6
5 mL pipette (to deliver)			2	12
test tube rack		1		12

Exercise B

	Per Student	Per Pair (2)	Per Group (4)	Per Class (24)
test tubes			6	36
test tube rack			1	6
Spectronic 20			1	6
Spectronic 20 tubes			6	36
lima bean mitochondria extract (14)				1
blender				1
1 mM DPIP, bottle (15)			1	6
0.2 M phosphate buffer, pH 7.2, bottle (16)			1	6
0.25 M succinate, bottle (17)			1	6
mercuric chloride ($HgCl_2$), bottle (18)			1	6
0.5 M malonic acid (19)			1	6

Let's Investigate

same as Exercise B, $HgCl_2$ not necessary

Exercise C

	Per Student	Per Pair (2)	Per Group (4)	Per Class (24)
vacuum (Thermos) bottle				1
lima bean seeds (100 g)				1
thermometer				1
cotton (roll)				1
one-hole rubber stopper (to fit vacuum bottle)				1

Exercise D

	Per Student	Per Pair (2)	Per Group (4)	Per Class (24)
soaked corn seeds, live (20)				200
soaked corn seeds, boiled (20)				200
tetrazolium (2, 3, 5-triphenyl-tetrazolium), dropping bottle (21)			1	6
Petri dish (100 mm)	1			24
dissecting needles	2			48

IV. PREPARATION OF MATERIALS AND SOLUTIONS

(1) stock yeast solution—

Prepare 1 liter of 10% molasses or syrup solution (100 mL syrup, 900 mL distilled water) and dispense 200 mL of the solution into each of three 250 mL Erlenmeyer flasks until they are half full. Add 2 g Fleischmann's dried yeast and 0.5 g peptone to each flask. Cotton stopper all flasks and refrigerate.

1. Approximately 12 hr before the start of the laboratory period, place one 250 mL flask in a 37° C oven and incubate for at least 12 hr. Keep stoppered with a cotton stopper. This will be used for Exercise A, Part 1.

2. Approximately 2-3 hr prior to the beginning of the laboratory, place one flask in a 37° C oven and warm it for several hours. This solution will be used for Exercise A, Part 2.

3. Approximately 24 hr before the start of the laboratory, place one 250 mL flask in a 37° C oven and incubate for at least 24 hours. Keep stoppered. This will be used for Exercise A, Part 4.

(2) neutral red—

Weigh out 0.2 g of neutral red. Add 100% (absolute) ethanol to make 100 mL.

(3) sugar and yeast suspension, flask—

Same as stock yeast solution prepared in **(1)**, step 2.

(4) 10% sucrose—

Weigh out 10 g sucrose. Add distilled water to make 100 mL.

(5) bromothymol blue—

Order prepared (0.04% solution) or grind 0.05 g bromothymol blue powder in 8 mL 0.01 N NaOH and add distilled water to make 125 mL of indicator solution.

(6) fermentation apparatus—

The Carolina Biological Supply Company's Basic Fermentation Biokit can be purchased once and then used year after year with new yeast purchased at the grocery store.

(7) and (8) yeast suspension—

Add two packages of dry yeast to 100 mL of warm tap water and mix. Make approximately 5 minutes before use. Boil a 10 mL sample for 5 minutes. Make sure that the yeast suspension itself is actually boiling.

(9) 5% glucose—

Dissolve 5 g glucose in 100 mL of distilled water. Each group will need approximately 20-25 mL.

(10) 5% sucrose—

Dissolve 5 g sucrose in 100 mL of distilled water. Each group will need approximately 10-25 mL.

(11) 24 hr. yeast culture—

See **(1)**, part 3.

(12) 10% NaOH—

Weigh 10 g NaOH. Add distilled water to make 100 mL.

(13) Lugol's solution—

Order prepared (Carolina Biological, # 87-2793) or dissolve 10 g potassium iodide in 100 mL distilled water and add 5 g of iodine (handle carefully—do not breathe fumes!).

(14) lima bean mitochondria extract—

Materials:

Homogenization medium—prepare 100 mL/class. Weigh out 13.69 g sucrose and add 0.2 M phosphate buffer (pH 7.2) to 100 mL. See **(16)** for phosphate buffer recipe. Readjust pH to 7.2.

Procedure:

Prepare extract in the classroom immediately prior to use. Soak 50 g white baby lima beans (obtain from grocery store) in tap water overnight. Keep in refrigerator. When ready to use, pour out the water. Obtain 50 g of the wet lima beans and put them into an electric blender. Add 100 mL homogenization medium. Homogenize 3 minutes at top speed. Filter through cheesecloth. Dispense 10-15 mL into each of six 50 mL beakers and give one beaker of extract to each group.

Boil a small amount (approximately 10 mL) for 5 minutes.

(15) 1 mM DPIP (or DCPIP, 2 4 dichlorophenol-indophenol)—

Dissolve 0.29 g DPIP in enough distilled water to make 1000 mL.

(16) 0.2 M phosphate buffer, pH 7.2—

Solution A. 0.2 M KH_2PO_4

Dissolve 27.22 g KH_2PO_4 in enough distilled water to make 1000 mL.

Solution B. 0.2 M KH_2PO_4

Dissolve 34.84 g K_2HPO_4 in enough distilled water to make 1000 mL.

For 1 liter of buffer, mix 280 mL of solution A plus 720 mL of solution B. Test pH and adjust with either 0.1 N NaOH or 0.1 HCl if necessary.

(17) 0.25 M succinate (succinic acid solution)—

Dissolve 29.5 g succinic acid and 15 g NaOH in 500 mL distilled water. Add distilled water to make 1000 mL and adjust pH to 7.0 using 2 N NaOH..

(18) mercuric chloride ($HgCl_2$) (0.01%)—

Dissolve 0.1 g $HgCl_2$ in 10 mL distilled water. Dilute 1:10 with distilled water. (Follow school protocol for disposal of hazardous chemicals—see below.)

(19) 0.5 M malonate (malonic acid solution)—

Dissolve 52 g malonic acid and 42 g NaOH in 500 mL distilled water. Add distilled water to 1000 mL and adjust pH to 7.0.

(20) corn seeds—

Soak corn seeds overnight in tap water. Boil half of the seeds for 15 minutes to kill embryos. Mark one set A and the other B.

(21) tetrazolium, 0.1%—

Weigh 1 g tetrazolium. Make up to 1 liter with distilled water.

V.   PREPARATION SUGGESTIONS

Exercise A (Part 1)

Yeast cultures for parts 1, 2, and 4 can all be prepared ahead and in the same manner.

Exercise A (Part 2)

In preparing the apparatus for part 2, a piece of glass tubing can be bent into a "U" to go from the yeast suspension or 10% sucrose flask to the flask of bromothymol blue. If glass tubing is not available, a piece of Tygon tubing will also work. Set this exercise up as a demonstration only.

Exercise A (Part 3)

The fermentation apparatus gives dependable results. This is a new design for the apparatus. If you have the old style apparatus, simply follow directions included in the kit. For the old style apparatus, it is best to fill the apparatus beneath water in a dishpan.

With the new style apparatus, students may have difficulty discerning the line that marks the top of the yeast solution in the small vial. If this is the case, carefully move the small vial sideways until it is up against the wall of the larger vial.

Exercise A (Part 4)

This reaction is fairly touchy. The yeast suspension must be at least 24 hours old to have enough alcohol in it so that the reaction is positive. Gentle shaking of tubes from side to side is enough for mixing.

Exercise B

Be sure to put directions for using the Bausch and Lomb Spectronic 20 next to the machines. It would be wise to have students practice using the Spectronic 20 before using it in this exercise. If not enough Spectronic 20 machines are available, split the laboratory into two groups of students and have half do Exercise A, Part 3, while the other half completes this exercise.

Results will be more precise if round-bottom cuvettes are used, but we get excellent results with plain Pyrex or Kimax glass tubes (see ordering information).

If the preparation of lima beans it too viscous, dilute it with pH 7 phosphate buffer. This may be particularly necessary with the boiled suspension in which denatured proteins tend to form a viscous mass.

Results will be best if two students sit on either side of the machine. One adds succinate and inverts the tube to mix it. The person reading the Spectronic 20 wipes finger marks off the tube and inserts it into the machine. A person standing behind the reader checks the reading. The person on the other side of the machine records the results.

$HgCl_2$ acts as a non-competitive inhibitor of the enzyme. This can be discussed further with the students if desired.

Please note that $HgCl_2$ is a regulated hazardous chemical and its disposal must be dealt with in the proper fashion. Have students place all tubes containing $HgCl_2$ in a labeled test-tube rack at a designated area. Wearing gloves, the instructor should pour the contents of the tubes into a milk bottle containing vermiculite. Label the bottle as to the type and amount of waste it contains (each tube will contain approximately 0.0003 g $HgCl_2$). Use a chromic acid bath to wash glassware—use test tube holders to dip the tubes into a large beaker of chromic acid wash. After washing, prepare the chromic acid for disposal and label it as containing trace amounts of mercury. Have both bottles of waste disposed of according to school regulations.

Chromic acid wash:

Make saturated potassium dichromate ($K_2Cr_2O_3$) by adding crystals to water until no more material dissolves. Add 90 mL saturated potassium dichromate to a 9 lb (4 liter) bottle of concentrated sulfuric acid (H_2SO_4). Place in glass container for wash. Dispose of the chromic acid wash in accordance with hazardous chemical regulations at your institution.

If you do not wish to use $HgCl_2$, you can run the experiment quite successfully using malonate. Malonate is a competitive inhibitor rather than a noncompetitive inhibitor like $HgCl_2$.

Let's Investigate

Since malonate is a competitive inhibitor of succinic dehydrogenase, increasing the amount of substrate (succinate) will overcome the effects of malonate. The more succinate present, the more likely the enzyme is to bind to succinate rather than malonate. Students can use the same procedure as that used for Exercise B, tube 5. Simply add increasing amounts of succinate to a series of tubes, keeping 0.2 mL malonate in all tubes. Be sure to adjust amounts of phosphate buffer to make the amounts of material in all tubes equal.

Students may wish to explore whether the same type of increase in substrate could overcome the inhibitory effects of $HgCl_2$. Since $HgCl_2$ is a non-competitive inhibitor, increasing the succinate concentration will not overcome the effects of the inhibition. Be sure that $HgCl_2$ is disposed of properly if students elect to test $HgCl_2$ effects as well as the effects of malonate

Exercise C

Soak lima bean seeds overnight and place them in moist cotton in the Thermos. Set up the vacuum bottle at least 3-4 days ahead of the laboratory period and record the temperature at 3-4 hr intervals (skip nights). Place graphed temperature data next to the Thermos when placed on demonstration.

Exercise D

Tetrazolium is a poison and should be handled carefully. The results of this experiment are very obvious and even help students locate the embryo of a corn seed more easily.

If cut seeds are placed cut surface down, the embryos can be viewed by looking through the bottom of the Petri dish if glass or plastic Petri dishes are used.

VI. ORDERING INFORMATION

peptone—Carolina Biological, # 79-4260
bromothymol blue—Carolina Biological, # 84-9163 (0.04%)
neutral red (1%)—Carolina Biological, # 87-6853
Fleischmann's dry yeast—grocery store; Carolina Biological, # 17-3234
basic fermentation kit—Carolina Biological, # 20-2200
Lugol's reagent—Carolina Biological, # 87-2793

DPIP—Carolina Biological, # 86-8600; Fisher, # S 286-5

succinate (succinic acid)—Fisher, # A294-500; Carolina Biological, # 89-2830 (500 g)

Spectronic 20 tubes:

    Pyrex (13 X 100 mm), Fisher # 14-957C

    Kimax (13 X 100 mm), Fisher # 14-923D

round cuvettes (13 X 100 mm), Fisher # 14-385-900B; Carolina Biological, # 73-1408

tetrazolium (2, 3, 5 triphenyl tetrazolium chloride), Fisher # T413-10; Carolina Biological, # 89-6930

malonate (malonic acid)—Fisher, # 170-100

sulfuric acid—Fisher, # A298-212

potassium dichromate ($K_2Cr_2O_7$)—Fisher, # LC 18950-1

LABORATORY 11   Photosynthesis

I.   FOREWORD

The progression of exercises in this laboratory allows students to first examine the effects of light intensity and light quality on photosynthesis. After studying the absorption of light by different pigments, an action spectrum is generated. The final exercise investigates how plants use trapped light energy for synthesis of photosynthetic products. Exercises can be split up to be done on separate days if desired.

II.   TIME REQUIREMENTS

Exercise A (Part 1)—class exercise; data collected at intervals
Exercise A (Part 2)—15 minutes
Exercise A (Part 3)—45 minutes
Exercise A (Part 4)—30 minutes
Exercise B (Part 1)—30 minutes
Exercise B (Part 2)—45 minutes
Let's Investigate—10 minutes
Exercise C—30 minutes
Let's Investigate—20 minutes
Let's Investigate—20 minutes (one week investigation)

III.   STUDENT MATERIALS AND EQUIPMENT

	Per Student	Per Pair (2)	Per Group (4)	Per Class (24)
Exercise A (Part 1—as class exercise)				
0.2% sodium bicarbonate (NaHCO₃) (1)				1
phenol red, bottle (2)				1
drinking straw				1
Elodea, sprig (see 1)				5
test tubes, large				5
aluminum foil				1
ring stand				5
3-prong clamp				5
photoflood lamp (150 w)				5
battery jars				5
meter stick				1
Exercise A (Part 2)				
equilateral or 90° right angle glass prism				1
slide projector				1
slit slide (3)				1

	Per Student	Per Pair (2)	Per Group (4)	Per Class (24)

Exercise A (Part 3)

	Per Student	Per Pair (2)	Per Group (4)	Per Class (24)
ring stand			1	6
photoflood lamp (150 w)			1	6
meter stick			1	6
2 liter beaker			1	6
Petri dish covered with colored filter (4)			1	6
250 mL side arm flask				1
1 hole rubber stopper (# 6 1/2)				1
fresh spinach				1
cork borer, #3			1	6
paper towels or Styrofoam board			1	6
vacuum tubing				1
vacuum pump, Nalgene				1

Exercise B (Part 1)

	Per Student	Per Pair (2)	Per Group (4)	Per Class (24)
chromatography paper (5)				1
capillary pipette	1			24
stoppered test tube, large			1	6
chromatography solvent, bottle (6)				1
chloroplast pigment extract (7)				1
test tube rack				1

Exercise B (Part 2)

	Per Student	Per Pair (2)	Per Group (4)	Per Class (24)
xanthophyll pigments, bottle (8)				1
chlorophyll a, bottle (8)				1
chlorophyll b, bottle (8)				1
carotenoids, bottle (8)				1
solvent blank for chlorophyll b and xanthophylls (8)				1
solvent blank for carotenoids and chlorophyll a (8)				1
Spectronic 20			1	6
Spectronic 20 tubes			1	6

Let's Investigate

	Per Student	Per Pair (2)	Per Group (4)	Per Class (24)
2 flats wheat seedlings (grown in dark and light) (9)				1

Exercise C

	Per Student	Per Pair (2)	Per Group (4)	Per Class (24)
variegated Coleus plant (10)				2
hot plate			1	6
250 mL beaker			1	6
hot 70% ethanol, bottle			1	6
Lugol's solution (I_2KI), dropping bottle (11)			1	6

	Per Student	Per Pair (2)	Per Group (4)	Per Class (24)

Let's Investigate

	Per Student	Per Pair (2)	Per Group (4)	Per Class (24)
potato				1
onion				1
Lugol's solution (I₂KI), dropping bottle (**11**)			1	6
test tube	3			72
Benedict's reagent, bottle (**12**)			1	6
pipette (2 mL)			1	6

Let's Investigate

	Per Student	Per Pair (2)	Per Group (4)	Per Class (24)
geranium plant			1	6
aluminum foil (piece)	1			24
scissors		1		12
alcohol (50 mL)	1			24
Lugol's solution (I₂KI), dropping bottle (**11**)			1	6
beaker	1			24
hot plate			1	6
forceps	1			24

IV. PREPARATION OF MATERIALS AND SOLUTIONS

(**1**) 0.2% sodium bicarbonate ($NaHCO_3$)—

Weigh 2.0 g $NaHCO_3$. Add distilled water to make 1 liter. Place shoots of *Elodea* in an enameled or glass pan containing 0.2% sodium bicarbonate. Place the tray under a good light source (window sill if possible) and aerate the water using a small fish-tank aerator. Soak *Elodea* for several hours before use.

(**2**) phenol red (0.1% stock solution)—

Dissolve 0.2 g phenol red in distilled water to make 100 mL of phenol red stock solution.

(**3**) slit slide—

Take a 35 X 38 mm piece of black paper or an exposed and developed piece of 35 mm film and make a slit in it, 1-2 mm wide. Mount this in a 2 X 2 slide mount.

(**4**) Petri dishes covered with colored filters—

Materials:

Filters— daylight blue # 851

medium green # 874

medium red (2 layers) #823

Procedure:

Cover the bottom and sides of the Petri dishes with black plastic (electrician's) tape. Cut circles from the large sheets of filters and cover the top of the Petri dish, taping the filter on with black tape around the sides. Be sure to use two layers of red filters.

(**5**) chromatography paper—

Use Whatman # 1 filter paper for chromatography. Cut strips 90 mm long for 100 mm tubes. This should give enough of an end to bend over and tack to the cork. Cut one end into a point so that the tapered portion is approximately 15-20 mm of the length of the strip.

(6) chromatography solvent—

For paper chromatography, use 9 parts petroleum ether to 1 part acetone. (**Caution**: this is a highly flammable mixture!)

(7) chloroplast pigment extract—

Use fresh spinach. Place 10 - 20 g of spinach in 50 mL of 100% acetone. Add a pinch of $CaCO_3$ to prevent Mg^{2+} loss from chlorophyll. Use a mortar and pestle to extract the green chlorophyll pigment. The extract should be dark green.

(8) pigment extracts for action spectrum—

You may wish to purchase the following extracts instead of separating your own as outlined below. If this is the case, order the following from Sigma Chemical Company: chlorophyll a, # C6144; chlorophyll b, # C5878; xanthophyll, # 6250; carotene, # C0126.

To prepare pigments from spinach, proceed as follows:

WORK UNDER A FUME HOOD

Gather together the following materials:

Chemicals and Solutions—

    acetone
    $CaCO_3$
    petroleum ether
    methanol
    diethyl ether
    30% KOH in methanol (30 g KOH: add methanol to 100 mL)

CAUTION: Petroleum ether and acetone are highly flammable solvents. Keep them cool and away from fire. Use only analytical grade petroleum ether. Chloroform is a carcinogen: be sure to dispose of it and other halogenated hydrocarbons using proper procedures approved by your institution.

Materials and Equipment—

    spinach (fresh) or parsley (dried)
    blender
    Buchner funnel and filter paper
    side arm filter flask
    aspirator or vacuum pump
    separatory funnel
    2 125 mL Erlenmeyer flasks
    1 100 mL graduated cylinders
    4 screw top test tubes

Procedure:

1. Place 3 g dried parsley in 40 mL 80% acetone or 10 g fresh spinach in 50 mL 100% acetone (latter preferred).
2. Add a pinch of $CaCO_3$ to prevent Mg^{2+} loss from chloroplasts.
3. Homogenize in blender for 3 minutes, top speed.
4. Vacuum filter through Buchner funnel to remove debris.
5. Readjust volume of filtrate to 40 mL.
6. Place in separatory funnel containing 60 mL petroleum ether.

7. Add 70 mL water to the pigment mixture by pouring the water down the side of the funnel.
8. Stopper and rotate slowly until the upper layer contains nearly all of the chlorophyll. Gas pressure will rise in the funnel—unstopper and vent carefully.
9. Permit the layers to separate.
10. Drain off the lower layer (acetone) and discard. The upper layer (petroleum ether) now contains the chlorophyll (all chloroplast pigments).
11. Add 20 mL distilled water to wash the petroleum ether and remove any traces of acetone. Do this twice.
12. Remove 5 mL of the petroleum ether-chlorophyll layer and put it in a test tube. Allow this to evaporate down to get a very concentrated extract (several hours or less). Stopper when three-fourths of the fluid has evaporated. This chlorophyll extract can be used for chromatography.
13. Add 50 mL of 92% methanol (92 mL methanol, 8 mL distilled water) to the petroleum ether extract and mix. Do not breathe the solvents.
14. Chlorophyll b and xanthophylls are polar enough to dissolve in the methanol while carotenes and chlorophyll a will remain in the petroleum ether (upper layer).
15. Draw off the two layers into two separate 125 mL flasks. Save the upper petroleum ether layer containing carotenes and chlorophyll a.
16. Place 50 mL of the bottom methanol layer (chlorophyll b and xanthophylls) back into the funnel and add 50 mL of diethyl ether (VERY FLAMMABLE and EXPLOSIVE!).
17. Add approximately 25 mL of distilled water, 5 mL at a time down the side of the funnel. Mix each 5 mL portion by inverting the funnel. This will remove the methanol, but the chlorophyll b and xanthophylls will remain in the upper ethyl-ether layer.
18. Discard the lower layer and place 30 mL of the diethyl ether layer into a 125 mL Erlenmeyer flask. Save.
19. Add 15 mL of 30% KOH in methanol to the 125 mL petroleum ether flask (carotenes and chlorophyll a) and to the 125 mL flask containing the diethyl ether extract (chlorophyll b and xanthophylls).
20. You are hydrolyzing the phytol tail off the chlorophyll molecules so that the chlorophyll pigments will dissolve in a more polar solvent. Swirl the flasks frequently (for at least 10 minutes or until the yellow upper layer in each flask is free of any green color.
21. Now add 30 mL of distilled water to each flask and mix by gently swirling.
22. Pour the contents of each of the flasks into separate graduated cylinders and allow the phases to separate.
23. The petroleum ether extract will contain carotenes in the upper layer and chlorophyll a in the lower layer. The diethyl ether extract will contain xanthophylls in the upper layer and chlorophyll b in the lower layer.
24. Separate the four layers with a pipette and dispense into four separate test tubes with plastic screw tops. Refrigerate.

   For blanks to use with spectrophotometry, you must use petroleum ether with carotenes and chlorophyll a and diethyl ether with xanthophylls and chlorophyll b.

You may need to dilute the pigments with the appropriate solvents for use with the Spectronic 20.

If you leave the pigments under the hood and significant evaporation occurs, simply add more solvent (this is not quantitative).

Acknowledgment: Ross, Cleon W. *Plant Physiology Laboratory Manual.* Wadsworth Publishing Co.

(9) wheat seedling—
Plant two flats of wheat seedlings approximately 4-5 days before the laboratory. Put one flat in the dark and leave the other in the light.

(10) *Coleus* plant—
Place a *Coleus* plant in the dark prior to use.

(11) Lugol's solution—
Order prepared or dissolve 10 g of potassium iodide in 100 mL of distilled water and add 5 g of iodine.

(12) Benedict's reagent—
Order prepared (see Ordering Information).

V.   PREPARATION SUGGESTIONS

Exercise A (Part 1)

Make sure that *Elodea* has been soaked in 0.2% sodium bicarbonate ($NaHCO_3$) with a good light source and aeration. Test the pH of your water and adjust to pH 7 before you begin. When you add phenol red to the water, the color should be a reddish orange. Use enough phenol red to make the color obvious. A student should be recruited to blow through a straw into the liquid. As soon as the liquid turns yellow, it is ready to use (approximately pH 6).

Discuss pH indicators with students. You could do the same exercise with cabbage juice as an indicator or use bromothymol blue. Perhaps some students will elect to try this—even a single tube could be used if exposed to a light source. Discuss how CO_2 acidifies water—or soda! (You might also discuss how oxygen produced by the first blue-green algae in the primitive earth's seas raised the pH enough to precipitate $CaCO_3$ in the oceans, forming ancient stromatolites.)

Be sure that a heat sink is used or lights will make the tubes too warm. Assign individual students or groups to monitor the change in color during the laboratory period.

Exercise A (Part 2)

Shine the light of a slide projector through a slit slide. Prop the prism up so that the light goes through it and rotate the prism until the light spectrum can be seen on a wall or piece of white poster board in the room. When you are ready to look at the effects of different wavelengths of light (Exercise A, Part 3), simply place the Petri dish covered by the filter in front of the projector and see which colors of light disappear from the spectrum. Discuss with the students what a green filter absorbs and what it transmits or reflects. Do the same with other colors of filters.

Exercise A (Part 3)

Have students cut out spinach disks. If you assign one filter color to a group of students (so there is a no filter group, a red group, a green group, a blue group, and a dark group), have all students place their disks into one flask and aspirate all disks at the same time. Students can then obtain disks from one common source. (The degree of aspiration will have an effect on the amount of time it takes for disks to float.) If a side arm flask is used, place a piece of masking tape over the hole in the one hole stopper. While aspirating, peel off the tape from time to time to see if the disks will sink. If they do not, replace the tape. Remember to release the vacuum in this manner before turning off the water. If using a two hole stopper with glass tubing for making the connection to an aspirator, then use the second hole as described. A hand operated vacuum pump (Fisher, # 01-070; Carolina Biological, # 71-1970) can be used in place of an aspirator.

Be sure to use filters only from Edmund Scientific. Using another red or blue filter will not give you the proper results since distances and amount of light have been calculated for these filters.

Preparation directions are written to assign one group to a filter color each to save on the number of lights and the preparation of Petri dishes with filters.

The design for this experiment was developed by Jean Dickey, Clemson University.

Exercise B (Part 1)

Cut strips of Whatman #1 filter paper to fit into large test tubes. Cut one end to form a point (like an arrow) and make sure that the paper is long enough to reach the solvent in the tube if the paper is pinned to the rubber stopper. You can simply place the paper, tip down, into the tube without pinning it to the stopper if desired. Put approximately 0.5 inch of solvent in the bottom of the test tube and use a rubber cork to close the tube tightly. Make sure that there is no solvent on the sides of the tube. While the air in the tube is saturating with solvent, apply a line (or dot) of chlorophyll extract to the paper strip above the pointed end. Reapply the extract in the same position several more times. (A simpler method requires that a leaf of ivy or spinach be placed bottom side on the paper and a dime can be rolled over the leaf to make the line of chlorophyll extract on the paper.) Place the paper strip into the solvent and allow the solvent to ascend until it is almost at the top. Remove the paper and mark the solvent front with a pencil. The order of pigments from top (solvent front) to bottom (pointed end) is: carotenes (orange-yellow pigments), xanthophylls (yellow pigments), chlorophyll a (bright green to blue-green pigment), chlorophyll b (yellow-green to olive-green). Some grayish breakdown products may also be associated with the xanthophylls. The Rf can be calculated for each pigment if paper is used:

$$Rf = (\text{distance pigment migrated})/(\text{distance solvent front migrated})$$

Exercise B (Part 2)

Separate Spectronic 20 tubes of extract should be provided for student use. Label the tubes to identify the pigment they contain and stopper each with a cork. Make sure proper blanks are used for each pigment and are labeled to correspond to pigment samples.

Have students use different colors of chalk (blackboard) or colored marker pens (transparency) to put all absorption spectra on one graph for class discussion.

The major point of this exercise is to compare the absorption spectra with the action spectrum developed from the spinach leaf disk experiment in Exercise A (Part 3). It should be obvious which pigments *absorb* to account for the *action* (photosynthesis) that made the leaf disks float.

Let's Investigate

Grow wheat seedlings for 4-5 days in Styrofoam pots. Place one pot in the dark and one in the light. Students can use prepared materials or this can be extended to a do-at-home exercise if students are given wheat seeds and some Styrofoam cups.

Exercise C

Coleus or geraniums can be used in this exercise. Do not let students boil the alcohol because it could start a fire. Boil leaves in a designated area. Use a double boiler; a large beaker of water with a beaker of alcohol contained in it. The leaves are placed in the alcohol. Be careful to use beakers that are the correct size so that the inner beaker of alcohol cannot tip over.

Place the variegated *Coleus* in the dark for two days prior to this experiment to make sure all starch has been translocated from the white or pink areas.

If variegated *Coleus* is not available, use plain green *Coleus* and cover parts of the leaves with foil for a week before use. Starch will be present in the uncovered leaves, but not in the areas covered by foil.

Let's Investigate

This investigation gives students the opportunity to further improve their hypothesis formation and experimental design skills. Potatoes store starch in their roots while onions store sugar. Onion will turn greenish and finally brick red when boiled with Benedict's reagent, indicating the presence of glucose. Is sucrose present too? This can be determined by mixing chopped onions and their juice with 10 mL distilled water. Add 1 mL of 5% cobalt nitrate solution (5 g cobalt nitrate dissolved in distilled water to make 100 mL). Then add 1 mL of a 10 N NaOH solution (40 g NaOH dissolved in distilled water to make 100 mL). A violet color indicates the presence of sucrose. Students might also ask what type of carbohydrate is made in the leaves. Allow the potatoes and onions to sprout and use the first green leaves to repeat the test. Most dicots (including potatoes) support starch production in leaves, while most monocots (including onions) support glucose production and storage.

Let's Investigate

This experiment is a manipulation of Exercise C. Students will have fun writing their initials, but must also think about some science. Does the plant need to be in the light before starting the experiment or in the dark? (It should be kept in the dark to use up all stored starch.) How long will it take for the plant to make enough starch to write a student's initials? (Usually two days in bright sunlight.) What happens if the plant is left too long? Can the products of photosynthesis be translocated? (Yes.) Results are easy to assess. Have students place their boiled leaves in plastic wrap and tape them onto their laboratory reports.

VI. ORDERING INFORMATION

clamp, 3 prong—Fisher, # 05-768-10; Carolina Biological, # 70-7376 or 70-7312
battery jar (aquarium)—Carolina Biological, # 67-0450
photoflood lamp and bulb—local hardware store; Carolina Biological, # 68-7000 or 68-7100
plastic dropping pipette—Carolina Biological, # 73-6898
Elodea (live, per 100)—Carolina Biological, # 16-2100
Parafilm—Fisher, # 13-374-10; Carolina Biological, # 21-5600
meter stick—Carolina Biological, # 70-2620
prism, 90°, variety of sizes—Carolina Biological, # 75-4950
daylight blue filter—Edmund Scientific, # H82,031
medium green filter—Edmund Scientific, # H82,041
medium red filter—Edmund Scientific, # H82,015
Nalgene, vacuum pump—Fisher, # 01-070; Carolina Biological, # 71-1970
1 hole rubber stopper (size 6 1/2)—Fisher, # 14-130K; Carolina Biological, # 71-2409
Lugol's solution—Carolina Biological, # 87-2793
Spectronic 20 tubes:
    Pyrex (100 X 13 mm)—Fisher, # 14-957C; Carolina Biological, # 73-1408
    Kimax (100 X 13 mm)—Fisher, #14-923D; Carolina Biological, # 73-1405A
round cuvettes (100 X 13 mm)—Fisher, # 14-385-900B; Carolina Biological # 73-1408
phenol red—Carolina Biological, # 87-9850; Fisher, P74-10
Benedict reagent—Carolina Biological, # 84-7111; Fisher, # LC11650-1
sodium bicarbonate ($NaHCO_3$)—Carolina Biological, # 88-8380; Fisher, # S233-500
petroleum ether—Carolina Biological, # 87-9580; Fisher, # E139-500
acetone—Carolina Biological, # 84-1500; Fisher, # A18-500

LABORATORY 12   Mitosis: Making Duplicates

I. FOREWORD

A simulation has been chosen as the focus of this exercise which is designed to teach the process of mitosis. Examples of mitotic events are examined using living materials such as the onion root tip, *Allium cepa*. The giant polytene chromosomes of *Drosophila* are also introduced as models for chromosome structure and function.

II. TIME REQUIREMENTS

Exercise A—30 minutes (home)
Exercise B—60 minutes
Exercise C—40 minutes
Exercise D—45 minutes
Exercise E—30 minutes

III. STUDENT MATERIALS AND EQUIPMENT

	Per Student	Per Pair (2)	Per Group (4)	Per Class (24)
Exercise A				
None				
Exercise B				
chromosome simulation kit (1)				2
Exercise C				
stained onion root tips (2)	1			24
compound microscope	1			24
microscope slides, box (75 X 25 mm)	1			24
coverslips, box (22 X 22 mm)	1			24
tap water, dropping bottle		1		12
Exercise D				
onion root tip, mitosis (prepared slide)	1			24
Exercise E				
Drosophila mojavensis, third instar larvae, vial (3)		1		12
aceto-orcein or aceto-carmine stain, dropper bottle (4)		1		12
microscope slides, box (75 X 25 mm)		1		12
coverslips, box (22 X 22 mm)		1		12
dissecting needles		2		24
insect Ringer's solution, bottle (5)		1		12

<u>Exercise E—continued</u>

bibulous paper, book		1	12

IV. PREPARATION OF MATERIALS AND SOLUTIONS

(1) chromosome simulation kit—

Two chromosome simulation Biokits can be purchased from Carolina Biological Supply Company and all necessary materials will be included. Although the original price is considerable ($103.80/kit), the same kit (# 17-1100) can be used year after year without additional purchases. The beads are also used in Laboratories 13 and 17.

If you prefer, you can purchase beads only (Carolina Biological Supply Company, # 17-112). Two sets cost $29.50 (two bags, 900 beads per bag with two colors in a set— this will be enough for a class of 30). Magnetic centromeres are expensive but can be made from amber rubber tubing (ID 3.2 mm, wall thickness 1.6 mm) with children's magnets placed inside. Centrioles can be made by cutting plastic drinking straws into 10 mm lengths.

Kits for individual students are made by attaching 10 beads to either side of a magnetic centromere. Two yellow "chromosomes" and two red "chromosomes" (four 20-bead strands in all) are then placed in a plastic bag to serve as an individual "kit."

Colored paper clips (vinyl coated) may be substituted for beads. Children's bar magnets can be inserted into narrow diameter amber rubber tubing (ID 4.8 mm, wall thickness 1.6 mm) and chains of paper clips can then be attached to opposite ends of the rubber tubing.

Colored pipe cleaners can also be used as an alternative. Paper clips can be used as centromeres to hold two chromatids together.

(2) stained onion root tips—

Gather together the following materials:

       camel-hair brushes

       plastic Petri dishes (100 mm diameter)

       tooth picks

       100 mL beakers (10)

       onion starts (10)

       single-edge razor blades

Solutions:

ALWAYS ADD ACID SLOWLY TO WATER WHILE STIRRING!
WEAR SAFETY GLASSES

3:1 EtOH-glacial acetic acid

Add 10 mL of glacial acetic acid to 30 mL of 100% (absolute) ethyl alcohol and mix. You will need approximately 40 mL of this solution.

6N HCl

Mix 50 mL of concentrated (12N) hydrochloric acid into 50 mL of distilled water.

Schiff Reagent

Purchase prepared solution.

Procedure:

1. Rooting the onions: first clean the bottom of the onion by rubbing it with your finger. Next insert a round tooth pick through the onion, placing the onion in the center of the tooth pick. Lower the onion down into a 100 mL beaker of tap water until the toothpick is resting across the top of the beaker. Allow two days for rooting. Alternatively, wrap in a wet paper towel and place in a plastic bag (not sealed). Keep in a warm, dark place overnight.

2. Removing the root tips: after the onions have rooted, harvest the root tips. Cut the root tips off using a razor blade, cutting approximately 5 mm from the tip itself. With a camel-hair brush, gently place the root tips into 3:1 95% ethanol:acetic acid solution. Let the root tips remain in this solution for at least 20 minutes.

3. With the camel-hair brush, transfer the root tips to a Petri dish of distilled water to rinse. Rinse for one minute.

4. With the camel-hair brush, transfer the root tips to a Petri dish of 6N HCl. Incubate for 5 minutes.

5. With the camel-hair brush, transfer the root tips to a Petri dish of distilled water to rinse. Rinse for one minute.

6. With the camel-hair brush, transfer the root tips to a Petri dish of Schiff Reagent for 15 minutes.

7. With the camel-hair brush, transfer the purple-stained onion root tips from the Schiff reagent to a Petri dish of distilled water. Root tips are now ready for use.

8. Onion root tips can be obtained by students from a central location on a demonstration bench. Each student should bring a glass slide with a drop of water on it. Be sure to provide a camel-hair brush to transfer root tips.

(3) *Drosophila mojavensis*, third instar larvae—

D. mojavensis larvae are larger than those of *D. melanogaster* and are ideal for studying polytene chromosomes. Larvae are usually larger if reared at 18° C with 1-2 drops of a thick yeast suspension added daily to the culture.

Fresh *Drosophila* medium can be prepared as follows:

To 3 liters of boiling distilled water add:

corn meal	300 g
brewer's yeast	76 g
agar	60 g

Add to the above a mixture of 800 mL of distilled water and 400 mL of molasses.

Let the suspension simmer for 10 minutes. Cool for 10 minutes. Add 26 mL proprionic acid and mix. Pour into vials and refrigerate (sufficient for about 200 vials with 20 mL/vial). It will take 6-8 days, depending on the temperature, for larvae to reach the third instar. The total life cycle takes 12 days.

Drosophila instant medium can also be purchased through Carolina Biological Supply Company (see Ordering Information).

(4) aceto-orcein and aceto-carmine stains—

aceto-orcein stain:

Gather the following materials:

aceto-orcein	2 g
glacial acetic acid	50 mL

Procedure:

   Mix and simmer gently for 10 minutes. Bring to a boil for 1 minute and add 50 mL of 85% lactic acid. Cool and filter. May also be purchased already made (see Ordering Information).

aceto-carmine stain:

   This stain can be prepared in the same manner. It can also be purchased already made (see Ordering Information).

   Both stains are intensified by small amounts of iron. Using non-stainless steel dissecting needles or insect pins (mounted in balsa wood for handles) is helpful.

(5) insect Ringer's solution—

   Mix 7.5 g NaCl, 3.5 g KCl, and 0.21 g $CaCl_2$ with enough distilled water to make 1 liter of solution.

V. PREPARATION SUGGESTIONS

Exercise A

The most important concept to be gained from this exercise and brought to the laboratory is the fact that the DNA content of the cell has doubled during interphase. All chromosomes are composed of two chromatids. Be sure that your students understand these concepts.

Exercise B

Although it may appear simple, we continue to use this exercise because it gives the instructor a chance to check on each student's progress. Watch as your students manipulate the chromosomes. Then, give them extra chromosomes—duplicates of red or yellow, duplicates in length, or give them an odd number of chromosomes. Make sure they understand that both haploid and diploid cells can divide by mitosis.

Exercise C

Have students observe a prepared slide of onion root tip before they view their own preparations. This way, students will be prepared to locate the correct area of the root tip and will know what mitotic figures should look like. You should always have a number of root tip slides on hand in case the live material does not prove satisfactory.

Exercise D

We have found that onion root tips prepared ahead and stained with Schiff's reagent give better results and are more reliable than root tips harvested and stained during the laboratory. Before harvesting all root tips, prepare several and take a look at them. If there are a great number of mitotic figures, harvest the remainder of the root tips. Otherwise wait for several hours and try again. Usually, the cycle is fairly well synchronized, taking 14-16 hours for completion.

   If students wish to prepare their own root tips, have them cut off the tip of a root and place it on a glass slide. Add 2-3 drops of 1 N HCl. Use a clothes pin or forceps to hold the slide and pass it over the flame from an alcohol burner (or Bunsen burner). Add a drop of stain (aceto-orcein, aceto-carmine, methylene blue, or toluidine blue), and reheat. Add a drop of fresh stain and a coverslip. If the students are lucky, they will have mitotic figures in abundance. You may wish to have some prepared slides of root tips available in case the student's slides are not satisfactory.

Exercise E

Third instar larvae should be used for this experiment. *Drosophila mojavensis* is recommended because of its larger size (and the larger size of its salivary glands). If *D. melanogaster* is used, larvae should be fed with extra yeast solution (see Preparation of Materials and Solutions section). Generally, 8 day old larvae should be used (if grown at 21° C). These will be the oldest and largest larvae available, since larvae will form pupae at about day 9. If you grow larvae at 18° C, they will be larger; use at day 10.

The lighting used for dissecting glands is crucial. If using transmitted light, the glands will appear to be more translucent (we prefer to use transmitted light reflected off a mirror below a clear glass stage). If a black stage and reflected light are used, the glands will appear whitish. If glands are filled with saliva, individual cells will be swollen and the glands will appear grape-like. If students are having difficulty identifying the salivary glands, gastric ceca, or Malpighian tubules, have them look for the piece of tissue in which they can actually see the individual cells (and even nuclei) using the dissecting microscope.

Use dissecting needles (non-aluminum) if possible to remove as much fat body tissue as possible (fat cells interfere with the production of good squashes). It is possible to place insect pins or steel needles into the ends of balsa wood strips or dowels to make dissecting needles. Some students can manipulate insect pins easily without the aid of handles.

It is important that the initial separation of the head from the body be done quickly, but then the students should NOT continue to try to pull the intestine out of the body. This leads to breakage and a general mess. Simply let the internal parts of the larvae flow out of the larval cuticle.

Be sure to keep an eye on the drop of stain on the glands while staining. It tends to dry up quickly (students should not leave the slide under the lights on the microscope stage). Stain for at least 10 minutes—the longer the better and the darker the bands. Save stain— the older the better. Simply filter the stain each year before use. If students have used too much stain, transfer the glands to a drop of 45% acetic acid to make the squash (only do this if the glands have stained darkly). If glands are in one piece, you may wish to cut them up with the dissecting needles before squashing, taking care that no pieces of gland stick to the needles. When squashing, use several thicknesses of bibulous paper and press with your thumb or use a small cork (or pencil eraser). Do not get discouraged if the first slide does not turn out well—it takes some time to learn how hard to press on the slide. If chromosomes are shattered into small pieces, press more lightly next time.

VI. ORDERING INFORMATION

Schiff reagent—Carolina Biological, # 88-7263
100% ethanol—Fisher, # A-407-500
camel-hair brush—Carolina Biological, # 70-6182
chromosome simulation Biokit—Carolina Biological, # 17-1100
microscope slides (75 X 25 mm)—Fisher, # 12-544-1; Carolina Biological, # 63-2000

coverslips (22 X 22 mm)—Fisher, # 12-524B; Carolina Biological, # 63-3095
onion sets—local seed store
Drosophila mojavensis—Carolina Biological, # 17-2870
aceto-orcein stain—Carolina Biological, # 84-1451
orcein—Sigma, # 09004; Carolina Biological, # 87-8471
aceto-carmine stain—Carolina Biological, # 84-1421
carmine—Sigma, # C-6752; Carolina Biological, # 85-3070
lactic acid—Carolina Biological, # 87-1690
dropping bottle—Fisher, # 02-980; Carolina Biological, # 71-6525
instant *Drosophila* medium:
    plain—Carolina Biological, # 17-3200
    blue—Carolina Biological, # 17-3210

LABORATORY 13   Meiosis: Reducing the Chromosome Number

I. FOREWORD

The exercises included in this laboratory are designed to help students understand the chromosomal events that occur during the process of meiosis. A simulation has been chosen because it provides the instructor with an opportunity to check each student's understanding of the process by simply observing the student's work displayed on the table.

Segregation and independent assortment are brought into the exercises to provide an introduction to the genetic consequences of meiosis.

Supplementing the laboratory simulations with slides of meiosis in lily or *Ascaris* is possible if slides are available. Crossing over and its consequences may also be examined in the fungus, *Sordaria fimicola*.

II. TIME REQUIREMENTS

Exercise A—30 minutes
Exercise B—60 minutes
Exercise C—45 minutes
Time for checking student work and problems—30 minutes

III. STUDENT MATERIALS AND EQUIPMENT

	Per Student	Per Pair (2)	Per Group (4)	Per Class (24)
Exercise A				
chromosome simulation kit (1)				2
Exercise B				
chromosome simulation kit (1)				2
labels for alleles, container (2)			1	6
colored pencils, red and yellow (1 each)	2			48
monohybrid cross, corn				48
dihybrid cross, corn (display box, plastic) (3)		1		12
Exercise C				
chromosome simulation kit (1)				2
dihybrid cross, corn (display box, plastic) (3)			1	6
dihybrid cross, corn (ears) (4)		1		12
colored pencils, red and yellow (1 each)	2			48
labels for alleles, container (2)			1	6

IV. PREPARATION OF MATERIALS AND SOLUTIONS

(1) chromosome simulation kit—
   If you completed Laboratory 12, Mitosis, you have all of the materials necessary for this laboratory. Student simulation kits should be assembled using the two large BioKits. Each student chromosome simulation kit should consist of 2 yellow strands of beads and two red strands of beads. Four centriole bodies will be necessary for meiosis. See Preparation of Materials and Solutions, section (1) in Laboratory 12 for a more detailed description of the chromosome simulation kit and possible modifications.

(2) labels for alleles—
   Do not let the students wrap tape around the beads—it is impossible to remove. We use sheets of white envelope labels from which we have cut small circles using a hole punch. Students can put a letter on a circle and peel the back off to attach the label to the beads.

(3)(4) plastic display boxes of corn—
   Plastic display boxes of monohybrid and dihybrid corn—order from Carolina Biological Supply Company. (See Ordering Information.)

V. PREPARATION SUGGESTIONS

Exercise A

Check the work on the table in front of each student to make sure that he or she has properly separated homologous pairs.

Exercise B

A discussion of how corn kernels are formed is advisable. Most students are not very knowledgeable concerning the biology of corn and, in order to understand the relationships of gametes to kernel color, some review is necessary. This will enhance the value of the exercise.

Exercise C

Check the work on the table in front of each student to make sure that the homologous chromosomes have been separated. Students tend to put two yellow chromosomes together and two red chromosomes together. Size is the difference which is important in identifying different chromosome types in this exercise, not color. Check all drawings and paper work to make sure that students understand the concept of independent assortment and can relate it to the meiotic process.

Sordaria (optional)

If you wish to explore crossing over as part of this exercise on meiosis, you are encouraged to try using *Sordaria fimicola*. Order a plate of crossed *Sordaria* (black × tan) from Carolina Biological Supply Company (# 15-5846). Students can remove perithecia (the fruiting bodies) with a toothpick and mount them as a wet-mount slide preparation. With a small amount of pressure on the coverslip, the asci will be extruded from the fruiting bodies. Each ascus contains 8 ascospores; the result of one meiotic division followed by mitosis.

71

Sordaria's haploid hyphae (*n*) fuse to form 2*n* dikaryotic cells. The nuclei then fuse to form a 2*n* nucleus which undergoes the meiotic and mitotic divisions. If hyphae from two different strains fuse (black × tan), then 4 ascospores will be tan and 4 will be black. If these are arranged in a 4 + 4 pattern (4 black and 4 tan), then no crossing over has occurred. However, a 2 + 2 + 2 + 2 pattern or a 2 + 4 + 2 pattern of ascospores can only occur if crossing over has occurred between chromatids of the two chromosomes carrying the spore color genes. Students should count the number of asci that are the result of crossing over and divide by the total number of counted hybrid asci (asci containing *any* combination of both black and tan) to give a per cent of the asci that show crossing over. Divide this number by 2 (because only 1/2 of the spores in each ascus are the result of crossing over). A 1% frequency of crossover is 1 map unit. In this way, students can map the color gene with reference to the centromere. (The tan gene is 26 map units from the centromere.) See optional materials for this exercise on p. 197-200 at the end of the Preparator's Guide.

VI.   ORDERING INFORMATION

chromosome simulation BioKit—Carolina Biological, # 17-1100 (order 2 kits if they are not available from Laboratory 12)

monohybrid cross, corn (display box)—Carolina Biological, # 17-6810

dihybrid cross, corn (display box)—Carolina Biological, # 17-6900

genetic corn ears, monohybrid (RR × rr)—Carolina Biological, # 17-6500

genetic corn ears, dihybrid (R/R Su/Su × r/r su/su)—Carolina Biological, # 17-6600

Sordaria demonstration cross plate (optional)—Carolina Biological, # 15-5846 (place order 3 weeks in advance)

LABORATORY 14   Human Genetic Traits

I.   FOREWORD

Basic concepts in human genetics are covered in this laboratory. Work with human
chromosomes is emphasized. Students work independently on all exercises.

II.   TIME REQUIREMENTS

Exercise A (home)—15 minutes (complete prior to laboratory; discussion in laboratory)
Exercise B—15 minutes
Exercise C (Parts 1 and 2)—45 minutes
Exercise D (Parts 1 and 2)—30 minutes
Exercise E—30 minutes

III.   STUDENT MATERIALS AND EQUIPMENT

	Per Student	Per Pair (2)	Per Group (4)	Per Class (24)
Exercise A				
written materials in laboratory manual				
Exercise B				
cheek scrapings, male (prepared slide)				1
cheek scrapings, female (prepared slide)				1
compound microscope				2
Exercise C (Parts 1 and 2)				
no preparation or materials needed				
Exercise D (Parts 1 and 2)				
blank karyotype	1			24
metaphase chromosome spread (photographs) (1)	1			24
scissors	1			24
tape or glue			1	6

IV.   PREPARATION OF MATERIALS AND SOLUTIONS

(1)   metaphase chromosome spread (photographs)—
      Specially prepared, reproducible photographs and karyotypes are included on p. 201-208
      at the end of the Preparator's Guide as follows:
          metaphase spread, normal male
          karyotype, normal male
          metaphase spread, Down's syndrome, male
          karyotype, Down's syndrome, male

metaphase spread, Down's syndrome, female
karyotype, Down's syndrome, female
metaphase spread, trisomy 18, female
karyotype, trisomy 18, female

A special note of thanks is given to Dr. Judy Capra and Dr. Arthur Robinson of the Genetics Unit, Health Sciences Center, University of Colorado, for sharing their excellent photographs with users of this laboratory manual.

V.   PREPARATION SUGGESTIONS

Karyotyping during Exercise E will proceed much more rapidly if students learn the technique during Exercise A. This should be tied to a discussion of amniocentesis techniques to make the exercise more meaningful. For additional studies of banding, polytene chromosomes can be examined (Laboratory 12).

Exercise B

This exercise is introduced as a contrast to Exercise A where sex is determined by the tedious process of karyotyping. It is possible for students to make their own Barr body slides from cheek scrapings if desired.

Exercise C (Parts 1 and 2)

This exercise is designed to be a simple introduction to some human genetic traits. The exercise in Part 2 is designed to investigate the unique genetic nature of individuals.

Exercise D (Parts 1 and 2)

Human chromosome abnormalities can be studied by karyotyping. If time does not permit students to complete this exercise, it can easily be done at home. It is also possible (and sometimes more fun) for students to work in pairs. Materials for this exercise are found on p. 201-208. This exercise can be supplemented by a study of human pedigrees and completion of pedigree forms as prepared by genetic counselors (Exercise E).

Exercise E

The family history presented in this exercise is adapted from an actual family history. You may wish to use other pedigree examples as take home problems for students to work on after familiarizing themselves with pedigree notations.

Laboratory Review Questions and Problems

Note that a discussion of blood types and several problems dealing with the inheritance of blood type have been included in this section. To avoid student and instructor contact with bodily fluids (in this case, blood), traditional blood typing exercises have been eliminated from this human genetics laboratory.

VI.   ORDERING INFORMATION

cheek scrapings, male (prepared slide)—Carolina Biological, # G506
cheek scrapings, female (prepared slide)—Carolina Biological, # G504
metaphase spreads and karyotypes used in Laboratory 14 are found in the back of this
Preparator's Guide.

LABORATORY 15   DNA Isolation and Protein Synthesis

I. FOREWORD

During the first part of this laboratory, students will be introduced to a simple technique for isolating DNA. By observing DNA, students will have a greater appreciation for the study of how such a molecule works. During the second part of the laboratory, students will use a cardboard and paper model to learn about the processes of transcription and translation. Model pieces are cut from poster board and paper, using patterns found at the end of the Preparator's Guide. The model is inexpensive and can be used over and over again by simply reproducing the paper parts on a copying machine.

Students will learn about semi-conservative replication and will see that polymerization takes place in a 5' to 3' direction. They will learn how amino acids are activated and how tRNA molecules are charged. Students will also learn how to use the genetic code and how specific codons in mRNA can specify the correct amino acids in a peptide. The processes of initiation, elongation, translocation, and termination, and the factors involved in each are covered in this laboratory using the hands-on model. Students should work individually with one model kit per student.

II. TIME REQUIREMENTS

Exercise A—30 minutes
Exercise B (Part 1)—20 minutes
Exercise B (Part 2)—15 minutes
Exercise B (Part 3)—30 minutes
Let's Investigate—15 minutes

III. STUDENT MATERIALS AND EQUIPMENT

	Per Student	Per Pair (2)	Per Group (4)	Per Class (24)
Exercise A				
onion (yellow)				1
blender				1
homogenization buffer, chilled (100 mL) (1)				1
cheesecloth (25 cm square) (2)				1
meat tenderizer, 6% solution (50 mL) (3)				1
test tubes	1			24
Pasteur pipette	1			24
95% ethanol, ice cold (500 mL) (4)				1
spooling pipette or glass rod (5)				24

76

	Per Student	Per Pair (2)	Per Group (4)	Per Class (24)

Exercise B (Parts 1, 2, and 3)

	Per Student	Per Class (24)
DNA model kit, (6) including	1	24
DNA molecule (white paper)		
deoxyribonucleotides (blue paper)		
ribonucleotides (green paper)		
amino acids (yellow paper)		
ribosome (black cardboard)		
4 amino-acyl tRNA molecules (green cardboard)		
1 ATP molecule (orange cardboard)		
transparency model (7)		1

Let's Investigate

written laboratory exercise

IV. PREPARATION OF MATERIALS AND SOLUTIONS

(1) homogenization buffer (100 mL)—

Add 1.5 g noniodized salt (NaCl) to 50 mL distilled water. Dissolve. Add 10 mL liquid *dishwasher* detergent. Mix gently. Bring up to 100 mL with distilled water. Chill in refrigerator.

(2) cheese cloth—

Cut 8 inch squares—four thicknesses will be adequate.

(3) meat tenderizer (6% solution)—

Add 3 g meat tenderizer to 50 mL distilled water. Make sure that the brand of meat tenderizer that you use contains papain to digest proteins. Check the label.

(4) 95% ethanol, ice cold—

Ethanol must be ice cold for this procedure to work. Place a plastic bottle of 95 % ethanol in the freezer overnight. Be sure that the cap is loose and the bottle is not completely full. Place the bottle on paper towels. It will not freeze.

(5) spooling pipette or glass rod—

To collect ("spool") the DNA, it is best to use a glass rod or pipette that has been scored with a diamond pencil. The rough surface helps the DNA strands adhere to the rod so they can be more easily "spooled."

(6) DNA model kit—

Patterns for constructing the DNA model kit are found at the end of the Preparator's Guide. Cut out all cardboard model parts and place in a brown envelope for distribution in the laboratory. If you make several cardboard patterns, a group of students or teaching assistants can trace around the patterns to make as many model kits as needed—one for each student.

Hand out green and blue sheets of nucleotides and yellow amino acids and ask students to cut these out, collect them in an envelope, and bring them to the laboratory. Distribute the white DNA molecule in the laboratory and explain how to cut it out into two wide pieces to be taped together, forming one long strand.

(7) transparency model—

You may wish to use reduced size model parts to make transparencies. These can be cut out to use on an overhead projector to help demonstrate how the model works. (If you have color transparencies available, use them to make the pieces in different colors. Patterns for the transparency model are also found at the end of this Preparator's Guide.)

V. PREPARATION SUGGESTIONS

Exercise A

This exercise allows students to isolate DNA without using chloroform or phenol and other substances prohibited in many classrooms. The DNA will not be very pure, but the strands can be seen and spooled from the mixture very easily. The major thing to remember is that everything must be kept cold. Keep the blender cup in the freezer until you are ready to use the blender. Make sure all tubes are ice cold. When students add the meat tenderizer (also cold), warn them to mix *gently*. Otherwise, they may shear the DNA into small pieces.

Adding ice-cold ethanol must be done slowly in order to create two layers. The DNA can be seen precipitating as long threads at the interface of the alcohol and the buffer. Spooling should be done as if one is winding yarn onto a knitting needle—spooling is different from mixing and must be done gently.

Exercise B (Part 1)

In this exercise, students study the process of semi-conservative replication. They will learn about the difference in nucleotides found in DNA and RNA, the role of hydrogen bonds and phosphodiester bonds, the direction of polymerization, the relation of template and complement, and the antiparallel structure of the DNA molecule.

The white DNA molecule is in two pieces and must be taped together to form one long strip. The 5' ends of the molecule are labeled I and II. Make sure that students understand that the zigzag line between bases represents the location of hydrogen bonds between bases and that bases within each single strand are held together by phosphodiester bonds. To replicate the DNA, students must cut the two strands apart along the zigzag line (this simulates the breakage of hydrogen bonds).

You will note that both the green and blue sheets of nucleotides contain all five nitrogen bases, A, T, G, C, and U, used in the synthesis of both DNA and RNA. Blue nucleotides (pattern copied onto blue paper) are used to synthesize DNA. The blue U nucleotides are included to make students choose the four nucleotides (A, T, G, C, and not U) to be used. Walk around the classroom and look for Us being placed in the new DNA strands and call this mistake to each student's attention. Next, look to see that students are synthesizing the new strand in a 5' to 3' direction on the 3' 5' template. This means that they will be forming new strands in opposite directions on the two templates. Understanding the fact that DNA polymerization takes place in a particular direction is basic to understanding the nature of replication and the need for forming short Okazaki fragments. Walk around the room and check to see in which directions students are working. Many students do not understand the 5' to 3' concept until after using this hands-on model. Be sure to clear up this point with students who are having trouble.

Many students try to use small pieces of tape to tape each nucleotide to the next. This will make it difficult to slide the mRNA (made in Exercise B (Part 2)) through the ribosome, so this should be discouraged at the start. Students should turn the ends of a long piece of tape under (so that the sticky side is up). After laying the template next to the strip of tape, the complementary nucleotides are put into place in a 5' to 3' direction. Alternatively, stick one end of a strip of tape to the table opposite the 3' end of the template and, holding the other end of the tape in the air, line up the complementary nucleotides by sticking them, face up, to the sticky underside of the tape (this produces a single smooth surface along the strip of nucleotides and makes it easy to slide mRNA through the ribosome). Some students will try to tape the nucleotide pairs together, blue to white, forming hydrogen bonds. While this does indeed happen, explain to students that polymerization comes first, and, in this model, we will keep the blue strand separate from the white (forming only imaginary hydrogen bonds) so that we do not have to cut the template and complement apart when we are ready to transcribe messenger RNA.

After completing this exercise, students should have two double stranded blue and white DNA molecules. Check to see that the 3' and 5' ends of each blue and white molecule are labeled to demonstrate the antiparallel orientation of the two polynucleotide strands in the DNA.

Exercise B (Part 2)

Students should use the green nucleotides to synthesize mRNA. Make sure that they use the correct strip of DNA (the newly synthesized I' blue DNA made from the I white strip). Be sure that the mRNA is being synthesized in a 5' to 3' direction. It is easy to check on this by wandering around the room to watch the students at work—the first three nucleotides should be AUG (the initiation codon). If you do not see these as the first nucleotides to be put down, then check to see what the students have done incorrectly.

Make sure that the polynucleotide chain has 1 long strip of tape covering its length on the upper surface (surface with letters). This will allow the mRNA to be pulled through the ribosome more easily.

Be sure to have students label the 5' and 3' ends of the message they have synthesized.

Exercise B (Part 3)

In this exercise, students will learn about the processes of transcription and translation, including the steps involved in initiation, elongation, translocation, and termination.

Have students remove all four green amino acyl tRNA synthetases from their kits and place them on the table in front of them.

Have them find the four blue tRNA molecules and the ATP molecule, also included in the kit, and place them on the table along with the four yellow paper amino acids that they cut out and brought to class. Show students the three binding sites on the enzyme, one for the R-group of the amino acid, one for the AMP, and one for the anticodon of the tRNA (you may need to interject a short discussion of tRNA structure if this has not been covered already in lecture).

Use the transparency model to show them how ATP is used to activate an amino acid, making sure that they understand the nature of the bond between AMP and the amino acid. Then, use the transparency model to demonstrate how the amino acid gets hooked to the tRNA molecule. Use your own paper model to show them how to cut off the –OH on the amino acid and review the nature of the ester bond formed between the amino acid and the tRNA.

After demonstrating how one tRNA is charged, ask students to charge the remaining tRNA molecules and then return the enzyme molecules and ATP molecule to the envelope.

The black ribosome is in one large piece to make the model easier to handle, but explain to students that, in the cell, subunits are separate and initiation of translation begins when an mRNA molecule attaches to the small ribosomal subunit. The large subunit only joins after the first tRNA molecule pairs with the initiation codon.

Use the transparency model to demonstrate how to position the mRNA on the ribosome and how the anticodons of the tRNAs match the codons on mRNA in both the P and A sites. You may wish to review the fact that codon and anticodon are antiparallel (left to right; the codon is 5' to 3' while the anticodon is 3' to 5' left to right—whenever two polynucleotide strands are complementary to one another, they must be antiparallel.) Use a paper model or extra transparency pieces to show how to make a peptide bond between amino acids. As students do this, walk around the class and it will be easy to identify those students who do not understand the peptide bond structure. Also, make sure students write the name of each amino acid on each yellow paper amino acid as it is put in place in the growing peptide chain. Again, if you walk around the classroom, it will be easy to identify students who are looking up the anticodon rather than codon (a common mistake) in the "genetic code chart" in order to identify amino acids. Once complete, students should have a chain of four amino acids, each identified. Be sure to review the use of protein factors and the fact that this is an energy demanding process, using GTP.

Once complete, have students return the ribosome to the kit's envelope and save kits for another time. We keep several kits on hand, including paper pieces, and allow students to check them out for review. Upper class students also use kits for review. Transfer students who have not completed this laboratory and seem to have difficulty with the specifics of the process are also referred to the kits by professors as a way of reviewing the concepts involved.

Let's Investigate

By re-examining the model, students have a chance to observe the effects of base substitution and frame shift mutations. This requires only pieces of the model already on hand and can be done as an at-home exercise, if preferred.

VI.   ORDERING INFORMATION

DNA Kit—all parts of the DNA kit can be made from patterns included at the back of the
    Preparator's Guide
dishwasher detergent—local grocery store
sodium chloride (NaCl)—Carolina Biological, # 88-8870; Fisher, # 640-500
meat tenderizer (Adolphs)—local grocery store
95% ethanol—Fisher, # A407-500
glass rods—Fisher, # 11-380C
cheesecloth—Fisher, # 06-665-17

LABORATORY 16   Molecular Genetics: Recombinant DNA

I. FOREWORD

In this laboratory, students are introduced to some common techniques in recombinant DNA technology. Knowledge of aseptic technique (Laboratory 7) is necessary, and students should be encouraged to review rules for working with bacteria. Exercise A (Part 1) can be completed prior to the laboratory. Students may work individually or in pairs during Exercise A (Parts 2 and 3) and Exercise B.

II. TIME REQUIREMENTS

Exercise A (Part 1)—30 minutes (can be completed prior to the laboratory)
Exercise A (Part 2)—60 minutes
Exercise A (Part 3)—60 minutes
Exercise B—2 to 3 hours (including running time for electrophoresis)
Exercise C—20 minutes

III. STUDENT MATERIALS AND EQUIPMENT

	Per Student	Per Pair (2)	Per Group (4)	Per Class (24)
Exercise A (Part 1				
scissors	1			24
tape (roll)	1			24
Exercise A (Part 2)				
microcentrifuge tubes or transformation tubes	2			48
inoculating loop	1			24
Escherichia coli MM294 plate (1)		1		12
0.05 M calcium chloride (CaCl$_2$), sterile tube (1 mL) (2)	1			24
plasmid pAmp (0.005 µg/µL) (3)	1			24
ice bucket with ice			1	12
marking pen			1	12
water bath (42° C) and beaker with Styrofoam float (4)			1	12
micropipette, 10 µL (5)	1			24
micropipette, 100 µL (5)	1			24
micropipette, 250 µL (5)	1			24
Luria broth, tube (1 mL) (6)	1			24
LB agar plate (7)	2			48
LB/Amp agar plate (8)	2			48
Bunsen burner			1	12
spreading rod	1			24

	Per Student	Per Pair (2)	Per Group (4)	Per Class (24)

Exercise A (Part 2)—continued

95% ethanol, beaker		1		12
masking tape, roll				1

Exercise A, (Part 3)

plasmid, pBLU™ (0.005 µg/µL), 200 µL vial (9)				1
microcentrifuge (Micro-Test) tubes		1		12
E. coli JM101 cells, plate (10)			1	6
micropipette (0-10 µL) (5)		1		12
micropipette (100-1000 µL) or sterile 1 mL pipette (5)		1 or 3		12 or 36
sterile inoculating loop		1		12
ice bucket with ice		1		12
water bath (42° C) and beaker with Styrofoam float (4)		1		12
Luria broth, tube (1 mL) (6)		1		12
LB/Amp/X-gal agar plates (11)		1		12
LB agar control plates (7)		2		24
LB/Amp agar plates (8)		2		12
spreading rod		1		12
95% ethanol, beaker		1		12
marking pen		1		12
masking tape				1

Exercise B

electrophoresis apparatus (12)		1		12
agarose, bottle (60 mL) (13)		1		12
Pasteur pipette		1		12
electrophoresis (TBE) running buffer (200 mL), bottle (14)		1		12
micropipette (50 µL)		1		12
Lambda DNA (EcoRI digest, 0.25 µg/µL) (200 µL), tube (15)		1		12
Lambda DNA (HindIII digest, 0.25 µg/µL) (200 µL), tube (15)		1		12
Lambda DNA (undigested, 0.4 µg/µL) (200 µL), tube (15)		1		12
bromophenol blue dye (16)				1
methylene blue stain (17)				1
semi-log paper (sheet)		1		12

Exercise C

written materials from laboratory manual

IV.   PREPARATION OF MATERIALS AND SOLUTIONS

General

Kits are available from Edvotek and from Carolina Biological Supply Company for both Exercise A (Parts 2 and 3) and for Exercise B. If you are inexperienced with recombinant

DNA, we suggest that you work with kits the first time through this laboratory. These kits come with all components, including cells, plasmids, agar, pipettes, and plates, for transformation. Electrophoresis kits contain buffer, stain, DNA, and pipettes.

For Exercise A (Part 2), the following kits are available:

Colony transformation kit (Carolina Biological Supply Company, kit # 21-1142). This kit uses the rapid transformation technique developed at Cold Spring Harbor as described in the directions of Exercise A. The plasmid used for transformation is pAmp.

Transformation of *E. coli* cells with plasmid pBR322 (Edvotek, kit # 201). This kit provides the reagents and directions for the transformation of *E. coli* cells with plasmid DNA that carries genes for antibiotic resistance. The plasmid used for transformation is pBR322. The protocol for its use differs slightly from that in Exercise A.

For Exercise A (Part 3), the following kits are available:

pBLU colony transformation kit (Carolina Biological Supply Company, kit # 21-1146). Transformation of *E. coli* strain JM101 with pBLU plasmid DNA. Contains all biologicals and plasticware necessary to complete this exercise. This kit contains enough materials for 20 students. (JM101 cells used in Exercise A (Part 3) must be maintained on minimal medium and are relatively difficult to propagate. For this reason, a kit is recommended (see Ordering Information).

Transformation of *E. coli* with pGAL kit (Edvotek, kit # 221). This kit contains the biologicals and labware necessary for Exercise A (Part 3).

For Exercise B, the following kits are available:

Restriction enzyme cleavage of DNA kit (Carolina Biological Supply Company, kit # 21-1149. *Lambda* DNA cleaved with *Eco*RI for electrophoresis with *Hind*III fragments. Methylene blue is included.

DNA restriction analysis kit (Carolina Biological Supply Company, kit # 21-1151). Students prepare their own restriction digests of *Lambda* DNA using *Bam*HI, *Eco*RI, and *Hind*III. Methylene blue stain is used. Ethidium bromide stain is also available (kit # 21-1150)

Analysis of *Eco*RI cleavage patterns of *Lambda* DNA (Edvotek, kit # 112). *Lambda* DNA predigested with *Eco*RI endonuclease. This kit contains undigested *Lambda* DNA, *Eco*RI digested *Lambda* DNA, and standard *Hind*III digested *Lambda* DNA fragments ready for electrophoresis. Agarose and micropipettes for loading samples and methylene blue stain are all included. Enough material is provided to run two gels as a classroom demonstration. Data can be distributed to each student for analysis.

Cleavage of *Lambda* DNA with *Eco*RI endonuclease (Edvotek, kit # 212). Cleaving of *Lambda* DNA with *Eco*RI endonuclease—an introduction to restriction enzymes. This kit provides *Lambda* DNA, restriction enzymes, and reaction buffers. Students prepare their own digests for electrophoresis. Agarose and micropipettes for loading samples are included. Enough materials are provided for a group of 1 to 10 students. Some materials must be shipped on ice.

Gel electrophoresis apparatus (Carolina Biological Supply Company). Electrophoresis apparatus, # 21-3668, and power supply, # 21-3673, can be ordered separately.

<u>Mini-lab station</u> (Edvotek, kit # 501). This is a complete horizontal gel electrophoresis system with a fixed current power pack for one apparatus. The apparatus will accommodate up to 12 samples. (Includes MiniGel Electrophoresis Apparatus, Model M12, Cat. #502, and MiniPower Pack, Cat. #503).

Catalogs for Edvotek, Carolina Biological Supply Company, and other companies that offer a variety of supplies, kits, and biologicals for recombinant DNA work can be requested from the following sources:

Bethesda Research Laboratories, 8717 Grovemont Circle, Gaithersburg, MD 20877 (800-638-8992)

Carolina Biological Supply Company, 2700 York Road, Burlington, NC 27215 or Box 187, Gladstone, OR 97027 (800-334-5551)

Edvotek, Inc., P. O. Box 1232, West Bethesda, MD 20827 (800-338-6835)

Fotodyne, New Berlin, WI 53151

Modern Biology, Inc., 290 Conjunction Street, P. O. Box 97, Dayton, IN 47941 (317-447-6577)

Wards Natural Science (Gelteach), Rochester, NY (800-962-2660)

We strongly suggest that you obtain catalogs from these companies before proceeding with these laboratories.

Development of this laboratory was completed with the assistance of Dr. Jack Chirikjian, Edvotek, Inc. and Drs. David Micklos, Mark Brown, and Greg Freyer of the DNA Learning Center, Cold Spring Harbor.

If a kit is not used, materials can be prepared as follows:

(1) *E. coli* plate—

From an agar slant of *E. coli* MM294 bacteria (see Ordering Information), prepare a fresh streak plate (see Laboratory 7, Exercise D (Part 2)) to isolate single colonies. (Alternatively, plates of *E. coli* are provided in both the Carolina and Edvotek kits.)

(2) 0.05 M calcium chloride ($CaCl_2$), sterile—

Dissolve 5.55 of anhydrous calcium chloride ($CaCl_2$) or 7.25 g of $CaCl_2 \cdot 2H_2O$ in distilled water to make a solution of 100 mL. Autoclave for 15 minutes, 15 pounds pressure, at 121° C in a loosely capped bottle covered with aluminum foil. Tighten cap after cooling. Alternatively, dispense into tubes of 1-2 mL each, cover with aluminum foil, and autoclave as above. This will allow each student to have his or her own sterile $CaCl_2$ solution.

(3) plasmid pAmp—

Plasmid pAmp (200 µL), 0.005 µg/µL, may be purchased separately from Carolina Biological Supply Company. (Plasmid pAmp is provided with the Carolina kit, 0.005 µg/µL; 0.2 mL.) This can be aseptically dispensed into microcentrifuge tubes for students, but we suggest that the instructor oversee dispensing the plasmid to avoid pipetting errors. Students should use 10 µL of the purchased plasmid pAmp (0.005 µg/µL) or 0.05 µg in the 250 µL of $CaCl_2$ and cells. (If this is the case, the transfer loop can be used to transfer 10 µL of plasmid from stock solution to the student's tube containing $CaCl_2$.)

If you wish to give each student a microcentrifuge tube containing plasmid, we suggest that you dilute the plasmid 1:1 with TE buffer and give each student 20 µL rather than 10 µL to be transferred to the $CaCl_2$. TE buffer can be purchased in prepared form from

Carolina Biological Supply company (see Ordering Information), or can be prepared as follows:

1 M Tris (pH 8.0)	1.0 mL
0.5 M EDTA	0.2 mL
distilled water	200.0 mL

(adjust to pH 8.0, see below)

1. For 1 M Tris (pH 8.0), dissolve 12.1 g Tris base in 80 mL distilled water. Add concentrated HCl to adjust the pH (about 4-4.5 mL). Add distilled water to 100 mL. **Be sure to wear a mask and cover your nose and mouth when working with Tris powder.** (1 M Tris can also be purchased in prepared form from the Carolina Biological Supply Company.)

2. For 0.5 M EDTA, add 18.6 g ethylenediamine tetraacetate (EDTA, disodium salt) to 80 mL of distilled water. Adjust the pH to 8.0 by adding approximately 2 g NaOH.

(4) water bath with Styrofoam float—

A beaker of water can serve as a water bath for an individual or a pair of students. Use a thin piece of Styrofoam and make a hole in it large enough to accommodate the microcentrifuge tube (or Micro-Test tube). Float the Styrofoam holding the tube of cells on the water bath to heat shock the cells. This can also be done in a large water bath regulated to 42° C, but make sure students label their floats with tape.

If you conduct the experiment in larger sterile transformation tubes (Carolina Biological, # 21-5080), be sure that students do not just put the tubes in the water bath expecting them to float—they leak!

(5) micropipettes (10 μL, 100 μL, and 250 μL)—

There are many different types of micropipettes available. The Carolina and Edvotek kits come with special capillary-type micropipettes. You can also purchase glass capillary pipettes calibrated in μ L amounts. The Ultramicro Accropet (see Ordering Information) is made for use with capillary pipettes and is like a miniature Pi-Pump. By turning the Accropet, you can pull up or deliver accurate amounts of solution. Be sure to sterilize capillary pipettes in covered glass tubes before use.

More expensive digital micropipettes are also available with special autoclavable, disposable tips. Groups of students can use a single pipette by changing tips. Pipettes are available from 2 to 10 μL, 10 to 100 μL, or 100 to 1000 μL (remember that 100 μL is 0.1 mL and sterile glass serological pipettes can be used for such larger amounts).

(6) Luria broth (provided in both kits)—

To make Luria broth for growing *E. coli*, use:

bacterotryptone	10 g
yeast extract	5 g
NaCl	10 g

1. Add ingredients to a 2 liter flask and add 1000 mL of distilled water. Swirl to dissolve.

2. Dispense into five 200 mL bottles. Cap loosely and cover the top with aluminum foil.

3. Autoclave 15 minutes, 15 pounds pressure, at 121° C.

4. Cool and tighten lids. Store at room temperature. (Cloudiness indicates contamination.)

5. Dispense 1 mL amounts into sterile, capped test tubes (enough for each student or pair of students) for use in recovery of transformed cells. Use disposable transformation tubes (Carolina Biological, # 21-5080).

(7) LB agar plates (plates and agar provided in kits; agar ready-to-pour)—
To make Luria broth agar (LB agar) plates, use:

bacterotryptone	10 g
yeast extract	5 g
NaCl	10 g
agar	15 g

1. Add ingredients to a 2 liter flask and add 1000 mL of distilled water to the flask. Swirl to dissolve lumps. Cover with aluminum foil.
2. Autoclave for 15 minutes, 15 pounds pressure, at 121° C. Let cool until you can pick up the flask with your bare hands. (If lumps are present autoclave again.)
3. Remove the cover from a sterile polystyrene Petri dish, but hold the cover at an angle above the dish and pour in the agar. Replace the cover immediately (never set the cover down on the counter top). Repeat for the rest of the plates.
4. After the agar has solidified, invert the plates and let them sit until condensation disappears. Label the plates "LB" and store in plastic bags in the refrigerator. Store inverted.

Alternatively, prepoured plates or ready-to-pour LB agar is available from Carolina Biological Supply Company (see Ordering Information).

(8) LB/Amp agar plates (plates, agar, and ampicillin provided in kits; agar ready-to-pour)—
To make LB/Amp agar plates:
1. Add 0.03 g ampicillin to 1000 mL of autoclaved LB agar (7). Add the ampicillin only after the agar has cooled enough to hold the flask in your hand.
2. Swirl and pour plates as described above.
3. Be sure to mark the Plates "LB-Amp."

Alternatively, prepoured plates or ready-to-pour LB agar containing ampicillin is available from Carolina Biological Supply Company (see Ordering Information).

(9) plasmid pBLU—

Plasmid pBLU (0.005 µg/µL), 0.2 mL, is included as part of the Carolina Biological Supply Company or Edvotek kits. If a kit is not used, the plasmid (1 µg) (200 µL; 0.005 µg/µL) can be purchased from Carolina Biological Supply Company or Edvotek, or from Bethesda Research Laboratories (see Ordering Information).

You will need 0.03 - 0.05 µg of plasmid per every 100 µL of cells to be transformed. If you order 200 µL; 0.005 µg/µL, this means that each student will use 10 µL. This amount (10 µL) is approximately what a transfer loop will hold and it can be dispensed by allowing each pair of students to obtain a loopful from the original vial. Thus, a vial (1 µg) (200 µL; 0.005 µg/µL) will be good for 18-20 pairs of students. Depending on the size of your class, order accordingly.

If you prefer to provide each student with a vial containing plasmid, dilute 10 µL of plasmid in 20 µL of sterile TE buffer.

(10) JM101 *E. coli* cells—

JM101 cells are provided with both Carolina and Edvotek kits. If a kit is not used, the cells can be purchased from Carolina Biological Supply Company or from Bethesda Research Laboratories (see Ordering Information). Purchase a slant culture of JM101.

The rapid colony transformation technique can be used. For this, prepare a fresh streak plate for each laboratory section (see Laboratory 7, Exercise D, Part 2). Use a sterile transfer loop to remove a small amount of bacteria from a slant tube culture. Spread this in a zig-zag motion over the surface of the plate, to one side. Turn the plate 90° and cross the first zig-zag once, making a new zig-zag pattern down the surface of the plate. Repeat twice more, never crossing an original zig-zag more than once. This dilutes the bacteria. Incubate overnight at 37° C. Single colonies should be isolated for the transformation. Each pair of students should use a colony about the size of the head of a round-headed straight pin. Caution students NOT to use too much cell material or the plasmid will be "overwhelmed" and transformation efficiency will be low. Also, caution students to avoid getting agar in the loop when they harvest a colony for transformation.

You can also make cells competent beforehand and ensure the density of cells for transformation. If you choose to do this, prepare cells the day before (remember that there is a possibility of damaging the cells during this procedure if you are not careful).

The rapid colony transformation technique can be used (14.7 g $CaCl_2 \cdot 2H_2O$/100 mL distilled water).

Approximately 24 hours ahead of the experiment:

Prepare 1000 mL of Luria broth (see (**6**)).

Prepare 100 mL of sterile 0.1 M $CaCl_2$

$CaCl_2 \cdot 2H_2O$	14.7 g
distilled water	100 mL

Prepare 100 mL of 0.1 M $CaCl_2$/15% glycerol as follows:

$CaCl_2 \cdot 2H_2O$	14.7 g
distilled water	85 mL
glycerol	15 mL

1. Add glycerol to water and dissolve $CaCl_2$ in the mixture.
2. Autoclave for 15 minutes at 121° C in a loosely capped bottle covered with aluminum foil. Tighten cap after cooling.
3. Store in a refrigerator.

Procedure:

1. Grow *E. coli* (JM101) in 100 mL of Luria broth, shaking at about 550 rpm at 37° C, until absorbance on the Spectronic 20 reads 0.2-0.3 at 660 nm. At 37° C, this will take about 2-3 hours. If you have a shaking water bath, the process will be faster. Otherwise, place the cells in an incubator or a 37° C water bath and simply shake from time-to-time.
2. Pour 15 mL of culture into each of 6 sterile conical centrifuge tubes and pellet cells at top speed in a clinical centrifuge (approximately 4-6 K or 5,000 rpm) for 10 minutes.
3. Pour off supernatant and pipette to resuspend cells in each tube in 5 mL of cold (4° C) 0.1 M $CaCl_2$. Combine cells from three tubes to give two tubes of 15 mL each. **Keep on ice at all times.** Let cells sit for 60 minutes.

4. Recentrifuge for 10 minutes as in Step 2. Pellets should be spread out with a hole in the middle, resembling a doughnut. If pellets are compact, resuspend and repeat the $CaCl_2$ treatment for 25 minutes.

5. Pour off the supernatant and resuspend in 0.1 M $CaCl_2$/15% glycerol using approximately 1.5 mL in each tube.

6. Store suspended competent cells overnight on ice or in the freezer. If using a low temperature (–80° C) freezer, cells will last for several months. Otherwise, use frozen cells within 2-3 days.

Transformation with plasmid pBLU can be carried out as described in Preparation Suggestions. Use 250 μL of competent cells for transformation.

(11) LB/Amp/X-gal agar plates—

To make LB/Amp/X-gal agar plates:

1. Prepare 1000 mL of LB/Amp agar as above (**8**).

2. After the agar has cooled enough to hold the flask, add 2.5 mL of 2% X-gal (see below). (In kits, the X-gal is combined with ampicillin. N,N' dimethylformamide is also in this mixture—this material is hazardous, so handle carefully.)

To make 2% X-gal:

1. Dissolve 0.16 g X-gal in 8 mL of N,N'dimethylformamide (DMF) in the hood. Please note: Because DMF is toxic, it must be used in a hood.

2. Pour agar into plates and mark LB/Amp/X-gal. Invert and store.

If you are using the plasmid pGal™ from Edvotek, you will also have to add the inducer, IPTG to the agar. This is available in the kit. If using the pGAL™ plasmid, but not from the kit, then add 0.5 mL of freshly made 100 mM IPTG to each liter of agar.

To make 100 mM IPTG:

Dissolve 0.07 g IPTG in 3 mL of sterile water. Swirl agar and pour plates as described above. Mark plates "X-gal," invert, and store in refrigerator.

(12) electrophoresis apparatus—

Any small electrophoresis apparatus can be used. If using one with many lanes, make sure that students write down lane numbers. See General Information (under Preparation of Materials and Solutions) and Ordering Information for suitable Edvotek and Carolina Biological Supply Company models.

(13) agarose—

In Carolina Biological Supply Company and Edvotek kits, agarose is supplied. If a kit is not used, a 1% agarose gel is made from a 1% agarose solution in 10X Tris borate EDTA buffer (TBE) as follows:

1. Prepare 10X Tris borate buffer (TBE)

Tris base	100 g
boric acid	55 g
EDTA (ethylenediamine tetraacetate disodium salt)	8.35 g

Add distilled water to make 1000 mL. Adjust to pH 8.0-8.2 by adding 1 M NaOH. The EDTA will dissolve only after the pH has been raised.

2. Prepare 1% agarose solution

agarose	1 g
Tris borate buffer	10 mL
distilled water	90 mL

Bring to a boil and dissolve the agarose completely.

Note: Kits use a 0.8% agarose gel. Follow kit directions.

This solution can be prepared immediately before use or it can be kept at room temperature and liquefied using a microwave oven. Place approximately 150-250 mL in sterile, screw cap media bottles when hot. Remember, when microwaving the solution for use, be sure to loosen caps.

(14) electrophoresis buffer—

Buffer for running agarose gels is prepared as follows:

10X Tris borate buffer	100 mL (13)
distilled water	900 mL

Alternatively, this buffer can be purchased already mixed or in a powdered form from Edvotek or Carolina Biological Supply Company (see Ordering Information).

(15) *Lambda* DNA—

Lambda DNA, undigested and digested with *Eco*RI and *Hind*III, can be purchased from Edvotek or Carolina Biological Supply Company (see Ordering Information). These are also included in appropriate kits (see General Information)

If you order a *Lambda* DNA and predigested *Lambda* DNA, you will want to use approximately 2 μg of DNA per gel if staining with methylene blue.

Lambda DNA—80 μg (200 μL, 0.4 μg/μL)

Mix 4 μL *Lambda* DNA and 4 μL loading dye plus 12 μL TBE buffer in a microcentrifuge tube. This will give a total of 20 μL. Load entire amount into a single lane.

Lambda DNA digested with *Eco*RI—50 μg (200 μL; 0.25 μg/μL)

Mix 8 μL DNA plus 8 μL TBE buffer plus 4 μL loading dye into a microcentrifuge tube. This will give a total of 20 μL. Load entire amount into a single lane.

Lambda DNA digested with *Hind*III—50 μg (200 μL; 0.25 μg/μL)

Mix 8 μL DNA plus 8 μL TBE buffer plus 4 μL loading dye in a microcentrifuge tube. This will give a total of 20 μL. Load entire amount into a single lane.

(16) bromophenol blue loading dye—

Bromophenol blue loading dye is available from Carolina Biological Supply Company or Edvotek (see Ordering Information). This is a special loading dye. Do not use other bromophenol blue solutions.

(17) methylene blue stain—

Methylene blue stain is available from Carolina Biological Supply Company or Edvotek (see Ordering Information).

V. PREPARATION SUGGESTIONS

Exercise A (Part 1)

All materials for this exercise are included in the laboratory manual. This exercise can be done at home prior to the laboratory in order to save time for experimentation. If the remainder of the laboratory is not used, this exercise will serve as an excellent supplement to lectures or reading on plasmids and recombinant DNA techniques. As a supplement, the text *DNA Science*, Micklos, David A, and Greg A. Freyer, Cold Spring Harbor Press, is available through Carolina Biological Supply Company. It is an excellent teacher supplement.

Exercise A (Part 2)

The easiest way to prepare for this exercise if you have small numbers of students is to order one of the kits described in the General Information section (see Preparation of Materials and Solutions). For large numbers, purchase bacteria, pAmp plasmid separately, and make Luria broth, LB agar, and LB/Amp agar plates according to directions (see (**6**), (**7**), and (**8**) in Preparation of Materials and Solutions). A solution of 0.05 M $CaCl_2$ will also be needed (see (**2**)) in Preparation of Materials and Solutions).

It is important to use a single colony of bacteria for transformation. The colony should be fairly large. This can be isolated from a fresh 24 hour streak plate. When the bacteria are introduced into the 0.05 M $CaCl_2$, be sure to agitate the inoculating loop to break up the colony before introducing the plasmid. Do not use too many cells—this is one of the most frequent errors. Otherwise, transformation will not be as effective. The heat shock must be fast and clean, moving from ice to heat to ice very quickly. Do not let students wander around the laboratory with tubes in hand.

Exercise A demonstrates the processes of transformation and selection, allowing for selection of ampicillin resistance, since only cells resistant to ampicillin can grow on agar containing this antibiotic. The Preparator's Guide is designed so that each student can carry out the exercise. You can also work in pairs or groups of 4 since there are 4 different plates to be inoculated at the end of the experiment. You will need 2 LB plates and 2 LB/Amp plates for each "group," See Materials Preparation (**7**) and (**8**) for directions for making agar plates.

Exercise A (Part 3)

In this exercise, the processes of transformation and selection for antibiotic resistance are, once again, investigated as in Exercise A (Part 2). However, a second gene which confers the Lac$^+$ phenotype to recipient bacteria is also present on the plasmid, pBLU (or pGAL), used in this exercise. (Note: this is a different plasmid from pAmp used in Exercise A, Part 2.) The recipient strain of bacteria is JM101 (note: this is also a different strain of bacteria from those used in Exercise A, Part 2, so do not mix materials from the two parts of this exercise). JM101 is a mutant strain and is not capable of making the α peptide of β galactosidase, but transformed bacteria can make the a peptide of β galactosidase and can, therefore, utilize lactose. However, this is not being selected for (as we select for ampicillin resistance) when bacteria are plated out. (If we wanted to select for this, we would need to use a medium containing only lactose as a food source.) In this experiment, X-gal is used as a histochemical substrate that substitutes for lactose. When cleaved by β galactosidase, a blue precipitate is formed and cells capable of using X-gal turn blue. Only transformed bacteria will turn blue. Other bacteria, assuming they are resistant to Amp, could grow on X-gal/Amp plates, but would not have the ability to utilize X-gal and would not turn blue. Thus, this exercise demonstrates a change in genotype by recognizing an alteration in phenotype (blue). Note that in this exercise, white colonies should not be present on X-gal plates. Ampicillin is included in the plates but only transformed bacteria picking up the pBLU plasmid can grow—both genes for Lac$^+$ and ampicillin resistance are on the same pBLU plasmid. Thus, ampicillin resistant cells will also turn blue. You may find small white colonies surrounding blue colonies, especially if growth is dense. These are "feeder colonies." The main colony (blue) has destroyed the ampicillin in the agar surrounding the colony so that untransformed JM101 cells can grow in the "halo" area.

As in Exercise A (Part 2), the simplest way to prepare for this exercise is to order one of the kits described in the General Information section (see Preparation of Materials and Solutions). For large numbers of students, JM101 cells and plasmid pBLU can be ordered separately. (Because JM101 cells must be maintained on minimal medium and are difficult to culture for any length of time, you will probably not want to try to maintain cultures from year to year.)

You can use the rapid colony transformation technique to make cells competent at the same time as they are transformed, or you can make them competent prior to the transformation (see (**10**)).

IF A KIT IS NOT USED the competent cells can be transformed with plasmid pBLU as follows:

1. Place a 200 µL sample of competent cells into a microcentrifuge tube and add 10 µL (approximately 0.05 µg of DNA) of pBLU for transformation. (Since this is such a small amount, the plasmid can be diluted using sterile TE buffer (**3**). The amount of plasmid added to competent cells should be increased by the same ratio used to dilute the plasmid; i.e., if 20 µL of plasmid is diluted by the addition of 40 µL of TE buffer, use 20 µL instead of 10 µL for the transformation of 200 µL of bacterial cells.)
2. Place the tube containing the competent cells and plasmid on ice for 60 minutes.
3. Heat shock the cells for 2 minutes in a 42° C water bath.
4. Return the cells to ice for 5 minutes.
5. Add 200 µL Luria broth to the cells and allow them to recover on ice for 15 minutes.
6. Plate out 200 µL of cells onto an LB agar plate and 200 µ onto an X-gal/ Amp plate.

If the Carolina Biological Supply or Edvotek kits are used, the instructor is responsible for preparing the control plates. This is done to save on the cost of kits. Before the day of the laboratory, the teacher must prepare sterile agar plates. They may be stored in the refrigerator for several days prior to lab.

Each group of students will need 2 LB plates (unless the instructor prepares control plates) plus 2 LB/Amp plates and 2 LB/Amp/X-gal plates. Make plates according to preparation directions (**7**), (**8**), and (**11**).

24 hours before the experiment:

If using the rapid colony transformation technique, prepare streak plates and incubate for 24 hours at 27° C.

On the day of the experiment:

If using frozen cells that you have made competent, carefully thaw, on ice, the frozen competent JM101 cells. Set up two control LB plates. Competent cells (100 µL) streaked on these plates should grow normally and produce a lawn. Also set up two control Amp-only plates. Competent cells (100 µL) streaked on these plates should not grow. Each student group should be provided with 10 µL of the dissolved pBLU plasmid solution. The students will transform the competent cells with pBLU (this may be diluted with TE buffer to make the plasmid easier to handle—see Preparation of Materials and Solutions (9)) and plate these cells onto the LB/Amp/X-gal plates according to the student directions.

Disposal of culture materials.

At the end of the laboratory period, the teacher should collect all bacterial cultures, tubes, pipettes, and other instruments that have come into contact with the cultures. Likewise, 12-24 hours is long enough to culture cells and check for recombinants. Dispose of these plates after 24 hours or other unwanted contaminating organisms may begin to grow on the plates.

Disinfect materials and glassware using a 10% bleach solution. This can be sprayed onto the surface of the plates using a plastic spray bottle. Soak all glassware in the same solution. Tape culture plates together in groups of three or four and close all tubes. Collect materials in a heavy brown bag to autoclave. For nondisposables (glassware and pipettes), disinfect with a 10% bleach solution.

Exercise B

Kits (described under Student Materials and Equipment; General Information) include all materials for this exercise. Alternatively, solutions can be prepared separately (see Student Materials and Equipment (13) and (14)) or purchased already made (see Ordering Information).

To cast agarose gels follow these suggestions.
1. Put absorbent paper under the gel box—some leaking may occur and cleaning solidified gel off lab tables and floors is no fun.
2. Extreme care should be emphasized by the instructor to ensure that the comb teeth are
   a. set completely down on their "shoulders" when placed on the gel box, and
   b. covered to the correct depth with the agarose gel.
   Too shallow a well will result in some DNA splashing out due to vigorous unloading of the micropipette by students with shaking hands. Wells should be able to accommodate 50 to 100 µL samples.

   Too deep a well may have a "shouldered connection" to the next well, allowing mixing with DNA cut by other restriction enzymes—not to mention the controls— and the resulting bands will be blurred and indistinct.
3. Pour the gels on unmovable counters—inevitably students bump tables while the gel is setting.
4. Recovering the comb after gel solidification must also be done very gently. Slowly lifting one end at a time reduces the number of ripped gel beds.

Follow these suggestions for loading gel beds:
1. You may wish to prepare some agarose in Petri dishes with wells made by the combs in order for students to practice loading their samples. (You could also use a 20% agar solution for practice in order to cut down on the expense of agarose.)
2. Be sure that students have identified their well sequence as starting from a particular side and have recorded this information in their lab books, as well as what they put in each well. Remind them to change pipette tips after loading each well.
3. Encourage students to "get down" and "eyeball" each well as closely as they can—a dark background may heighten the contrast.

4. If a digital micropipette is used for loading, two hands on the pipette will help, but not together (one should be close the base and the other on the handle with a thumb on the button). Slowly expel the contents of the pipette, being sure that the tip is not stabbing through the bottom of the well.

In order to electrophorese the gel, follow these directions:
1. Be sure to cover the tank. It is essential, to ensure safety during this procedure, that the electrophoresis unit be used with the cover properly in place.
2. With the power supply turned off and the plug not in the outlet, connect the red lead to the positive pole (anode—red) and the black lead to the negative pole (cathode—black). Then plug in and turn the power on. If using an Edvotek chamber, set the voltage to 50 volts. For the Carolina apparatus, use 80 volts and check.
3. Be sure to watch for dye movement as the experiment begins to ensure that the apparatus is working properly. It should take 1.75 to 2 hours to complete electrophoresis at this setting.
4. When finished, turn the power off first; unplug the power supply from the outlet, and then unplug the leads to the electrophoresis chamber.
5. Gingerly move the gel to a disposable plastic tray for staining. Make sure that students wear gloves. If a kit is not used, gels can be stained with 0.25% methylene blue and destained with water. Remember, gloves should always be worn when handling the staining and destaining of gels.

Once gels are stained, wrap them in plastic wrap and mark the bands using a waterproof felt tip marker. Also mark the location of the corners of the gels and the wells. Alternatively, cut transparencies into quarters. Place the gel on an overhead projector and lay a piece of transparency film on top of the gel. Mark all bands using a waterproof marker. Tape the transparency or plastic wrap to a piece of white paper and copy it on a copying machine. (If the electrophoresis is done as a demonstration, copies can be distributed to all students.) If some students are unsuccessful, copies of data from other experiments can be shared.

You may wish to do the electrophoresis experiment as a separate laboratory or have students carry out the experiment as an extra credit project. Since the running time does not require student involvement, students can be doing other activities or can leave and return later.

Exercise C

This is a paper and pencil exercise that can be completed at home. It introduces the concept of DNA fingerprinting and builds on knowledge of electrophoresis and restriction enzyme digestion of DNA from Exercise B.

VI.   ORDERING INFORMATION

E. coli MM294, slant culture—Carolina Biological, # 21-1530
E. coli MM294, streaked plate—Carolina Biological, # 21-1531
E. coli JM101 cells—Carolina Biological, # 21-1561 (slant) or # 21-1562 (plate)
plasmid pAmp (0.005 μg/μL)—Carolina Biological, #, 21-1438 (1 μg, 200 μL)
plasmid pBLU (0.005 μg/μL)— Carolina Biological, # 21-1427 (1 μg; 200 μL)

phage *Lambda* DNA—Carolina Biological, # 21-1410

phage *Lambda* DNA, *Hind*III fragments—Carolina Biological, # 21-1473

phage *Lambda* DNA, *Eco*RI fragments—Carolina Biological, # 21-1474

*Eco*RI endonuclease—Carolina Biological, # 21-1670; Edvotek[*], # 715

Luria broth (powdered)—Edvotek, # 611

Luria broth agar plates (LB agar), prepoured—Carolina Biological, # 21-6610

Luria broth agar, ready to pour—Carolina Biological, # 21-6620

Luria broth agar + ampicillin (LB-Amp) plates, prepoured—Carolina Biological, # 21-6611

Luria broth agar + ampicillin, ready-to-pour—Carolina Biological, # 21-6621

Luria broth agar + ampicillin + X-gal, ready-to-pour—Carolina Biological, # 21-6624

X-gal—Carolina Biological, # 21-7190; Edvotek, # 614; Bethesda Research Laboratories[**]

IPTG—Carolina Biological, # 21-7930; Edvotek, # 613; Bethesda Research Laboratories, # 5529UA

N,N'dimethylformamide—Carolina Biological, # 21-7350; Edvotek, # 614

ampicillin— Carolina Biological, # 21-6880; Sigma, # A-9393

bromophenol blue loading dye— Carolina Biological, # 21-8200; Edvotek, # 606

methylene blue stain— Carolina Biological, # 21-8290; Edvotek, # 609

Tris-EDTA (TE) buffer—Carolina Biological, # 21-9026

Tris-borate-EDTA (TBE), conc. buffer—Carolina Biological, # 21-9027; Edvotek, # 607

agarose (low EEO)— Carolina Biological, # 21-7080; Edvotek, # 605; Sigma, # A-3768

bacterotryptone—Carolina Biological, # 79-4420

yeast extract—Carolina Biological, # 79-4780

(Bacto) agar— Carolina Biological, # 79-6240; Fisher, # DF0140-02-9

glycerol (redistilled)—Carolina Biological, # 21-7730; Bethesda Research Laboratories, # 5514UA

calcium chloride (CaCl$_2$)—Carolina Biological, # 85-1950; Fisher, # C79-500

Tris base (Trizma base)—Sigma, # T-1503

boric acid—Carolina Biological, # 84-8440; Fisher # A74-500

EDTA, disodium salt—Carolina Biological, # 86-1790; Fisher 5311-100

0.5 M EDTA—Carolina Biological, # 21-7432

microcapillary pipettes, 10 µL—Carolina Biological, # 21-4512

microcapillary pipettes, 100 µL—Carolina Biological, # 21-4517

Ultramicro Accropet—Carolina Biological, # 21-4688

Eppendorf digital micropipettes—

2-20 µL—Carolina Biological, # 21-4641

10-100 µL—Carolina Biological, # 21-4642

100-1000 µL—Carolina Biological, # 21-4644

micropipette tips, 1-200 µL—Carolina Biological, # 21-5120

micropipette tips, 100-1000 µL—Carolina Biological, # 21-5123

microtransfer pipettes for loading samples on gels—Edvotek, # 632

---

[*] Edvotek, Inc., P.O. Box 1232, West Bethesda, MD 20817 (800-338-6835 or 800-EDVOTEK)

[**] Bethesda Research Laboratories, P.O. Box 6009, Gaithersburg, MD 20877 (800-638-8992; in Maryland and outside USA, 301-840-8000)

transformation tubes (17 X 100 mm; Falcon 2059), disposable—Carolina Biological, # 21-5080

Micro-Test tubes— Carolina Biological, # 21-5220; Edvotek, # 632

Micro-Test tube rack—Carolina Biological, # 21-5572

centrifuge tube, conical glass—Carolina Biological, # 73-2014; Fisher, # 05-500

centrifuge tube, conical, disposable—Fisher, # 05-538-530

gel electrophoresis apparatus—Carolina Biological, # 21-3668; Edvotek, # 502

electrophoresis power supply—Carolina Biological, # 21-2673; Edvotek, # 503

visible light gel visualization system—Carolina Biological, # 21-6214; Edvotek, # 552

Kit; Exercise A (Part 2)— Carolina Biological, # 21-1142; Edvotek, # 201

Kit; Exercise A (Part 3)— Carolina Biological, # 21-1146; Edvotek, # 211

Kit; Exercise B (predigested DNA—Carolina Biological, # 21-1149; Edvotek, # 112

Kit, Exercise B (restriction endonuclease digestion)—Carolina Biological, # 21-1151; Edvotek, # 212

Petri dishes, sterile disposable—Carolina Biological, # 74-1350

LABORATORY 17   The Genetic Basis of Evolution

I.   FOREWORD

This laboratory demonstrates various aspects of quantitative genetic variation and sexual dimorphism that can be encountered when studying phenotype differences. Use of the Hardy-Weinberg equation allows students to investigate the dynamics of population isolation and the mechanisms that lead to evolutionary change in gene frequencies. Concepts of sample size and sampling error can be emphasized. An outdoor exercise adds fun to the laboratory while providing the opportunity to study the selection process. The roles of variation and adaptation as they relate to selection pressure are explored by students acting as predators on a population of "wooly worms."

The Bio-Bytes computer simulation, DUELING ALLELES, provides an excellent supplement to extend this laboratory. The program simulates the effect of genetic drift and selection on the frequency of an allele.

II.   TIME REQUIREMENTS

Exercise A (Parts 1 and 2)—40 minutes
Exercise B—30 minutes
Exercise C—50 minutes
Exercise D—50 minutes
Exercise E—60 minutes (outside environment)

III.   STUDENT MATERIALS AND EQUIPMENT

	Per Student	Per Pair (2)	Per Group (4)	Per Class (24)
Exercise A (Part 1)				
calipers			1	6
metric ruler (30 cm)			1	6
Exercise A (Part 2)				
meter stick (1 m)			1	6
Exercise B				
PTC taste test papers	1			24
Exercise C				
beads from chromosome simulation kit OR beans (1)				2
pint jar or 500 mL beaker			1	6
small boxes or Petri dishes (100 mm)			10	60
Exercise D				
beads from chromosome simulation kit OR beans (1)				2

	Per Student	Per Pair (2)	Per Group (4)	Per Class (24)

Exercise D—continued

pint fruit jar or 500 mL beaker			1	6
Styrofoam plate or dissecting pan			2	12

Exercise E

yarn "woolly worms" (2)				100

IV. PREPARATION OF MATERIALS AND SOLUTIONS

(1) chromosome simulation kit—
The chromosome simulation kits used in Laboratories 12 and 13 contain red and yellow beads that can be separated and used in these exercises. See Laboratory 12 for more information on these kits.

(2) yarn "woolly worms"—
For a class of 15-30, you will need at least 100 pieces of yarn for each of 16 different colors (1,600 pieces). Yarn pieces should be 2-3 inches long. Wrap yarn around 4 fingers and then cut to make 3 inch lengths. Distribute the yarn on a grassy lawn, 50-100 feet on a side, depending on class size.

V. PREPARATION SUGGESTIONS

Exercise A

If the instructor wishes to determine if the difference in cephalic index of males and females is significant, proceed as follows. List all measurements for males in a column on the left side of a page and all measurements for females in a column in the middle of the page. Total all measurements for each sample (to give the sum of Xs or ΣX). Divide each total by the number of observations ($\Sigma X/n$) to give the arithmetic average or mean. Subtract the smaller mean from the larger and record the result as the difference (d).

There are a variety of ways to test this difference to see if it is "significant." One standard test involves the calculation of the sums of squares (SS). Square each measurement in each sample and total the squares (ΣX^2) separately for males and for females. Square the sum of the original observations, divide the sum by the number of observations, and subtract this result from the total of the squares to give the sums of squares—thus

$$SS = \Sigma X^2 - (\Sigma X)^2/n$$

Do this for both groups or samples. Add the two sums of squares. Divide this total by the sum of each sample size minus 1, multiplied by the sum of the two sample sizes minus 1 divided by their product, and take the square root of the result. This is the standard error of the difference (s_d). Expressed as an equation, this series of operations is as follows:

$$s_d = \sqrt{((SS_1 + SS_2)/((n_1 - 1)(n_2 - 1)) \times ((n_1 + n_2)/(n_1 n_2))}$$

While this equation looks formidable, it is easy to solve if the calculations are performed inside each level of parentheses in order. To test the difference, calculate Student's t by dividing the difference between the two sample means and the standard error of the difference:

$$t = d/s_d$$

For a class of 24, a value equal to or greater than 2.074 indicates a 1-in-20 chance (or less) that the difference observed is due to chance. A value greater than 2.819 indicates a one-in-100 chance (or less) that the difference is due to chance. For other sample sizes, consult a statistics book for a "t table" (Cumulative Student's t Distribution). Add the two numbers of observations in each group and subtract 2 to determine the degrees of freedom (df).

This calculation of t assumes a normal distribution of observations and that the variances in each sample are equal. Other versions of the t test can be used under certain conditions (note that the t test *cannot* be used to compare more than two means). A variety of other tests are available and can be adapted to other experimental situations. Consult standard statistical references. Sampling, estimates of central tendency, and testing of hypotheses (along with types of errors) can be introduced as useful tools using these calculations if desired.

Exercise C

For each group, start with 400 beads (pull beads in the chromosome simulation kit apart) in a pint fruit jar or 500 mL beaker. Place 360 of one color ($p = 0.9$) and 40 of another ($q = 0.1$) The bead of the rarer color is to represent the rarer allele. To show a more dramatic founder effect, increase the number of beads in the parent population relative to the numbers in the founder population. If beads are not available, you can use beans of different colors, but make sure that these are the same size and shape so that student sampling techniques will not be affected.

Exercise D

Students may work alone if desired, but the number of setups will need to be increased. The starting frequencies of beads in the two trays are the same: 35 common beads and 15 rare. The common bead is red in Tray A and yellow in Tray B. Individual beads represent genes (alleles). Trays A and B are experimental populations where gene flow takes place without regard to genotype as students exchange beads. For each gene pool, immigration equals emigration so that the size of the gene pool stays the same. In tray A, selection operates against one homozygote, demonstrated by the removal of one individual (two beads) during each generation (iteration). In tray B, the other homozygote is selected against, one individual (two beads) per generation. These individuals are replaced by adding beads to simulate births, but in proportion to the adjusted allele frequencies. Each repetition or iteration is equivalent to one generation in which one individual is lost from the population due to natural selection and one individual joins the population as a potential reproducer.

Exercise E

The purpose of this exercise is to introduce students to the concepts of variation, adaptation, selection pressure, and cryptic coloration (a specific adaptation). Pieces of colored yarn represent "wooly worms" distributed throughout the ecosystem. Students represent predators (birds) that feed on the worms. Depending on the colors of wool pieces used, some will be harder to find than others. When the colored yarn pieces that have been found are tallied as data, a Chi-square test is used to determine if the wool pieces are collected randomly or by a selection process.

Allow students to work in teams of 3 or 4. Students should "feed" on the wooly worms for 10 minutes (make sure that at least 10 pieces of the hardest to find colored yarn are collected). It is best to conduct this activity outside. If you have a rainy day, a quick substitute can be made by using "holes" from a paper hole punch. We have successfully used a room with a mottled pattern floor tile. Different colored holes can be quickly produced. Transparencies make excellent "hard to find" holes. Students can pick up the "holes" with a wet finger. On occasion, more pieces of wool are collected than originally distributed. Check to see if some of the pieces have become unraveled so that one piece becomes two.

If the experiment is repeated using only those pieces of wool that were collected, then gene frequencies will change from one generation to the next with a subsequent reduction in variation within the species in time. Drastic changes in the environment can lead to extinction, but this is the exception rather than the rule.

VI. ORDERING INFORMATION

anthropometric calipers—Carolina Biological, # 69-6245
metric ruler—Carolina Biological, # 70-2616
meter stick—Carolina Biological, # 70-620
PTC taste test papers—Carolina Biological, # 17-4010
chromosome simulation Biokit—Carolina Biological, # 17-1100
colored yarn—local store

LABORATORY 18   Behavior

I.   FOREWORD

This laboratory is designed to introduce students to the behavior of animals. Students work in pairs as they study simple responses to external stimuli and behaviors involved in courtship, and learning. Exercise B requires isolation of crickets several days before laboratory. Exercise C requires that students return on subsequent days to complete the training of their mealworm larvae. Alternatively, additional laboratory sections may extend Exercise C throughout the week, sharing their results at the beginning of the following week.

II.   TIME REQUIREMENTS

Exercise A—40 minutes
Exercise B (Part 1)—60 minutes
Exercise B (Part 2)—30 minutes
Exercise B (Part 3)—20 minutes
Exercise C—30 minutes for each training session, each session separated by 60 minutes
Let's Investigate—20 minutes

III.   STUDENT MATERIALS AND EQUIPMENT

	Per Student	Per Pair (2)	Per Group (4)	Per Class (24)
Exercise A				
paper lids (opaque)		2		24
plastic lids (clear)		1		12
aluminum dissecting pan		1		12
pill bugs (isopods) **(1)**		10		120
Exercise B (Part 1)				
plastic shoe box			1	6
male crickets, marked **(2)**			4	24
matchbox **(3)**			1	6
Exercise B (Part 2)				
same materials as in Exercise B (Part 1)				
Exercise B (Part 3)				
plastic shoe box			1	6
male crickets, marked **(2)**			4	24
female crickets, marked **(2)**			2	12

100

	Per Student	Per Pair (2)	Per Group (4)	Per Class (24)
Exercise C				
shallow black box		1		12
T-maze		1		12
mealworm larvae, marked (**4**)		1		12
flashlight		1		12
Let's Investigate				
live termites (**5**)			6	36
ball-point pens, several brands and colors (**6**)			3-4	18-24
box lid (**7**)			1	6

IV. PREPARATION OF MATERIALS AND SOLUTIONS

(**1**) pill bugs (isopods)—

Pill bugs (sow bugs or "rolly pollies") are easily collected in many regions of the country from under bricks, stones, boards, or other derbies lying on the soil in damp areas around your house or in the woods. Place them in a plastic refrigerator container with some moist moss or leaf litter until needed. These crustaceans are generally available year round in many parts of the country. They may also be purchased (see Ordering Information).

(**2**) crickets, marked—

Order crickets from a cricket farm. Do not purchase them from a bait store because you will not know age and they will have already established dominance patterns. Suggested vendor—Fluker's Cricket Farm, 2623 Beach Street, Baton Rouge, LA 70821 (504-343-7035).

Sex crickets when they arrive and separate males into one aquarium and females into another. Females can be identified by the long, needle-like ovipositor extending from their abdomens.

Place cardboard-type egg cartons upside down in the bottom of the aquarium giving enough room for the crickets to move around. Fill a Petri dish with aquarium gravel and add water. Place this in the tank. Do not use a container of open water. Keep the cage as dry as possible. Place small wedges of potato on a Petri dish as food. Change food and water about every 4 days. Crickets have a life span of 2 weeks.

Approximately 3-4 days before using the crickets for experiments, you must isolate both males and females. Pick the crickets up carefully using small paper cups. We use urine specimen cups with small holes poked in the top. Place a small wedge of potato in each cup for food and moisture. The day before use, take tempera paint and a small point brush. Place a dot of colored paint (red, yellow, blue, or green) on the back of each cricket. Place a corresponding dot on the cup. Only the males need to be color marked. You will need 4 male crickets (each of a different color) for each group of students. You will need 2 females for each group of students.

Have enough crickets isolated so that each set is used for only one laboratory. Have students place "used" crickets back into the aquarium.

(3) matchbox—

Use the outer sleeve from small, safety match boxes.

(4) mealworm larvae, marked—

Mealworm larvae can be obtained in most pet stores or they can be ordered from Carolina Biological Supply Company (see Ordering Information) or obtained from a local culture.

To develop a culture, use a flat, opaque plastic or metal storage container. Place a 1" layer of uncooked Cream of Wheat or bran meal and four layers of paper towels in the pan and add larvae (and adults if available). The towels should be sprinkled lightly with water every 4-5 days and replaced as necessary. Add cereal when the level decreases (every several months). A slice of apple or other fruit also adds moisture to the colony which can be maintained indefinitely. Start your colony well in advance of use and maintain it from year to year.

Individual larvae should be marked with dots of model paint in different color combinations for individual identification. Keep mealworms "in training" in a small separate culture dish with only a small amount of food so they can be easily located.

Mealworms will also be used in Laboratory 23, Exercise B (Part 5).

(5) live termites—

Collect termites from rotten logs on the floor of the woods. Find areas that are not too wet. Open the log using a hatchet or other suitable tool. Use workers or soldiers for this exercise and not the winged, reproductive adults. Termites can also be ordered from Carolina Biological Supply Company (see Ordering Information). (Termites will also be used in Laboratory 19, Let's Investigate.)

(6) ball point pens, several brands and colors—

Furnish a variety of ball point pens for this experiment and allow students to try their own. Be sure to include PaperMate pens in the selection (they work!).

(7) box lid—

Provide a suitable arena for observing termites' following behavior.

V.   PREPARATION SUGGESTIONS

Exercise A

Collect opaque lids from pint ice cream containers, Wendy's chili cartons, or other food containers for use in this exercise. Cut 2 "doors" in opposite sides of the lip. The lids should be approximately the same diameter. Plastic Petri dishes can be used as clear shelters. Cut "doors" in the sides opposite one another. Clean, empty dissecting pans without wax or vinyl or aluminum trays can be used to hold the experiments—they should not be larger than necessary so that the isopods are constrained to some extent and cannot wander off.

Exercise B (Parts 1, 2, and 3)

Use a plastic or translucent Rubbermaid shoebox as a container for your experiment. Some students may wish to make a grid the size of the bottom of the box to help map territories. In this case, you must be able to see through the box. The grid can be labeled A through K or L along the top and 1 to 5 or 6 down the side.

Crickets prefer low light, so keep the room light dimmed. Crickets are also sensitive to vibrations—do not move the plastic container during the experiment and do not bump the table it is sitting on. Give students small paper cups to handle crickets.

Students will have fun with this lab. When one group established its most dominant cricket, you may wish to have crickets from different groups "face off." If you allow students to do this, use other males for Part 3, Courtship.

The design for this exercise was developed by Joseph R. Larsen, University of Illinois.

Exercise C

You will need to construct the training apparatus used in this exercise. Use a box measuring about 8 X 10 X 1-2" to hold the T-maze. This can be made from 0.25" plywood or cardboard (small, flat gift boxes are adequate). It should be sprayed with flat black paint on the inside surfaces and allowed to dry thoroughly to dissipate all paint odor.

A floorless T-maze should be constructed with an alley (the upright member of the "T") measuring 5" (13 cm) by 1/8" (3 mm) and the two arms measuring 4" (10 cm) by about 0.5" (1.3 cm). The maze should be about 0.5-0.75" high (1.3-2 cm). The mealworm larva should not be able to turn around in the alley but should be able to do so in the arms of the "T." The maze should be made of plywood and should be spray-painted flat black.

Be sure that the room lights are kept dim and offer no directional information that can affect behavioral tendencies during the training period.

Let's Investigate

Make sure that you have a USDA permit if you live in HI, TN, or VT. Keep termites in a Rubbermaid box. Warn students to try "mazes" by placing the paper with its ink markings inside a box (or a Rubbermaid container) so the termites can be confined. Termites will follow markings made with Paper-Mate pens because they contain an analog of the trail pheromone (ink color will not matter). Be sure that the trail is not too complicated. Dispose of the termites in an appropriate manner—take them back to the woods from which they were collected and return them to their colony.

This is a fun activity for students to assist with development of hypothesis formation and decision making concerning appropriate experiments.

The design for this exercise comes from the work of Sheryl Shanholtzer, De Kalb College, Dunwoody, GA, and Marsha Fanning, LeNoir Rhyne College, Hickory, NC.

VI.   ORDERING INFORMATION

aluminum dissecting pan—Carolina Biological, # 62-9010
pill or sow bugs—Carolina Biological, # L 624
mealworm larvae, *Tenebrio*—Carolina Biological, # L 891 (or # L 893 for starting a new culture)
crickets—Fluker's Cricket Farm, 2623 Beach St., Baton Rouge, LA 70821 (504-343-7035); Carolina Biological, # L715

LABORATORY 19   Diversity—Kingdoms Monera and Protista

I. FOREWORD

This is the first of three laboratories designed to study diversity of three kingdoms: Monera, Protista, and Fungi. Live material should be used as often as possible. By selecting parts of exercises, the laboratory can be shortened and combined with one or both of the other diversity laboratories.

II. TIME REQUIREMENTS

Exercise A—10 minutes
Exercise B (Part 1)—15 minutes
Let's Investigate—30 minutes
Exercise B (Part 2)—10 minutes
Exercise C—40 minutes
Exercisc D—30 minutes
Let's Investigate—30 minutes
Exercise E—20 minutes
Exercise F—30 minutes
Exercise G—30 minutes
Exercise H—15 minutes

III. STUDENT MATERIALS AND EQUIPMENT

	Per Student	Per Pair (2)	Per Group (4)	Per Class (24)
Exercise A				
bacilli bacteria (prepared slide)				1
cocci bacteria (prepared slide)				1
spirilla bacteria (prepared slide)				1
compound microscope (demonstration)				3
nutrient agar, Petri dish (1)	1			24
Exercise B (Part 1)				
antibiotic agar Petri dish containing *Escherichia coli* bacteria and five different antibiotic sensitivity disks (2)				1
antibiotic agar Petri dish containing *Staphylococcus aureus* bacteria and five different antibiotic sensitivity disks (3)				1
Escherichia coli, gram stain (prepared slide)	1			24
Staphylococcus aureus, gram stain (prepared slide)	1			24

104

	Per Student	Per Pair (2)	Per Group (4)	Per Class (24)

Let's Investigate

	Per Student	Per Pair (2)	Per Group (4)	Per Class (24)
S. aureus broth culture (**4**)			1	6
E. coli broth culture (**5**)			1	6
nutrient agar, Petri dish (**1**)	1			24
paper disks (**6**)	2			48
cleaning solutions (student selected), bottles (**6**)			1	6
forceps	1			24
wax pencil		1		12
ruler		1		12
cotton swabs (Q-Tips)	2			48

Exercise B (Part 2)

	Per Student	Per Pair (2)	Per Group (4)	Per Class (24)
soybean plants, pot (inoculated with *Rhizobium*) (**7**)				1
soybean plants, pot (not inoculated with *Rhizobium*) (**7**)				1
Rhizobium (prepared slide)				1
compound microscope (demonstration)				1

Exercise C

	Per Student	Per Pair (2)	Per Group (4)	Per Class (24)
microscope slides, box (75 X 25 mm)			1	6
coverslips, box 22 X 22 mm)			1	6
Nostoc (live culture)				1
Cylindrospermum (live culture)				1
Oscillatoria (live culture)				1
Anabaena (live culture)				1
Gloeocapsa (live culture)				1
compound microscope	1			24

Exercise D

	Per Student	Per Pair (2)	Per Group (4)	Per Class (24)
Trypanosoma (prepared slide)	1			24
Amoeba proteus (live culture)				1
Paramecium caudatum (live culture)				1
Plasmodium vivax (prepared slide)	1			24
microscope slides, box (75 X 25 mm)			1	6
coverslips, box (22 X 22 mm)			1	6
compound microscope	1			24

Let's Investigate

	Per Student	Per Pair (2)	Per Group (4)	Per Class (24)
insect Ringer's solution, dropping bottle (**8**)			1	6
termites (larvae) (**9**)	3-5			up to 120
microscope slides, box (75 X 25 mm)			1	6
coverslips, box (22 X 22 mm)			1	6
dissecting needle	2			48
Giemsa stain, dropping bottle (**10**)			1	6

	Per Student	Per Pair (2)	Per Group (4)	Per Class (24)

Let's Investigate—continued

	Per Student	Per Pair (2)	Per Group (4)	Per Class (24)
glycerol, dropping bottle (**11**)			1	6

Exercise E

	Per Student	Per Pair (2)	Per Group (4)	Per Class (24)
agar Petri dishes (**12**)	1			24
Physarum on agar plate (**13**)	1			24
Physarum, dried plasmodium starts (**14**)	1			24
oat flakes, box				1

Exercise F

	Per Student	Per Pair (2)	Per Group (4)	Per Class (24)
Euglena, live culture				1
diatomaceous earth, bottle				1
diatoms (prepared slide)		1		12
Peridinium (prepared slide)		1		12
Fucus (preserved, complete plant)				1
Laminaria (preserved, complete plant)				1
Ectocarpus (live culture)				1
Polysiphonia (live culture)				1
Corallopsis (coralline algae, live culture)				1
Dasya (preserved)				1
microscope slides, box (75 X 25 mm)			1	6
coverslips, box (22 X 22 mm)			1	6
compound microscope	1			24

Exercise G

	Per Student	Per Pair (2)	Per Group (4)	Per Class (24)
Chlamydomonas (live culture)				1
Spirogyra (live culture)				1
Gonium (live culture)				1
Volvox (live culture)				1
Zygnema (live culture)				1
Stigeoclonium (live culture)				1
Ulva (preserved)				1
Ulothrix (live culture)				1
desmids (live culture)				1
microscope slides, box (75 X 25 mm)			1	6
coverslips, box (22 X 22 mm)			1	6
compound microscope	1			24

Exercise H

	Per Student	Per Pair (2)	Per Group (4)	Per Class (24)
plankton sample (**15**)				1
microscope slides, box (75 X 25 mm)			1	6
coverslips, box (22 X 22 mm)			1	6
compound microscope	1			24

Exercise H—continued

Ward's dichotomous key to free-living protozoa	1			24

IV. PREPARATION OF MATERIALS AND SOLUTIONS

(1) nutrient agar Petri dishes—

Using a 500 mL Erlenmeyer flask, dissolve 3.1 g of nutrient agar (see Ordering Information) in 100 mL of distilled water. Heat to a boil to dissolve nutrient agar. Autoclave for 15 minutes at 15 pounds pressure (121° C). Place a cotton plug covered with cheesecloth in the flask before autoclaving. After autoclaving, let the agar solution cool (but not enough to gel), and then pour enough solution to cover the bottom of each Petri dish.

(2) and **(3)** Petri dishes for antibiotic sensitivity tests

Gather the following materials:

> antibiotic agar
> Difco antibiotic disks
> tryptic soy broth
> sterile Petri dishes (100 mm)
> 500 mL Erlenmeyer flask (cotton plugged)
> two 250 mL Erlenmeyer flasks (cotton plugged)
> inoculating loop
> sterile spreader
> Bunsen burner
> incubator (37° C)

Procedure:

1. Antibiotic agar Petri dishes. Using a 500 mL Erlenmeyer flask, dissolve 3.05 g of antibiotic agar (see Ordering Information) in 100 mL of distilled water. Heat to a boil to dissolve the agar before autoclaving at 121° C for 15 minutes at 15 pounds pressure. After autoclaving, let the solution cool, then pour enough antibiotic agar solution to cover the bottom of each Petri dish. (See alternative method.)

2. Tryptic soy broth solution. Using two 250 mL Erlenmeyer flasks, each flask containing 100 mL of distilled water, dissolve 3 g of tryptic soy broth in each. Heat slightly to dissolve the tryptic soy broth before autoclaving for 15 minutes at 15 pounds pressure (121° C). After autoclaving, let both flasks cool.

3. After the flasks of tryptic soy broth have cooled, flame and break open a vial of *E. coli* freeze-dried bacteria, and empty the vial into a flask of tryptic soy broth after flaming the top of the flask. Alternatively, use a loop of bacteria from a bacterial slant (see Ordering Information). Do the same with *S. aureus*. Allow to incubate 24 hours. If inoculating loops are not available, a sterile Pasteur pipette can be used to transfer a few drops of culture. The drops can then be spread. Use a sterile bent glass rod to spread the bacteria in a film to cover the entire Petri dish. Keep the lid over the culture dish while spreading to insure sterility. With sterile forceps, place five appropriate antibiotic disks (your choice) on the surface of

plates of *E. coli* and *S. aureus*. Use the same kinds of disks on both plates. Allow 24-28 hours of incubation (37° C).

Alternate method:

Antibiotic agar can be poured into sterile capped tubes instead of Petri dishes. When ready to inoculate, the agar can be melted at 45-48° C and can then be inoculated with bacteria (approximately 0.3 mL or several loops full). Pour the inoculated agar onto a plate and let it harden. Place antibiotic disks on the surface of the agar as above.

(4) *S. aureus* broth culture—

Follow steps 2 and 3 in **(2)** to prepare a tryptic soy broth culture of *S. aureus*. Use freeze-dried *S. aureus* or a loopful of bacteria from a prepared slant (see Ordering Information). Spread the bacteria onto the surface of a nutrient agar Petri dish, prepared as in **(1)**. Place approximately 0.1 mL of a 24 hour tryptic soy broth culture onto the center of the agar plate and use a glass spreading rod to spread the bacteria. Alternatively, students can use a sterile Q-Tip to spread the bacteria. You may also wish to use *S. epidermidis* (living culture), a non-pathogenic staphylococcus found on the skin instead of *S. aureus*..

(5) *E. coli* broth culture—

Prepare as in **(4)** above, but use freeze-dried *E. coli* (see Ordering Information).

(6) paper disks with cleaning solutions—

Use blank paper disks for preparing commercial cleaning or soap solutions (see Ordering Information). Students should allow their disk to soak in a solution for 1-2 minutes. These should be drained by touching one edge to a sterile paper towel (sterile gauze squares may be used to blot off excess fluid).

(7) soybean plants, pot (inoculated with *Rhizobium*)—

Either soybeans or clover can be used for this demonstration. Seeds are simply coated with the *Rhizobium* inoculum by gently shaking them in a plastic bag containing the inoculum. The inoculum which we have found to be particularly good is from Nitragin Company (Milwaukee, WI 53209, phone 414-462-7600) and can be ordered by phone. Carolina Biological Supply Company also provides the inoculum with clover seeds as an inexpensive package (see ordering information). ALLOW EIGHT WEEKS FOR GROWTH.

(8) insect Ringer's solution—

Dissolve 7.5 g NaCl, 3.5 g KCl, and 0.21 g $CaCl_2$ in enough distilled water to make 1 liter of solution.

(9) termites—

Collect termites from rotten logs on the floor of the woods. Find areas that are not too wet. Open the log using a hatchet or other suitable tool. Use the larvae for this exercise and not the winged adults. Termites can also be ordered from Carolina Biological Supply Company (see Ordering Information).

(10) Giemsa stain—

It is easiest to order this stain already prepared (see Ordering Information). If you have powdered Giemsa on hand, dissolve 0.5 g Giemsa powder in 33 mL glycerin (this will take 1-2 hours). Add 33 mL of acetone-free absolute methyl alcohol. To use, dilute this stock solution 1:10 with distilled water.

(11) glycerol (50%)—

> Add 50 mL glycerin (glycerol) to 50 mL distilled water. Place in dropping bottle for easy use in mounting coverslips.

(12) (13) and **(14)** (Bacto) agar Petri dishes—

> Using a 500 mL Erlenmeyer flask, dissolve 2 g of (Bacto) agar into each 100 mL of distilled water. Autoclave for 15 minutes at 15 pounds pressure (121° C). After autoclaving let the agar solution cool, then pour enough agar solution to cover the bottom of each Petri dish.
>
> When you autoclave the agar, also autoclave a bottle of distilled water (100 mL), a pair of forceps, and a few Pasteur pipettes.
>
> *Physarum* is available in two forms—a culture of the plasmodium growing on agar and as the dried resting stage called a sclerotium. After agar has cooled, place the plasmodium on a small piece of filter paper and place it in the center of the agar dish. Place four oat flakes close to the material and wet the filter paper and oat flakes with the sterile distilled water using a sterile Pasteur pipette. Start the slime mold two days before the laboratory. Hold it at room temperature in the dark. Feed as it moves away from the oat flakes. Exposure to light triggers the formation of fruiting bodies (start cultures one week ahead for fruiting bodies).
>
> You can increase the numbers or save for later by simply drying out the agar with the plasmodium by placing the plate in a fume hood. The agar can then be cut into small pieces to give new starts. Alternatively, the plasmodium can be scraped off the agar and transferred to wet filter paper. Refeed with oat flakes until it spreads out and then simply dry out the filter paper and slime mold by exposing it to the air. Cut up the filter paper to make new cultures.

(15) plankton sample—

> A plankton net can be made from a pair of support hosiery. Cut the hose off at the ankle and attach it to a small plastic jar (those in which protozoan cultures are shipped by Carolina Biological Supply Company are ideal) with a rubber band. Usually the top of the stocking is a double thickness. Put a hole in it on the top rim and slide an opened coat hanger through the hole and around the rim. Fold the coat hanger to make a suitable opening to the net and a handle. You may wish to centrifuge the sample at low speed to concentrate the sample.
>
> Ward's Natural Science Establishment has an excellent key for free-living protozoa (4 pages) entitled "Dichotomous Key to Free-living Protozoa." If the use of keys has been taught prior to the beginning of the diversity laboratories, this will reinforce the student's learning. Otherwise, the key is simply useful for identification purposes.

V.   PREPARATION SUGGESTIONS

Exercise A

This exercise needs to be started one week ahead of time. Students are encouraged to sample many different types of possible sources of bacteria, including feet of animals, shoes, parts of the body, etc. Agar plates for this experiment should be poured very thin to avoid costly expenses for agar.

Exercise B

If you do not wish to prepare your own antibiotic study plates, Carolina Biological kit # 15-4737 or 15-4740 can be substituted.

Let's Investigate

This is a fairly simple exercise that allows students to practice their aseptic techniques learned during Laboratory 7. Make sure that everything is kept sterile. Autoclave forceps and use autoclaved paper towels (wrap in foil) or sterile gauze pads to drain disks. Let students select disinfectants. Cleaning solutions and facial scrubs or medicines are best. If liquid soap is to be used, dilute the soap until you have a thin rather than thick liquid.

Exercise B (Part 2)

For soybeans inoculated with *Rhizobium*, we emphasize that plants will take eight weeks to grow and show *Rhizobium* infection.

Exercises C and D

A box of microscope slides and a box of cover slips should be provided for every four people (or whatever is logistically simple for your seating arrangement). Slides are used in Exercises C and D. Encourage students to rinse slides between wet mounts and reuse them. Provide a dirty slide container for used slides at the end of the laboratory period.

Living materials or preserved materials and prepared slides can be used for Exercises C and D. Substitutions can easily be made to use what is available in your laboratory. A plankton sample from a pond will provide some good examples of many organisms, both plant and animal.

Let's Investigate

Termites are easily found in the wild. Supply students with a Petri dish and have them collect their own, but warn them to tape the dish around the edges to prevent escape. Termites will live overnight even if the edges of the dish are taped. We collect termites along with a piece of their decayed wood in a Rubbermaid container. The termites will stay in the wood. Place a damp paper towel in the container for moisture.

The flagellates that students will observe in this exercise are very numerous and are easily observed.

Exercise E

Experiments with *Physarum* are easy for students to carry out in their dormitory rooms. This exercise can also give students a chance to work with the scientific method and it fosters some discovery learning.

Exercises F and G

A box of microscope slides and a box of coverslips should be provided for groups of students. Encourage students to rinse slides and reuse them during the exercise. Provide a container for used coverslips.

Exercise H

A plankton sample will usually be rich in algae and protozoans. If a plankton sample is not available, you may wish to substitute material from a microecosystem culture (see Laboratory 6, Exercise C).

VI. ORDERING INFORMATION

bacilli slide—Carolina Biological, # #Ba 050

cocci slide—Carolina Biological, # Ba 040

spirilla slide——Carolina Biological, # Ba 030

nutrient agar—Carolina Biological, # 78-5301 (1 lb)

antibiotic agar—Fisher, # DF 0163-01-1

Difco antibiotic disks—Carolina Biological, # 80-5080

tryptic soy broth—Carolina Biological, # 78-8440

Escherichia coli (freeze-dried vial)—Carolina Biological, # 85W-1860

Staphylococcus aureus (freeze-dried vial)—Carolina Biological, # 85W-1941

E. coli, gram stain (prepared slide)—Carolina Biological, # Ba-049

S. aureus, gram stain (prepared slide)—Carolina Biological, # Ba-038

E. coli, living culture—Carolina Biological, # 85W-0400

S. aureus, living culture—Carolina Biological, # 85W-1178

S. epidermidis—Carolina Biological, living culture, # 85W-1035; freeze dried, # 85W-1940

paper disks—Carolina Biological, # 38W 1600

Rhizobium inoculant for soybeans—Nitragin Company, Milwaukee, WI 53209; Carolina Biological, # 15-4720

soybean seeds—Nitragin Company; Carolina Biological, # 17-8200

clover seed—Carolina Biological, # 15-8540

Rhizobium meliloti (prepared slide)—Carolina Biological, # Ba 169M

16 X 100 mm culture tubes, glass—Carolina Biological, # 73-1462; Fisher, # 14-923K

caps for 16 X 100 mm culture tubes—Carolina Biological, # 73-1472; Fisher, # 14-127-28B

17 X 100 mm culture tubes, disposable—Carolina Biological, # 73-1520A; Fisher, # 14-956-6B

Nostoc (live)—Carolina Biological, # 15-1845

Cylindrospermum (live)—Carolina Biological, # 15-1755

Oscillatoria (live)—Carolina Biological, # 15-1865

Anabaena (live)—Carolina Biological, # 15-1710

Gloeocapsa (live)—Carolina Biological, # 15-1800

Trypanosoma gambiense (prepared slide)—Carolina Biological, # PS-310

Amoeba proteus (live)—Carolina Biological, # L-1 (class of 30)

Paramecium caudatum (live)—Carolina Biological, # L-2A (class of 30)

Plasmodium vivax—Carolina Biological, # PS 620

Physarum (live)—Carolina Biological, # 15-6198 or *Sclerotium* (live), # 79-6201

agar (Difco)—Fisher, # DF-0140-02-9; Carolina Biological, # 79-6201

Giemsa stain—Carolina Biological, # 86-5171

glycerol—Carolina Biological, # 86-5530

termites—Carolina Biological, # L743

Euglena (live)—Carolina Biological, # L3 (class of 30)
diatomaceous earth—Carolina Biological, # PB 115
diatoms (prepared slide)—Carolina Biological, # B21
Peridinium (prepared slide)—Carolina Biological, # B83P
Fucus (preserved)—Carolina Biological, # PB 133C
Laminaria (preserved)—Carolina Biological, # PB 136
Ectocarpus (live)—Carolina Biological, # 15-3360
Polysiphonia (live)—Carolina Biological, # 15-3580
coralline algae (preserved)—Carolina Biological, # PB 154
Dasya (preserved)—Carolina Biological, # PB 154B
Chlamydomonas (live)—Carolina Biological, # 15-1245
Spirogyra (live)—Carolina Biological, # 15-1320
Gonium (live)—Carolina Biological, # 15-1270
Volvox (live)—Carolina Biological, # 15-1335
Zygnema (live)—Carolina Biological, # 15-1345
Stigeoclonium (live)—Carolina Biological, # 15-1325
Ulva (preserved)—Carolina Biological, # PB 90
Ulothrix (live)—Carolina Biological, # 15-2640
desmids (live)—Carolina Biological, # 15-1260

LABORATORY 20 Diversity—Fungi and Nonvascular Plants

I. FOREWORD

This laboratory is designed to introduce students to the divisions within the Kingdom Fungi and to a few of the divisions in the Kingdom Plantae. Students work individually, but the entire laboratory can be set up as a series of stations (two per exercise) and students can do the exercises in any order. This saves on cost of prepared slides, preserved materials, and reduces the number of live specimens required.

II. TIME REQUIREMENTS

Exercise A—30 minutes
Let's Investigate—15 minutes
Exercise B—20 minutes
Exercise C—30 minutes
Exercise D—20 minutes
Let's Investigate—10 minute set-up, 2-3 day incubation
Exercise E—15 minutes
Exercise F—15 minutes
Exercise G—15 minutes
Exercise H—30 minutes

III. STUDENT MATERIALS AND EQUIPMENT

	Per Student	Per Pair (2)	Per Group (4)	Per Class (24)
Exercise A				
Rhizopus stolonifer (bread mold, live) (**1**)	1			24
dissecting microscope	1			24
microscope slides, box (75 X 25 mm)			1	6
coverslips, box (22 X 22 mm)			1	6
distilled water (dropping bottle)			1	6
Rhizopus (prepared slide)	1			24
Let's Investigate				
bread molds grown by students (**2**)	1			24
compound microscope	1			24
Exercise B				
water mold, live (demonstration) (**3**)				1
water mold, wet mount of mycelium (demonstration) (**4**)				1
Saprolegnia (prepared slide)	1			24

	Per Student	Per Pair (2)	Per Group (4)	Per Class (24)
Exercise B—continued				
compound microscope	1			24
Exercise C				
Sordaria (live) (**5**)			1	6
microscope slides, box (75 X 25 mm)			1	6
coverslips, box (22 X 22 mm)			1	6
distilled water, dropping bottle			1	6
yeast culture (**6**)				1
Schizosaccharomyces (prepared slide)	1			24
compound microscope	1			24
Exercise D				
edible mushroom (**7**)	1			24
microscope slides, box (75 X 25 mm)			1	6
coverslips, box (22 X 22 mm)			1	6
distilled water, dropping bottle			1	6
Coprinus (prepared slide)	1			24
basidiomycetes (demonstration) (**8**)				1
compound microscope	1			24
Let's Investigate				
fresh basidiomycetes (student collected)	1			24
glass dish	1			24
heat source (100 w light)	1			24
Exercise E				
Aspergillus (prepared slide)		1		12
Penicillium (prepared slide)		1		12
compound microscope	1			24
Exercise F				
fungus collection—prepared by students (**9**)				1
3 X 5 inch cards	1			24
Exercise G				
selection of crustose, foliose and fruticose lichens (**10**)				1
lichen thallus (prepared slide)	1			24
compound microscope	1			24
Exercise H				
moss plants, live (sporophyte and gametophyte) (**11**)			1	6
moss antheridium (prepared slide)		1		12

	Per Student	Per Pair (2)	Per Group (4)	Per Class (24)

Exercise H—continued

	Per Student	Per Pair (2)	Per Group (4)	Per Class (24)
moss archegonium (prepared slide)			1	12
Polytrichum antheridia, moss (preserved)				1
Polytrichum archegonia, moss (preserved)				1
Marchantia antheridia, liverwort (preserved)				1
Marchantia archegonia, liverwort (preserved)				1
Marchantia, live (12)				1
compound microscope	1			24

IV. PREPARATION OF MATERIALS AND SOLUTIONS

(1) *Rhizopus*, live—

Gather together the following materials:
> *Rhizopus* culture
> corn meal agar
> dextrose
> yeast extract
> Petri dishes (100 X 15 mm)

Procedure:

Maintaining a *Rhizopus* culture can be accomplished using corn meal agar plates. Into each 100 mL of distilled water, put 1.7 g of corn meal agar, 0.2 g of dextrose, and 0.1 g of yeast extract. Autoclave for 15 minutes at 15 pounds pressure (121° C). After autoclaving, let the corn meal agar cool and pour in Petri dishes. Using a sterile inoculating loop place some sporangia of two strains (+ and –) of Rhizopus (from purchased cultures) onto the corn meal agar plates, keeping the lid over the dish as much as possible to prevent contamination. The asexual spores begin forming around the edge of the mycelial mat two days after inoculation: zygospores form a day or two later on the line where the hyphae of the two strains meet.

To see zygospores, you will need to part the mycelium. The zygospores will be on the agar surface and may be seen even better by looking at the bottom of the dish by holding it up to the light.

Sporangia can also be placed on bread. Put the bread in a plastic bag to keep it moist.

(2) bread molds—

At the end of the preceding laboratory, distribute a piece of bread (without preservatives), a 3 X 5 inch index card, and three plastic bags to each student. Students should design an experiment to test conditions necessary for fungus growth. (You may wish to ask students to take a few minutes to plan their experiments so that you do not dispense more bags or bread than necessary.) Warn students to not breathe mold spores. Keep bags closed.

(3) live water mold—

Use a medium size culture dish containing a small amount of dirt. Fill the dish half full of pond water (the dirt and water used for growing water mold should come from a brook or pond). Boil several radish seeds for 5 minutes. Use two dissecting needles to break the seeds into small pieces and place them on top of the water so that the float. Do not include the seed coats with the seeds. Allow four days at room temperature for growth.

(4) water mold mycelium demonstration—
Prepare water mold as in (3). Use this culture to provide the mycelium for a wet mount slide. Put petroleum jelly or nail polish around the coverslip so the slide can be used during the entire period.

(5) *Sordaria*—

Gather together the following materials:

        corn meal agar plates—see preparation in (1)
        Sordaria (live culture)

Procedure:

    After agar plates have solidified, inoculate one or several plates with *Sordaria fimicola*. Obtain a culture of *Sordaria fimicola*, wild type. Cut out a small agar block with mycelia and place this upside down on an agar plate. Place a second block into a new sterile tube of agar to keep the culture going (put this tube in the refrigerator). It will take about 8 days from inoculation to see perithecia. Alternatively, purchase *Sordaria* on a plate if you do not wish to keep a stock culture in the laboratory (see Ordering Information).

(6) yeast culture—
Prepare 200 mL of a 10% molasses or syrup solution. Add 2 g of Fleischmann's dried yeast and 0.5 g peptone to the flask. Incubate in a warm place (25-30° C or 77-86° F) for approximately 12 hr before use and check for budding. Methylene blue (0.1g in 1 liter) or neutral red (0.1 g in 1 liter) can be used as vital stains to make observation easier.

(7) edible mushrooms—
Obtain mushrooms from a grocery store.

(8) selected basidiomycetes—
These can be collected during wet weather and are best preserved in FAA fixative (formalin-acetic acid):

95% ethanol	50 mL
glacial acetic acid	2 mL
formalin (40% formaldehyde)	10 mL
water	40 mL

(9) and (10) fungus and lichen collections—
These should be collected by students and preserved dry or in FAA fixative (see (8)). The collection should be augmented by your own specimens.

(11) and (12) moss and liverwort collections—
Mosses, *Marchantia* (liverworts), and hornworts can be obtained from a woodland area nearby or from a supply house (see Ordering Information).

V. PREPARATION SUGGESTIONS

Exercise A

Leave *Rhizopus* cultures in plastic bags or keep the lids on the cultures. Students should not inhale spores. If *Rhizopus* is grown on bread, the same cultures can be used for Let's Investigate.

Let's Investigate

This investigation on conditions necessary for fungus growth can be used to give students further practice with hypothesis formation and the scientific method. Each student should include a card stating his or her hypothesis, procedure, results, and conclusions. Warn students not to open bags and to avoid breathing mold spores.

Exercise B

Students have probably seen water molds before if they have ever tended an aquarium. The whitish spots of "ick" often seen on fish are a water mold. Students may want to grow their own water molds and experiment with conditions necessary for growth.

Exercise C

Sordaria are simple to grow but the cultures must be set up 8-10 days prior to the laboratory period. Alternatively, order prepared plates of *Sordaria*. Yeast cultures can be best studied using vital stains (methylene blue or neutral red) which will slowly be taken up by the living cells. (See Preparation of Materials and Solutions (6)).

Exercise D

Fresh mushrooms can be collected by students or can be obtained from the local grocery store. If not available, live or preserved examples of all fungi can be obtained from Carolina Biological Supply Company. FAA fixative can be used to preserve fungi (see Preparation of Materials and Solutions (8)). Wash fixed specimens with water before allowing students to handle them (due to formaldehyde content of fixative).

Let's Investigate

Use fresh materials for this experiment. Place the light (heat source) about 8 inches above the fungus. A small glass aquarium bowl works well as a cover. White paper is best for most species.

Exercise E

Prepared slides are used for this experiment. Make sure that students realize that this is a group of fungi (sometimes not even called a Division) which have "lost" the ability to reproduce sexually.

Exercise F

Student collections can be made using dry or fixed fungi (see FAA in Preparation of Materials and Solutions (8)). Be sure to tell students to place dry materials in bags. Spores will be released as the materials dry further. These should not be inhaled.

Exercise G

Lichens can be collected dry and kept from year to year. Have students list the places and types of lichens they find around the school or campus.

Exercise H

Depending upon the time of year during which this laboratory is done, it might be difficult to find mosses and liverworts with both sporophyte and gametophyte obvious. A combination of live materials (vegetative forms) and preserved materials (showing archegonia and antheridia) or slides can be used. To obtain live *Marchantia* archegonia and antheridia in season (January to spring), orders must be placed at least four weeks in advance since sexual stages are artificially induced.

VI. ORDERING INFORMATION

Rhizopus (prepared slide)—Carolina Biological, # B224

Rhizopus (live)—Carolina Biological, # 15-6223 (+) and # 15-6224 (–)

corn meal agar—Carolina Biological, # 78-2461

yeast extract—Carolina Biological, # 79-4781

dextrose—Fisher, # D16-500; Carolina Biological, # 74-1350

Petri dishes (100 X 15 mm)—Fisher, # 08-757-12

Sordaria fimicola——Carolina Biological, # 15-6290 (tube); # 15-6291 (plate)

Schizosaccharomyces (prepared slide)—Carolina Biological, # B261B

Coprinus (prepared slide)—Carolina Biological, # B270

Aspergillus (prepared slide)—Carolina Biological, # B234

Penicillium (prepared slide)—Carolina Biological, # B252

lichen thallus (prepared slide)—Carolina Biological, # B293

Polytrichum (moss, live)—Carolina Biological, # 15-6730

Polytrichum antheridia (preserved)—Carolina Biological, # PB385 or *Mnium* antheridia (preserved)—Carolina Biological, # PB375A

Polytrichum archegonia (preserved)—Carolina Biological, # PB386 or *Mnium* archegonia (preserved)—Carolina Biological, # PB376A

moss antheridium (prepared slide)—Carolina Biological, # B361

moss archegonium (prepared slide)—Carolina Biological, # B363

Marchantia vegetative (live)—Carolina Biological, # 15-6540

Marchantia antheridia (live)—Carolina Biological, # 15-6544 and *Marchantia* archegonia (live)—Carolina Biological, # 15-6546 (available January through spring)

Marchantia antheridia (preserved)—Carolina Biological, # PB320

Marchantia archegonia (preserved)—Carolina Biological, # PB321

Anthoceros (live)—Carolina Biological, # 15-6520

LABORATORY 21   Diversity—Vascular Land Plants

I.   FOREWORD

This laboratory is designed to introduce students to the vascular plants. As much live material as available should be used. The exercises could be set up as stations to cut down on expenses. Students could do the exercises in any order if necessary.

II.   TIME REQUIREMENTS

Exercise A—60 minutes
Let's Investigate—20 minutes
Exercise B—60 minutes
Exercise C—60 minutes

III.   STUDENT MATERIALS AND EQUIPMENT

	Per Student	Per Pair (2)	Per Group (4)	Per Class (24)
Exercise A				
Psilotum (live or preserved)				1
Psilotum stem (cross section, prepared slide	1			24
Lycopodium (club moss, live or preserved)				1
Selaginella (live or preserved)				1
Equisetum (live or preserved)				1
fern prothallus (live, class of 12)				1
water, dropping bottle			1	6
microscope slides, box (75 X 25 mm)			1	6
coverslips, box (22 X 22 mm)			1	6
compound microscope	1			24
fern prothallus with antheridia and archegonia (prepared slide)	1			24
fern prothallus with attached sporophyte (live, class of 12)				1
Let's Investigate				
fern leaves with sori (live) (1)				1
herbarium sheets (several)				1
gooseneck lamp (100 w bulb)			1	6
Exercise B				
representative gymnosperm branches (2)				1
male cones		1		12
water, dropping bottle			1	6

119

	Per Student	Per Pair (2)	Per Group (4)	Per Class (24)

Exercise B—continued

	Per Student	Per Pair (2)	Per Group (4)	Per Class (24)
microscope slides, box (75 X 25 mm)			1	6
coverslips, box (22 X 22 mm)			1	6
compound microscope	1			24
male cone (longitudinal section, prepared slide)		1		12
female cones		1		12
female cone (longitudinal section, prepared slide)		1		12
cycads, male (live or preserved)				1
cycads, female (live or preserved)				1

Exercise C

	Per Student	Per Pair (2)	Per Group (4)	Per Class (24)
flower types (assorted for dissection) (3)				1
forceps	1			24
dissecting microscope	1			24
10 % sucrose solution, dropping bottle (4)			1	6
microscope slides, box (75 X 25 mm)			1	6
coverslips, box (22 X 22 mm)			1	6
compound microscope	1			24

IV. PREPARATION OF MATERIALS AND SOLUTIONS

(1) fern leaves with sori (live)—
These can be obtained from a greenhouse. Carolina Biological Supply Company will guarantee several fertile fronds.
(2) representative gymnosperm branches—
Obtain locally. If male and female cycads are available, place these on demonstration.
(3) flower types—
Obtain from gardens or from florist. Include examples of both monocots and dicots for dissection. Suggestions include:
> **dicots**—morning glory, azalea, water lily, rose, snap dragon, chrysanthemum, dogwood, buttercup, daisy, violet, etc.
> **monocots**—daylily, yucca, orchid, iris, gladiolus, tulip, etc.
(4) 10 % sucrose solution—
Weigh 10 g sucrose. Add water to make 100 mL. As an alternative, mix 25 mL of white Karo syrup with 75 mL of distilled water.

V. PREPARATION SUGGESTIONS

Exercise A

Provide each student with a soaked peat pellet (used to germinate seeds). You can put these in a bucket at the beginning of the laboratory so they swell. Students should place their fern prothallia on their peat pellet. Spores from the sori can also be placed on the pellet. Place the pellet on a Petri dish bottom and cover it with a clear plastic cup. Students can take the materials home and can watch the development of the young sporophyte plant and look for growth of new prothallia during the following weeks.

Let's Investigate

Have students try to carry out their investigations using a dissecting microscope. Place a gooseneck lamp by the microscope to heat the sori. Make sure that students have observed prothallia so they will know what to look for on the peat pellets.

Exercise B

Have students make a dichotomous key to the pines on display. This is usually quite straightforward and will give them good practice.

Exercise C

Since this exercise comes at the end of the laboratory period, you may wish to tell students to select a flower for dissection early in the period. The students should then tap the anthers to see if any pollen can be obtained. If placed on a slide in a sugar solution early in the period, pollen germination can be observed during the period. If *Impatiens* is available in the greenhouse, use their flowers for obtaining pollen—they usually work well for this.

Have students work in a group of four with each student dissecting a different type of flower. After dissecting a flower, each student should demonstrate the structure to the other students in his or her group.

This exercise could be supplemented with a study of flower adaptations for pollination.

VI. ORDERING INFORMATION

Psilotum (live or preserved)——Carolina Biological, # 396A
Psilotum stem (prepared slide)—Carolina Biological, # B396
Lycopodium (live)—Carolina Biological, # 15-6980
Selaginella (live)—Carolina Biological, # 15-7015
Equisetum (live or preserved)—Carolina Biological, # 15-6960 OR # PB494
fern with sori—Carolina Biological, # 15-6902
fern prothallia (antheridia and archegonia)—Carolina Biological, # 15-6878
fern prothallia (young sporophytic stage)—Carolina Biological, # 15-6880
fern prothallus with antheridia and archegonia (prepared slide)—Carolina Biological, # B410
pine staminate cone—Carolina Biological, # PB560
pine ovulate cones—Carolina Biological:
    at pollination, # PB561
    first winter, # PB562
    second summer, # PB563C
    second autumn, # PB564
pine winged seed—Carolina Biological, # PB565
pine staminate cone (prepared slide)—Carolina Biological, # B495
pine ovulate cone (prepared slide)—Carolina Biological, # B499
Cycas revoluta (live)—Carolina Biological, # 15-7140

LABORATORY 22   Diversity—Porifera, Cnidaria, and Wormlike Invertebrates

I. FOREWORD

This laboratory begins a series of three laboratories (22, 23, and 24) that survey animal diversity. One of the goals of these exercises is to interest students in the overall diversity of body forms and adaptations—alternative solutions to recurring selective opportunities. To this end, added specimens should be used freely to augment or expand the basic overview of animals presented in these laboratories.

II. TIME REQUIREMENTS

Exercise A—10 minutes
Exercise B—30 minutes
Let's Investigate—30 minutes
Exercise C (Part 1)—30 minutes
Let's Investigate—20 minutes
Exercise C (Part 2)—10 minutes
Exercise C (Part 3)—30 minutes
Let's Investigate—15 minute set-up; incubate 24 hours
Exercise C (Part 4)—60 minutes

III. STUDENT MATERIALS AND EQUIPMENT

	Per Student	Per Pair (2)	Per Group (4)	Per Class (24)
Exercise A				
sponges (demonstration specimens)				
Grantia (preserved)			1	6
Grantia (prepared slide)	1			24
compound microscope	1			24
Exercise B				
Hydra, live	1			24
culture dish (1 1/2 inches)	1			24
Obelia (whole mount—prepared slide)	1			24
Physalia, Portuguese man-of-war				1
Aurelia (plastic mount)				1
Metridium (preserved)				1
corals (demonstration specimens), set				1
Pleurobranchia, comb jelly				1
compound microscope	1			24

	Per Student	Per Pair (2)	Per Group (4)	Per Class (24)

Let's Investigate

	Per Student	Per Pair (2)	Per Group (4)	Per Class (24)
Hydra, live	1			24
Daphnia (culture) (**1**)				1
brine shrimp (culture) (**2**)				1
culture dish	1			24

Exercise C (Part 1)

	Per Student	Per Pair (2)	Per Group (4)	Per Class (24)
planaria, live	1			24
Petri dish (100 mm)	1			24
pond water, flask (2000 mL)				1
food for planaria (**3**)				
Clonorchis, liver fluke (whole mount, prepared slide)			1	6
Taenia, tapeworm (preserved)			1	6
Taenia (whole mount, prepared slide)	1			24
compound microscope	1			24

Let's Investigate

	Per Student	Per Pair (2)	Per Group (4)	Per Class (24)
Dugesia, live	1			24
Petri dish (glass)	1			24
spring water (gallon)				1
aluminum foil (12 inch square)	1			24
dropper (plastic or eye dropper)	1			24
carmine powder (bottle)			1	6

Exercise C (Part 2)

	Per Student	Per Pair (2)	Per Group (4)	Per Class (24)
Cerebratulus, ribbon worm (preserved)			1	6

Exercise C (Part 3)

	Per Student	Per Pair (2)	Per Group (4)	Per Class (24)
Turbatrix, vinegar eel, live	1			24
0.2% neutral red, dropping bottle (**4**)			1	6
microscope slides, box (75 X 25 mm)	1			24
coverslips, box (22 X 22 mm)	1			24
Trichinella (prepared slide)	1			24
compound microscope	1			24

Let's Investigate

	Per Student	Per Pair (2)	Per Group (4)	Per Class (24)
ring stand	1			24
funnel with rubber tubing extension	1			24
beaker, 250 mL	1			24
cheese cloth	1			24
soil sample	1			24
pinch clamp	1			24
microscope slides, box (75 X 25 mm)	1			24

	Per Student	Per Pair (2)	Per Group (4)	Per Class (24)
Let's Investigate—continued				
coverslips, box (22 X 22 mm)	1			24
tap water, bottle	1			24

Exercise C (Part 4)

	Per Student	Per Pair (2)	Per Group (4)	Per Class (24)
Lumbricus, earthworm (preserved)	1			24
dissecting trays	1			24
dissecting pins	20			480
fine scissors or razor blades			1	6
dissecting needles	2			48
Lumbricus, earthworm (cross section, prepared slide)	1			24
Lumbricus, earthworm (live)			1	6
segmented worms (preserved)				
compound microscope	1			24

IV.   PREPARATION OF MATERIALS AND SOLUTIONS

(1) *Daphnia*, culture—

A culture of *Daphnia* can be used to seed an aquarium for raising more *Daphnia*. Simply put pond water and some aquarium plants in the aquarium. Provide a regular aquarium lamp and some nutrients (small amounts of fish food).

(2) brine shrimp, culture—

Brine shrimp can be hatched from eggs. Do this 2-3 days before use in laboratory.

Make a 3.5%–5% salt water solution (use non-iodized NaCl or lab grade NaCl) and place it in a 1 liter Erlenmeyer flask. Add approximately 1 teaspoonful of eggs to the water. Aerate with an aquarium pump. To collect hatched shrimp, place a lamp to one side and above the flask. The brine shrimp will swim toward the light. Collect the brine shrimp with a turkey baster. Put these into a beaker for students to use in feeding *Hydra*. Unhatched eggs will sink to the bottom.

Make sure unused eggs are stored in a cool place to be viable from one year to the next.

(3) food for planaria—

Fresh liver (0.5 lb or 500 g) should be purchased and diced into small cubes using a single-edged razor blade (2-3 mm in each dimension). Dried liver or egg yolk that has been stained with red food coloring can be used and is effective in staining the gastrovascular cavity red. Fed planaria should be returned to a separate culture bottle marked "fed." They can be reused in later labs (after 1-2 days).

(4) 0.2% neutral red—

Weigh out 0.2 g of neutral red. Add absolute (100%) ethanol to make 100 mL.

V. PREPARATION SUGGESTIONS

Exercise A

Chalina, a Demospongiae with spongin, and a collection of dry specimens are suggested as demonstration specimens in the section on ordering information. In courses that have been taught through the years, many other demonstration specimens may be available. Slides of spicules or other materials may be made available as time and resources permit.

Exercise B

Individual *Hydra* can be transferred to any small dish (Stender, Petri, etc.) for study under the dissecting microscope. Transfer the *Hydra* using a wide-tip plastic transfer pipette. Whatever dish is available for student use should be deep enough to allow the *Hydra* to extend and expand its arms without encountering the surface film.

Whole and dissected preserved anemones should be available in the demonstration area. *Metridium* is commonly used.

A variety of corals should be on demonstration. To show the relation of a living polyp to the dried skeleton, a preserved coral might be available for demonstration under a dissecting microscope.

Let's Investigate

Cladocera, Daphnia, Artemia, or other food should be provided for observation of feeding behavior. Introduce only 2 or 3 *Daphnia* or brine shrimp into the culture dish containing the *Hydra*. Return fed *Hydra* to a collecting dish.

Exercise C (Part 1)

Have a supply of pond water available (lake, river, artificial pond water, spring water, or dechlorinated tap water allows to stand for 24 hours should suffice).

For artificial pond water, make a stock solution as follows:

NaCl	0.1 g
KCl	0.004 g
$CaCl_2$	0.006 g

Add distilled water to 1 liter and adjust pH to 6.9-7.0 using 0.1 N HCl or 0.1 N NaOH.

If you use egg yolk that has been stained with red food coloring, students will be able to see the outlines of the entire gastrovascular cavity as it fills up with the red coloring that comes from the egg yolk.

Let's Investigate

Planaria lay down a slime trail as the move around in the dish. The carmine powder is sprinkled onto the surface of the water in the dish (after removing the planarian). Allow time for the carmine to sink to the lower surface of the dish and become attached to the slime trail. Swirl the dish quickly and decant the water. If you place the Petri dish on a white piece of paper, you will be able to determine whether the taxis response of planaria is toward or away from light (planaria move away from the light). Be sure that students have drawn a line down the middle of the Petri dish—on the bottom—to show which side was light and which was dark (label D and L). Interestingly, most students will hypothesize that the planaria will move toward the light.

Exercise C (Part 2)

Most students are unfamiliar with ribbon worms. Make sure that students are acquainted with the evolutionary advances demonstrated by members of this phylum; two digestive openings, closed circulatory system, and protonephridia that are excretory rather than osmoregulatory. The rhynchocoel is not a true coelom—it is lined by endoderm.

Exercise C (Part 3)

Vinegar eels are only one type of roundworm that students can observe. If you do not plan for students to do the Let's Investigate that follows, you may want to provide students with nematodes from a soil sample. Follow the Let's Investigate directions to obtain a sample of soil nematodes. Also, *Ascaris* is a common nematode that can be purchased as a preserved specimen. If you obtain live *Ascaris* from a veterinarian or local abattoir, make sure that you have thoroughly washed your hands after handling the material or any of the containers associated with it. The eggs remain viable for a lengthy period of time even outside the *Ascaris* body.

Let's Investigate

Use soil from local areas. Rich organic soil usually has the highest number of nematodes. Compare student samples taken from different locations. Students may want to test soil pH. If a local laboratory performs soil tests, you may wish to have some of the samples tested for mineral content. Alternatively, a soil test kit that tests for pH, nitrogen, phosphorous, and potash is available from Carolina Biological Supply Company (see Ordering Information). Students may make hypotheses that link nematode diversity to soil type or specific soil characteristics such as pH or nitrogen content.

Exercise C (Part 4)

Lined dissecting pans and pins should be available. Dissecting needles should also be provided if students do not have their own dissecting kit. Provide scissors with fine, sharp blades for opening the earthworms (a single edged razor blade will also work if students are careful to cut only the outer body wall). Some of the internal organs of the earthworm may be better visualized if the dissected specimen is covered with a thin layer of water.

Various annelids should be available on demonstration. Oligochaetes such as *Lumbricus* lack the segmental appendages (parapodia) typical of polychaetes, are hermaphroditic, and are a less diverse group. Several polychaetes, including *Nereis* (live if possible) should be available on demonstration. Leeches should also be on demonstration.

VI.   ORDERING INFORMATION

Grantia (preserved)—Carolina Biological, # P20
Grantia (cross section, prepared slide)—Carolina Biological, # Z505
Chalina (Demospongiae with spongin)—Carolina Biological, # P40

commercial sponge set (dry)—Carolina Biological, # P49

Hydra (live)—Carolina Biological, # L55 (green Hydra, # L60)

Daphnia (live)—Carolina Biological, # L565

Obelia (whole mount, prepared slide)—Carolina Biological, # Z690

Physalia (Portuguese man-of-war, preserved)—Carolina Biological, # P115

Aurelia (plastic mount)—Carolina Biological, # POM825

Metridium (preserved)—Carolina Biological, # P160C

corals—Carolina Biological, # P175B (deerhorn coral), # P180A (brain coral), # 26-1350 (sea fan), # 26-1324 (mushroom coral), # 26-1330 (pipe organ coral), or # 26-1312 (cluster coral)

Pleurobranchia, comb jelly (preserved)—Carolina Biological, # P200F

planaria, flatworm (live)—Carolina Biological, # L210

carmine alum lake (powdered carmine)—Carolina Biological, # 85-3070; Fisher, # C579-25

Clonorchis, human liver fluke (whole mount, preserved slide)—Carolina Biological, # PS 1210

Taenia, tapeworm (preserved)—Carolina Biological, # P245C

Taenia, tapeworm (preserved slide)—Carolina Biological, # PS 1810

Cerebratulus, ribbon worm (preserved)—Carolina Biological, # P255C

Tubatrix, vinegar eel (live)—Carolina Biological, # L258

garden soil test kit—Carolina Biological, # 66-5410

Trichinella (teased muscle, prepared slide)—Carolina Biological, # Z1040

Trichinella (whole mount, prepared slide)—Carolina Biological, # Z1050

Lumbricus (preserved)—Carolina Biological, # P403 or P405

dissecting trays—Carolina Biological, # 62-9004

dissecting pins (2 inch)—Carolina Biological, # 62-9122

dissecting needles—Carolina Biological, # 62-7200

fine dissecting scissors—Carolina Biological, # 62-1820

Lumbricus (cross section, preserved slide)—Carolina Biological, # Z1250

Lumbricus (live)—Carolina Biological, # L400

worms—Carolina Biological:

    leech (preserved), # P416

    Nereis (preserved), # P412C

    sabellid plume worm (preserved), # P431C

    Aphrodite (sea mouse, preserved), # P432C

    Arenicola (lug worm, preserved), # P434C

    Chaetopterus (preserved), #P436C

LABORATORY 23   Diversity—Mollusks, Arthropods, and Echinoderms

I. FOREWORD

This laboratory continues our survey of animal diversity. If live material is available, it can be substituted for preserved specimens. If a marine aquarium is available, point out and discuss feeding in clams and the use of tube feet in locomotion in echinoderms, etc. Supplement with other available specimens as time permits.

Shells and preserved specimens used in this laboratory are not dissected. There will be some wear and tear in their use, but if students are careful, organisms can be reused for a number of laboratories (over several years).

II. TIME REQUIREMENTS

Exercise A (Part 1)—5 minutes
Exercise A (Part 2)—20 minutes
Let's Investigate—30 minutes
Exercise A (Part 3)—20 minutes
Exercise A (Part 4)—15 minutes
Exercise B (Part 1)—30 minutes
Exercise B (Part 2)—20 minutes
Exercise B (Part 3)—20 minutes
Exercise B (Part 4)—15 minutes
Exercise B (Part 5)—20 minutes
Exercise B (Part 6)—15 minutes
Exercise C—30 minutes

III. STUDENT MATERIALS AND EQUIPMENT

	Per Student	Per Pair (2)	Per Group (4)	Per Class (24)
Exercise A (Part 1)				
Katharina, chiton (preserved)			1	6
salt water aquarium (1)				1
Exercise A (Part 2)				
clam, oyster, or mussel shell (dry)	1			24
venus, clam (preserved)			1	6
pelecypod shells, dry (demonstration)				1
Let's Investigate				
freshwater mussels, live (2)			1	6
clams, live (2)			1	6

128

	Per Student	Per Pair (2)	Per Group (4)	Per Class (24)

Exercise A (Part 3)

	Per Student	Per Pair (2)	Per Group (4)	Per Class (24)
snail shell, dry			1	6
pulmonate snail, live			1	6
gastropod shells, dry (demonstration)				1

Exercise A (Part 4)

	Per Student	Per Pair (2)	Per Group (4)	Per Class (24)
Loligo, squid (preserved)			1	6
cuttlebone or pen, dry				1
octopus (preserved)				1
Nautilus, shell (whole or split)				1

Exercise B (Part 1)

	Per Student	Per Pair (2)	Per Group (4)	Per Class (24)
crayfish (preserved)	1			24
dissecting tray with wax	1			24

Exercise B (Part 2)

	Per Student	Per Pair (2)	Per Group (4)	Per Class (24)
spider (preserved)	1			24
cotton pad	1			24
Petri dish (100 mm)	1			24
forceps			1	6
dissecting microscope	1			24

Exercise B (Part 3)

	Per Student	Per Pair (2)	Per Group (4)	Per Class (24)
Romalia, grasshopper (preserved)	1			24

Exercise B (Part 4)

	Per Student	Per Pair (2)	Per Group (4)	Per Class (24)
spiracle (whole mount, preserved slide)	1			24
tracheal system (whole mount, preserved slide)	1			24
compound microscope	1			24

Exercise B (Part 5)

	Per Student	Per Pair (2)	Per Group (4)	Per Class (24)
Oncopeltus, milkweek bugs (life cycle) (**3**)				1
Tenebrio, mealworms (life cycle) (**4**)				1
Manduca, tobacco hornworms (life cycle) (**5**)				1
Vanessa, painted lady butterflies (life cycle) (**6**)				1

Exercise B (Part 6)

	Per Student	Per Pair (2)	Per Group (4)	Per Class (24)
Spirobolus, millipede (preserved)			1	6
Scolopendra, centipede (preserved)			1	6

Exercise C

	Per Student	Per Pair (2)	Per Group (4)	Per Class (24)
sea lily (preserved or dry)				1
starfish (preserved or dry)				1
brittlestar (preserved)				1

	Per Student	Per Pair (2)	Per Group (4)	Per Class (24)

Exercise C—continued

sea cucumber (preserved)				1
sea urchin (preserved)			1	12
sea urchin shell			1	12
sand dollar shell			1	12

IV. PREPARATION OF MATERIALS AND SOLUTIONS

(1) saltwater aquarium—

A 30 gallon aquarium can be set up with an undergravel filter or a filter-pump combination. Make sure to specify that gravel is for a marine aquarium when you purchase your supplies—this gravel is composed of $CaCO_3$ and contains pieces of shells and corals. Instant Ocean can be used for making salt water. Start with a single fish while setting up the tank. Several additives can be purchased to "seed" the tank. Make sure to purchase a kit for testing water quality—pH and ammonia levels must be checked regularly. You must also test specific gravity. The aquarium will give students an excellent opportunity to study nutrient cycling in an ecosystem—especially the nitrogen cycle. You can order an assortment of marine animals from Gulf Marine Specimen Company. These are shipped overnight by Parcel Post. Be sure not to put too many organisms into a single tank (general rule—"an inch of fish per two gallons"). Have students adopt an organism and do some research on its life cycle and feeding habits. Brine shrimp from a local pet store or pieces of raw shrimp can be used to feed most organisms.

(2) freshwater mussels, live clams—

Live clams or oysters can be obtained from a local grocery store or freshwater mussels can be obtained from Carolina Biological Supply Company (see Ordering Information). To open bivalve mollusks, insert a scalpel into the shell next to the hinge and cut the adductor muscles. Be careful not to insert the scalpel too far because you do not want to damage the visceral mass. Carbon particles can be prepared ahead of time. Black chalk dust, charcoal powder from a charcoal rubbing, or even small fibers can be used to watch filter feeding and the movement of water over the gill surface.

(3) milkweed bugs—

Milkweed bugs (*Oncopeltus fasciatus*) are excellent for demonstrating incomplete metamorphosis. These can be maintained in a large glass jar. Place a paper towel (cut to fit the bottom) into the jar. Use shelled sunflower seeds (purchased at a health food store and free of insecticides) as a food source—several to a jar. Place a cotton plug in a small glass jar (obtain prescription bottle from drugstore), filled with water. The cotton will act as a wick and provide moisture. The first instar nymphs are red and are fairly difficult to see. Five instars, with molts, produce adults (see Ordering Information).

(4) mealworms—

For complete metamorphosis, mealworms can be easily cultured on oat bran (see Ordering Information).

(5) tobacco hornworms—

Tobacco hornworms are fun for students to observe. The transition from larva to pupa to adult is pronounced and usually amazes students who are unfamiliar with this organism. Tobacco hornworms can be cultured on a special medium (see Ordering Information) or on green pepper plants.

(6) painted lady butterflies—

Painted lady butterflies (see Ordering Information) also provide excellent material for observing metamorphosis, including chrysalis formation (see Ordering Information).

V.   PREPARATION SUGGESTIONS

Exercise A (Parts 1 and 2)

If a marine aquarium is present in the laboratory, small chitons are excellent for cleaning the algae off the sides. Students enjoy being able to see live specimens from all phyla (see Preparation of Materials and Solutions (1)).

An assortment of mollusk shells should be kept on hand. These will give students some idea of the diversity of shell types. If live clams are available, have groups of students observe their anatomy "on the half-shell." You may want to have individuals participate in the Let's Investigate activities with the clams or conduct the activities as a demonstration.

The Carolina Biological video on *The Anatomy of the Freshwater Mussel* (# 49-2364V) is an excellent supplement to Exercise A (Part 2).

Let's Investigate

If live clams, oysters, or mussels are available (see Ordering Information), insert a one-piece scalpel into the shell and cut both adductor muscles against one of the shells, leaving the gills and visceral mass intact. Place the dissected clam in a finger bowl covered with water (pond water for a freshwater clam and seawater for a marine specimen) and place it on demonstration under a dissecting microscope. Students can watch a very small (<1 mm in diameter) piece of paper or a small fiber move across the gills. Students can also dilute India ink 10:1 with water and place a small drop near the gills—follow the circulation of water over and through the gills. Observe how particles are trapped by mucus and are moved by cilia in the process.

Exercise A (Parts 3 and 4)

A selection of gastropod shells can be used to show differences in shell coiling patterns. Show right-hand and left-hand examples. Have students differentiate between a whelk and a conch shell. Dried whelk egg cases can be found on nearby beaches. Split one of the casings open to show the students the tiny whelks inside.

Display a chambered nautilus shell cut longitudinally. Have students understand why this is an example of a cephalopod and not a gastropod. Cuttlebones can be purchased in most pet stores or pet sections in larger food stores. The "pen" of a squid can be dissected out and dried for demonstration.

Exercise B (Parts 1, 2, and 3)

Dissections can be done as demonstrations. You can supplement with excellent videotape dissections of the crayfish and grasshopper (Carolina Biological, # 49-2399V and 49-2402V). For spider dissections, have students collect their own spiders (use the freezer to euthanize specimens) or order preserved specimens (see Ordering Information).

Exercise B (Part 4)

Have an enterprising student capture a live adult cockroach. Pin the body firmly to the wax in a dissecting pan and spread the wings on one side of the body, pinning them to hold them extended. Place the insect under a dissecting microscope focused on the proximal veins of the second (metathoracic) wing illuminated with a bright dissecting light. Have students watch blood flow through the wing. Have them note respiratory movements of the abdomen.

Exercise B (Part 5)

Place examples of insect life cycles on demonstrations (see Preparation of Materials and Solutions (3), (4), (5), and (6)).

Exercise B (Part 6)

Collect examples of centipedes and millipedes from the yard or woods. Have students add to the collection—preserve in 70% alcohol. Warn students to be careful when collecting centipedes. Some are fairly toxic and students may react to having these organisms on their skin.

Exercise C

If a marine aquarium is available, have students watch the actions of tube feet as a starfish moves. If a specimen attaches to the side of the tank, feed it a small piece of raw shrimp by placing the food between two of its arms. Students will be able to watch the feeding behavior, including the extrusion of the stomach to digest the shrimp.

VI. ORDERING INFORMATION

Caro-Safe (preservative)—Carolina Biological, # 85-3341 (4 l)
Katharina (chiton, preserved)—Carolina Biological, # P460C
Mercenaria, venus (preserved)—Carolina Biological, # P513C
clams, live—local grocery store
freshwater mussels—Carolina Biological, # L500
video, *The Anatomy of the Freshwater Mussel*—Carolina Biological, # 49-2364-V
clam shell—beach, local seafood store, etc.
gastropod shell collection—Carolina Biological, # 26-1791
pulmonate snails (live)—Carolina Biological, # L480
Loligo (squid, preserved)—Carolina Biological, # P532C
cuttlebone or pen—pet shop, dissection
octopus (preserved)—Carolina Biological, # P539C

Nautilus shell—Carolina Biological, # 26-1854 (split) or # 26-1856 (whole)
mollusc shell collection—Carolina Biological, # 26-1788 or # 26-1790
crayfish (preserved)—Carolina Biological, # P590D
dissecting trays—Carolina Biological, # 62-9002
dissecting pins (2 inch)—Carolina Biological, # 62-9122
video, *The Anatomy of the Crayfish*—Carolina Biological, # 49-2399-V
spider (preserved)—Carolina Biological, # P659
spiders, live—Carolina Biological, # L658A
Romalia, grasshopper preserved)—Carolina Biological, # P727
video, *The Anatomy of the Grasshopper*—Carolina Biological, # 49-2402-V
Spirobolus, millipede preserved)—Carolina Biological, # P644
Scolopendra, centipede (preserved)—Carolina Biological, # P642
spiracle (whole mount, prepared slide)—Carolina Biological, # Z1860
tracheal system (whole mount, prepared slide)—Carolina Biological, # Z1850
milkweed bug culture kit—Carolina Biological, # L840
mealworm culture kit—Carolina Biological, # L895
tobacco hornworm eggs—Carolina Biological, # L907A
ready-to-use hornworm medium—Carolina Biological, # L908K
painted lady butterfly kit—Carolina Biological, # L912
fossil crinoid (sea lily)—Carolina Biological, # GEO6681
starfish (preserved)—Carolina Biological, # P331S
brittlestar (preserved)—Carolina Biological, # P351
sea urchin (preserved)—Carolina Biological, # P359
sea urchin (test)—Carolina Biological, # P363
sand dollar (preserved)—Carolina Biological, # P377
sand dollar (shell)—Carolina Biological, # 26-1552
sea cucumber (preserved)—Carolina Biological, # P380C

LABORATORY 24   Diversity—Phylum Chordata

I. FOREWORD

This laboratory completes our survey of multicellular animals. Specimens are not dissected and should last for many laboratories and over several years if they are handled carefully and stored properly.

Students should be encouraged to pay careful attention to the Overview introducing this Laboratory—the classification scheme and phylogeny presented will form the basis for Laboratories 26-29.

II. TIME REQUIREMENTS

Exercise A—20 minutes
Exercise B—20 minutes
Exercise C—20 minutes
Exercise D—30 minutes
Exercise E—30 minutes
Exercise F—45 minutes

III. STUDENT MATERIALS AND EQUIPMENT

	Per Student	Per Pair (2)	Per Group (4)	Per Class (24)
Exercise A				
Balanoglossus (acorn worm, preserved or plastic mount)			1	6
Balanoglossus (acorn worm, median longitudinal section, prepared slide)		1		12
compound microscope	1			24
Exercise B				
tunicate tadpole larva (whole mount, prepared slide)			1	6
Molgula, sea squirt (preserved) or *Corella*, glass tunicate (preserved)			1	6
compound microscope	1			24
Exercise C				
Branchiostoma, lancelet (preserved) or (whole mount, prepared slide)		1		12
Branchiostoma (cross section, pharyngeal region, prepared slide)		1		12
compound microscope	1			24

	Per Student	Per Pair (2)	Per Group (4)	Per Class (24)
Exercise D				
Entosphenus, lamprey (preserved)			1	6
Squalus, shark (preserved)			1	6
perch (preserved)			1	6
blunt probe			1	6
hand lens			1	6
Exercise E				
frog (preserved)				1
Necturus (preserved)				1
garter snake (preserved)				1
Caiman (preserved)				1
turtle (preserved)				1
frog skeleton (optional)				1
turtle skeleton (optional)				1
frog eggs (cluster of 12)				1
turtle eggs (group of 12)				1
Exercise F				
pigeon skeleton			1	6
cat skeleton			1	6
OR human skeleton				1

IV. PREPARATION OF MATERIALS AND SOLUTIONS

None

V. PREPARATION SUGGESTIONS

Exercise B

Cut the tunic away from one side of a preserved tunicate to expose internal organs.

Exercise E

While frog and turtle skeletons would be helpful, they are not essential.

Exercise F

If a human skeleton is purchased for this exercise, it is worthwhile to obtain one hanging in a cabinet. Be sure students touch skeletons only with their fingers and only when necessary—warn them not to point with probes, dissecting needles, pencils, or pens!

VI. ORDERING INFORMATION

Balanoglossus, acorn worm (preserved)—Carolina Biological, # P 1206

Balanoglossus, acorn worm (plastic mount)—Carolina Biological, # POM 2690

acorn worm (median longitudinal section)—Carolina Biological, # Z 2625

tunicate tadpole larva (whole mount, prepared slide)—Ward's, # 92W8400; Carolina Biological, # E958

Molgula, sea squirt (preserved)—Carolina Biological, # P1226C

 OR *Corella*, glass tunicate (preserved)—Carolina Biological, # P1224C

Branchiostoma (preserved)—Carolina Biological, # P1250C

 OR *Branchiostoma* (whole mount, prepared slide)—Carolina Biological, # Z2706

Branchiostoma (cross section, pharyngeal region, prepared slide)—Carolina Biological, # Z2720

Entosphenus, lamprey (preserved)—Carolina Biological, # P1263D

Squalus, shark (preserved)—Carolina Biological, # P13055

perch, teleost fish (preserved)—Carolina Biological, # P1410AD

frog (preserved)—Carolina Biological, # P1496D

Necturus (preserved)—Carolina Biological, # P1429D

garter snake (preserved)—Carolina Biological, # P1639AD

Caiman (preserved)—Carolina Biological, # P1623C

turtle (preserved)—Carolina Biological, # P1608D

frog skeleton (optional)—Carolina Biological, # 24-3710

turtle skeleton (optional)—Carolina Biological, # 24-4120

frog eggs (fertilized)—Carolina Biological, # P1530AF

turtle eggs—Carolina Biological, # P1609C

pigeon skeleton—Carolina Biological, # 24-5120

cat skeleton—Carolina Biological, # 24-5850 or human skeleton—Carolina Biological, # 24-6860

LABORATORY 25   Animal Tissues

I. FOREWORD

This laboratory is designed to introduce students to different types of animal tissues. Some comparisons are made with living tissues to add interest to the laboratory. All exercises can be enhanced by using color transparencies of slides for the tissue types being studied. This facilitates discussion and identification of structures which students will need to locate on different slides.

II. TIME REQUIREMENTS

Exercise A (Parts 1, 2, and 3)—45 minutes
Exercise B (Parts 1, 2, 3, 4, and 5)—75 minutes
Exercise C—30 minutes
Exercise D—15 minutes

III. STUDENT MATERIALS AND EQUIPMENT

	Per Student	Per Pair (2)	Per Group (4)	Per Class (24)
Exercise A (Parts 1, 2, and 3)				
frog (live)				7
forceps				1
frog Ringer's solution, bottle (1)				1
stratified squamous epithelium, dog esophagus (prepared slide)		1		12
simple columnar epithelium, human kidney (prepared slide)		1		12
simple cuboidal epithelium, human thyroid (prepared slide)		1		12
microscope slides, box (75 X 25 mm)			1	6
coverslips, box (22 X 22 mm)			1	6
compound microscope	1			24
board (8 X 8 inches)			1	6
string, ball			1	6
cork particles, container (2)			1	6
methylene blue, dropping bottle (3)			1	6
board covered with cheese cloth				1
scalpel				1
tweezers				1

	Per Student	Per Pair (2)	Per Group (4)	Per Class (24)

Exercise B (Parts 1, 2, 3, and 4)

	Per Student	Per Pair (2)	Per Group (4)	Per Class (24)
hyaline cartilage, human trachea (prepared slide)		1		12
elastic cartilage, human fetus (prepared slide)		1		12
decalcified bone, human (prepared slide)		1		12
chicken bones (demineralized) (4)		1		12
areolar tissue, rat or cat (prepared slide)		1		12
tendon, human (prepared slide)		1		12
adipose tissue, cat, osmium (prepared slide)		1		12
adipose tissue, fat dissolved (prepared slide)		1		12
human blood smear, Wright's stain (prepared slide)		1		12
blood film, frog, Giesma stain (prepared slide)		1		12
microscope slides, box (75 X 25 mm)			1	6
coverslips, box (22 X 22 mm)			1	6
compound microscope	1			24
Wright's stain, dropping bottle (5)			1	6
buffer for Wright's stain (6)			1	6
frog Ringer's solution, bottle (1)			1	6
single edge razor blades				1
live frog (same as in A)				1

Exercise C

	Per Student	Per Pair (2)	Per Group (4)	Per Class (24)
skeletal muscle, dog, cat, rat or rabbit (prepared slide)		1		12
cardiac muscle, dog, cow, or sheep (prepared slide)		1		12
smooth muscle, cat or frog (prepared slide)		1		12
pithed live frog (optional)				1
dissecting needles				2
methylene blue, dropping bottle (3)			1	6
frog Ringer's solution, dropping bottle (1)			1	6
microscope slides, box (75 X 25 mm)			1	6
coverslips, box (22 X 22 mm)			1	6
compound microscope	1			24

Exercise D

	Per Student	Per Pair (2)	Per Group (4)	Per Class (24)
neuron, cow (prepared slide)		1		12
compound microscope	1			24

IV. PREPARATION OF MATERIALS AND SOLUTIONS

(1) frog Ringer's solution—
   Weigh 0.42 g KCl, 9.0 g NaCl, 0.24 g $CaCl_2$, and 0.20 g $NaHCO_3$. Make up to 1 liter with distilled water.

(2) cork particles—
   Use a kitchen grater to break a cork into fine particles.

(3) methylene blue—
    Order prepared solution or weigh 0.01 g methylene blue and add absolute alcohol (100%) to make 100 mL.
(4) demineralized chicken bones—
    Soak chicken bones in vinegar for at least one week. Smaller bones require less time. If not bendable after a week, change the vinegar and treat for an additional week.
(5) Wright's stain—
    Order prepared stain.
(6) buffer for Wright's stain—
    Weigh 1.63 g KH_2PO_4 and 3.2 g K_2HPO_4. Add distilled water to make 1 liter.

V.   PREPARATION SUGGESTIONS

Note: the use of live vertebrate animals must be approved by your institution's animal care and use committee (IACUC). Be sure to submit a protocol and obtain approval for this laboratory in advance so that you may proceed with this experiment.

Exercise A

If frogs have been kept in an aquarium for a few days, some of the epidermis is usually shed or becomes loosely attached to the body. This can be removed easily. If frogs are in short supply, make a single slide at the beginning of the laboratory and place it on demonstration.

Exercise B

Examples of different types of bones are helpful in this exercise. A human femur (longitudinally sectioned—Carolina Biological, # 24-7811) or a cross section of a femur (Carolina Biological, # 24-7820), are excellent for studying compact and spongy bone tissue. If funds are scarce, road killed rodents and birds provide a source of bones which you can section. All types of bones, including chicken bones can be demineralized by soaking them in vinegar for 1-2 weeks (or until soft). Larger bones will require additional time. They can then be cut longitudinally or in cross section more easily.

Make sure that bone slides are decalcified bone. Also, be sure to order adipose tissue slides both stained with osmium and with fat dissolved so students will have a complete understanding of fat cell structure.

In order to avoid exposing students and instructors to human bodily fluids, prepared slides of human blood are used in this exercise. You may wish to prepare fresh blood smears from a frog or other animal and stain them with Wright's stain under appropriate conditions (see Ordering Information). If you use a frog as a blood source, nick one of the toes with a clean scalpel to obtain a drop of blood.

To prepare a blood smear from the frog, place a drop of blood plus a drop of frog Ringer's solution on the end of a glass slide (the slide should be on a paper towel). Pull a second glass slide, held at a 45° angle, down the length of the flat slide (alternatively, you can push the slide). Let the slide dry and then stain as follows.

To stain a blood smear, place the slide on several layers of paper towels to absorb spills. Cover the dried blood film completely with Wright's stain for 1-3 minutes. This fixes the blood film. Next add Wright's buffer solution, drop by drop, until a metallic greenish scum forms on the surface of the stain. Continue until the stain is diluted in half and then let the slide stand for approximately 2 minutes (lengthen to 3 minutes if staining is light). Tip the slide and allow stain and buffer to drain onto the paper towels. Place the slide in a Coplin jar of distilled water for 2-3 minutes and air dry. Inspect without a coverslip. Use oil immersion for closer study (focus under high power and rotate the objective away from the slide, apply immersion oil to stained spear directly and rotate the objective into the drop and focus). Basophilic granules should be bright blue, eosinophilic granules should be red, and neutrophil granules should be lilac or purple. Rotate the oil immersion objective away from the slide and clean the objective tip. Blot the slide with lens paper (do not wipe) and store it if you wish to keep good smears for future use. Be sure that the students are not confused by the nucleated red blood cells found in the frog.

Exercise C

Use of a pithed frog for this exercise is optional. Substitute prepared slides if desired.

Make sure that the muscle tissue removed from the frog's thigh is an extremely thin strip. You will need to tease it away and use methylene blue stain to see the muscle cell structure.

To pith a frog—

Place a live frog on crushed ice in a dish pan at least an hour before it is to be pithed—this induces cold narcosis and reduces or eliminates any pain that might be caused to the frog by the following operation.

If right handed, grasp the chilled frog firmly in your left hand, anchoring the body with your thumb and holding the tip of the snout firmly between your second and third fingers (reverse this if your are left handed). Bend the head down slightly to emphasize the posterior margin of the cranium. Draw an imaginary line across the back of the head connecting the anterior edges of the tympanic membranes on each side of the head. Insert a dissecting needle into the spinal column precisely in the middle of this line—muscle tremors will indicate that you have severed the spinal cord. Keep the tip of the dissecting needle in the neural canal and point it backwards. Gently push it to the posterior, keeping it in the neural canal (if you have to force it, it is in the wrong place). Withdraw the needle, keeping the tip in the neural canal and push it forward into the brain and rotate it within the cranium to destroy brain tissue. Withdraw the needle—the frog should be flaccid. You may wish to do this out of sight of the class.

If appropriate, you may wish to discuss the use of live vertebrate animals in teaching and research, indicating that there are certain experiences and experiments that can only be done with live animals. However, the ethical use of live animals requires procedures which minimize pain and suffering (such as chilling or anesthetizing the frog before the central nervous system is destroyed in this exercise).

VI. ORDERING INFORMATION

frog (live)—Carolina Biological, # L1502
stratified squamous epithelium, dog esophagus (prepared slide)—Carolina Biological, # H230
simple columnar epithelium, human kidney (prepared slide)—Carolina Biological, # H6008

simple cuboidal epithelium, human thyroid (prepared slide)—Carolina Biological, # H6006
hyaline cartilage, human trachea (prepared slide)—Carolina Biological, # H6022
elastic cartilage, human fetus (prepared slide)—Carolina Biological, # H6026
decalcified bone, human (prepared slide)—Carolina Biological, # H6320
areolar tissue, rat or cat (prepared slide)—Carolina Biological, # H570
tendon, human (prepared slide)—Carolina Biological, # H6275
adipose tissue, osmium, cat (prepared slide)—Carolina Biological, # H610
adipose tissue, fat dissolved (prepared slide)—Carolina Biological, # H600
human blood smear, Wright's stain (prepared slide)—Carolina Biological, # H1155
blood film, frog, Giesma stain (prepared slide)—Carolina Biological, # H1060
skeletal muscle, dog, cat, rat, or rabbit (prepared slide)—Carolina Biological, # H1310
cardiac muscle, dog, cow, or sheep (prepared slide)—Carolina Biological, # H1350
smooth muscle, cat or frog (prepared slide)—Carolina Biological, # H1260
neuron, cow (prepared slide)—Carolina Biological, # H1660
Wright's stain solution—Carolina Biological, # 89-8533
buffer solution for Wright's stain—Carolina Biological, # 84-9751
methylene blue—Carolina Biological, # 87-5684 (powder), or # 87-5911 (liquid)

LABORATORY 26   The Basics of Animal Form—
Skin, Bones, and Muscles

I. FOREWORD

This laboratory is designed to introduce students to the support systems of the body. It is the first in a series of four laboratories that explore the anatomy and physiology of vertebrate systems. Human anatomy and physiology are emphasized throughout the series. In this laboratory, students will study the origins and diversity of epithelial coverings and will explore how muscles and bones work together to allow movement. Muscle contraction is studied at both anatomical and biochemical levels.

II. TIME REQUIREMENTS

Exercise A—20 minutes (at home)
Exercise B—60 minutes
Exercise C (Part 1)—20 minutes
Exercise C (Part 2)—20 minutes
Exercise D (Part 1)—30 minutes
Exercise D (Part 2)—45 minutes
Let's Investigate—30 minutes
Exercise E—45 minutes

III. STUDENT MATERIALS AND EQUIPMENT

	Per Student	Per Pair (2)	Per Group (4)	Per Class (24)
Exercise A				
materials contained in manual				
Exercise B				
shark skin, placoid scales (whole mount, prepared slide)		1		12
frog skin (cross section, prepared slide)		1		12
snake skin (cross section, prepared slide)		1		12
turtle skeleton				1
bird feather, contour (1)		1		12
bird feather, down (1)		1		12
human skin (cross section, prepared slide)		1		12
microscope slides (75 X 25 mm)	1			24
coverslips (22 X 22 mm)	1			24
glycerol, dropping bottle			1	6
ethanol (100%), 125 mL beaker (optional) (1)			1	6
xylene, 125 mL beaker (optional) (1)			1	6
balsam, Canada, dropping bottle (optional) (1)			1	6

	Per Student	Per Pair (2)	Per Group (4)	Per Class (24)
Exercise B-continued				
compound microscope	1			24
Exercise C (Part 1)				
human bone (plastic mount)				1
demineralized bones (**2**)				1
Exercise C (Part 2)				
materials contained in manual				
Exercise D (Part 1)				
tape measure		1		12
tape (roll)			1	6
Exercise D (Part 2)				
rubber ball (tennis ball size)		1		12
Let's Investigate				
chicken wings (fresh, uncooked)	1			24
diagram of chicken wing (**3**)	1			24
forceps	1			24
probe	1			24
scissors	1			24
Exercise E				
glycerinated rabbit psoas muscle (**4**)				1
ATP solution, containing Ca^{2+} (5 mL) (**5**)				1
$MgCl_2$ + KCl solution (5 mL) (**5**)				1
ATP + $MgCl_2$ + KCl solution (5 mL) (**5**)				1
ATP—muscle kit				1
microscope slides (75 X 25 mm)	1			24
coverslips (22 X 22 mm)	1			24
glycerol, 50% (dropping bottle) (**6**)			1	6
dissecting needles	2			48
millimeter ruler (clear plastic)	1			24
lens paper, pieces			1	6
compound microscope	1			24

IV. PREPARATION OF MATERIALS AND SOLUTIONS

(**1**) bird feathers—
Students can prepare their own feather slides for study. Temporary mounts can be prepared using glycerine. To make permanent slides, cut a 3-4 mm long section from the

vane or one side of each feather that includes the central shaft (down feathers can be mounted whole). If a flight feather (wing or tail feather) is available, pull the barbs apart in at least one place along the length of the section before mounting the feather. Rinse the piece of feather in absolute (100%) ethanol and then in xylene. Place on a microscope slide and cover with a drop of Canadian balsam in xylene. Hold a cover slip at a 45° angle to the slide and move it until one edge touches the balsam (the cover slip could be dipped in xylene before using). Gently lower the coverslip, using care to avoid bubbles under the feather and coverslip. Keep slides flat until the mounting medium sets. These slides can be used in subsequent years.

The same technique can be used to mount hairs or vibrissae from mammals if desired.

(2) demineralized bones—
Long bones from a chicken or other small bones from squirrels or other types of "road kills" (be sure to wear gloves when removing bones) can be demineralized by soaking the bones in vinegar for 3-10 days, depending on the size of the bone. With minerals removed, the bones become fairly rubbery and can be cut longitudinally with ease.

Alternatively, ask the butcher in your local grocery to use a bone saw to cut a larger beef bone longitudinally. After students have examined the bone, clean off any remaining tissue (marrow can be rinsed out with hot water). Place the bone on a window sill to dry. Direct sunlight will also bleach the bone. Keep dried bones for use in following years.

(3) diagram of chicken wing—
Copy the diagram at the end of this Preparation of Materials and Solutions section for class distribution.

(4) glycerinated rabbit psoas muscle—
This material is perishable. Have shipped close to the date of use and store in the freezer at –20° to –10° C. Keep at this temperature. The muscles can be used for up to 6 months.

(5) ATP, KCl, and MgCl$_2$ solutions—
The ATP solution containing Ca^{2+} must be used within 7 days after arrival or activity will be lost. Store in the refrigerator at 4°-10° C. Refrigerate all three solutions: ATP; MgCl$_2$ + KCl; and ATP + MgCl$_2$ + KCl. Solutions must be kept on ice during the experiment.

(6) glycerol, 50%—
Add 50 mL glycerol to 50 mL distilled water, mix, and pour into a dropping bottle.

V. PREPARATION SUGGESTIONS

Exercise A

Have students complete exercise A before coming to class. Give a brief oral quiz using a cat skeleton and a member of your class for comparison.

Exercise B

Supplement this exercise with additional specimens showing modifications of epidermal coverings—hoofs, nails, claws, porcupine quills, horns. Compare horns to antlers that are formed by bone formed under a covering skin which is shed after growth of the antlers (the "velvet"). Slides of dermal fish scales (ganoid, cycloid, and placoid—Carolina Biological, #

Z3115) or snake skins (epidermal scales) can also be used (ask students to bring in shed snake skins for study). Examine a turtle shell if available.

Have students look at hairs of different colors and textures.

Also examine feathers of different colors. Study slides under both reflected light (dissecting microscope) and transmitted light (compound microscope). If the color is due to melanin, it will appear dark brown to black in transmitted light (but viewed with reflected light, feather structure and other pigments may modify the brown color of melanin to provide green, blue, purple, and iridescent colors). If the color is due to a true pigment (as in the case of brown, yellow, red, or orange feathers), the feather will appear to be the same color in both transmitted and reflected light. Visit your local pet store and collect feathers molted from parakeets, canaries, or other captive birds.

Have students examine and explain the interlocking mechanisms revealed by the flight feather slide. Why does a bird "preen?"

Exercise C (Part 1)

Use a bone mounted in plastic for comparison of longitudinal and cross-section pieces. Have the butcher cut beef long bones longitudinally or demineralize bones (see Preparation of Materials and Solutions). Visit your state's medical school and request specimens of dried bones. Supplement this exercise with bones that have been broken and repaired (also from local medical schools) and with X-rays of bones with fractures, cancer, etc. from local doctors or medical schools.

If students did not look at the histology of bones during Laboratory 25 (Animal Tissues), you might want to have students refer to Exercise B and examine a cross section of decalcified bone (Carolina Biological, # 740).

Exercise C (Part 2)

Supplement this exercise with X-rays of joints obtained from a local hospital. Show both healthy joints and joints with arthritis. Discuss what it means to have a "torn" ligament—something that seems to be common among young, athletic students.

Exercise D (Parts 1 and 2)

This investigation is designed to get students to think about exercising. Many students talk about isometrics but have no idea what is meant. Make sure that the ball used for Part 2 is a spongy rubber bulb so that the hand muscles actually squeeze the ball.

Let's Investigate

Simple, but messy. Have plenty of paper towels and soap on hand—the chicken is greasy. As students examine the chicken wing and try to locate the different muscles (see diagram included on p. 209 at the end of the Preparator's Guide), have them compare these muscles to those present in the human arm. Discuss what muscles and tendons are involved in moving the human arm and decide what the counterpart is in the chicken wing. Note the comparison of the upper arm, lower arm and hand to the upper and lower parts of the wing plus the "hand," composed of fused digits. Primary feathers attach to the hand while the secondaries attach to the posterior bone of the forelimb (ulna).

If available, have students study a skeleton of a bird. This is also a very good time to review homologies—look at the wing of a bat or flipper of a whale for comparison. Cover diagrams or reference materials in plastic for protection.

Exercise E

Glycerinated muscles should be ordered in advance of the laboratory and should be stored in the freezer. All solutions must be kept cold during the experiment. The ATP solution will lose its effectiveness after 7 days.

Instructors should try this exercise before introducing it to your class. Students must have some idea of what the muscle looks like and some notion of what they might see as the muscle contracts. They cannot read directions and descriptions at the same time they are looking through the microscope! Clean microscope objectives and oculars are essential as well as good lighting. You may wish to supplement this exercise with a video demonstration (Carolina Biological Supply Company, # 49-8349-V: *What is a Muscle?*).

VI. ORDERING INFORMATION

shark skin, placoid scales, whole mount (prepared slide)—Carolina Biological, # Z2905

frog skin, (prepared slides)—Carolina Biological, # H2060 (cross section); # Z4195 (whole mount to show pigment cells)

snake skin, cross section (prepared slide)—Carolina Biological, # H2065

turtle skeleton—Carolina Biological, # 14-4120

bird feather (prepared slides)—Carolina Biological, # Z4975 (contour); # Z4980 (down); # Z4985 (feather types—coutour, down, filoplume)

human skin (prepared slides)—Carolina Biological, # H7475 (cross section); # H7455 (scalp, longitudinal section of hair shafts)

microscope slides (75 X 22 mm)—Carolina Biological, # 63-2000; Fisher, # 12-544-4

coverslips (22 X 22 mm)—Carolina Biological, # 63-3075; Fisher, # 2865-22

glycerol—Carolina Biological, # 86-5560; Fisher, # G-33-500

widemouthed glass balsam bottle, 45 mL—Carolina Biological, # 71-6690

balsam, Canada, in xylene—Carolina Biological, # 84-6558 (30 g); # 84-8560 (100 g)

ethanol, absolute (100%)—Carolina Biological, # A-962-4 (denatured); Fisher, # A-407-500

xylene—Carolina Biological, # 89-8743; Fisher, # X3S-4

human bone (Plastomount)—Carolina Biological, # POM 9100

tape measurers—local hardware store

rubber ball—local store

chicken wings—local grocery store

glycerinated rabbit psaos muscle—Carolina Biological, # 20-3520

ATP solution—Carolina Biological, # 20-3530

$MgCl_2$ + KCl solution—Carolina Biological, # 20-3530

ATP + $MgCl_2$ + KCl solution—Carolina Biological, # 20-3530

ATP muscle kit—Carolina Biological, # 20-3525

video—*What is a Muscle*—Carolina Biological, # 49-8349-V

LABORATORY 27   The Physiology of Circulation

I.   FOREWORD

This laboratory is designed to give students an opportunity to learn about the structure and function of the circulatory system. The structural features of the blood vessels and pumps that circulate this fluid through the body are studied with prepared slides and preserved materials. Heart rate and pulse rate are measured. Additionally, the effects of temperature and hormones on heart rate are measured. Exercises from Laboratory 27 can be combined with related exercises in Laboratory 28.

II.   TIME REQUIREMENTS

Exercise A—30 minutes
Exercise B—45 minutes
Exercise C—20 minutes
Exercise D—10 minutes
Exercise E—30 minutes
Exercise F (Parts 1 and 2)—20 minutes
Exercise G (Parts 1 and 2)—45 minutes

III.   STUDENT MATERIALS AND EQUIPMENT

	Per Student	Per Pair (2)	Per Group (4)	Per Class (24)
Exercise A				
human blood (prepared slide)	1			24
human blood, sickle cell anemia in crisis (prepared slide)	1			24
human blood, mononucleosis (prepared slide)	1			24
frog blood (prepared slide)	1			24
compound microscope	1			24
Exercise B				
sheep heart (1)		1		12
scalpel	1			24
probe	1			24
scissors	1			24
Exercise C				
artery, cat (cross section, prepared slide)		1		12
vein, cat (cross section, prepared slide)		1		12
atherosclerosis (human)		1		12
compound microscope	1			24

	Per Student	Per Pair (2)	Per Group (4)	Per Class (24)

Exercise D

	Per Student	Per Pair (2)	Per Group (4)	Per Class (24)
goldfish, live				2
cotton (box)				1
microscope slides, box (75 X 25 mm)				1
coverslips (22 X 22 mm)				1
compound microscope				1

Exercise E

	Per Student	Per Pair (2)	Per Group (4)	Per Class (24)
sphygmomanometer				4
stethoscope				4

Exercise F

	Per Student	Per Pair (2)	Per Group (4)	Per Class (24)
stethoscope		1		12

Exercise G

	Per Student	Per Pair (2)	Per Group (4)	Per Class (24)
Daphnia magna (live culture) (**2**)				1
Pasteur pipette	1			24
petroleum jelly, jar			1	6
finger bowl or Petri dish	1			24
ice bucket with ice			1	6
thermometer	1			24
glass file			1	6
acetylcholine, dropping bottle (**3**)			1	6
epinephrine (adrenalin), dropping bottle (**4**)			1	6

IV. PREPARATION OF MATERIALS AND SOLUTIONS

(**1**) sheep heart—
Purchase preserved (see Ordering Information) or obtain from local abattoir. Use gloves when handling fresh material.

(**2**) *Daphnia magna*, live culture—
Order only *Daphnia magna*. Other species of *Daphnia* are so small that they cannot be trapped as easily in the Pasteur pipettes and their heart rate is more difficult to observe.

(**3**) acetylcholine, dropping bottle—
Order prepared (see Ordering Information). Keep refrigerated.

(**4**) epinephrine (adrenalin), dropping bottle—
Order prepared (see Ordering Information). Keep refrigerated.

V. PREPARATION SUGGESTIONS

Exercise A

Because it is not advisable to use human bodily fluids in a general biology laboratory, prepared slides have been substituted.

Exercise B

Sheep hearts can be purchased from Carolina Biological Supply or Ward's Biology. These are preserved hearts. Fresh hearts can be obtained from the local abattoir. If fresh material is used, make sure that students wear gloves. Have a flexible knitting needle and some string on hand. It is fairly easy to follow the blood vessels as they go to and from the heart (even before you dissect the heart) by probing with the needle.

Exercise C

If you dissect a fresh heart, have students observe the difference in the thickness of the walls of the aorta and vena cava. Relate this to the prepared slides used for this exercise.

Exercise D

The goldfish can be wrapped in cotton and taped directly to the microscope stage or it can be laid out in a Petri dish, wrapped in cotton and taped to the dish. In this case, only one glass slide or coverslip will be necessary to observe the tail. If the fish does not move its tail very much, no covering will be necessary.

Exercises E and F

The stethoscopes, which come with the sphygmomanometers if purchased in kit form, can supplement the number of stethoscopes needed in Exercises E and F. To save on funds, have half of the class do Exercise G while the other half does Exercises E and F. If you have a smoker in the room, do you see any differences in heart rate or pulse?

If you do not plan to have students do Laboratory 28, The Physiology of Respiration and Immunity, you may wish to combine this exercise with Exercise D from Laboratory 26—The Effect of Exercise on Heart and Respiratory Rates.

Exercise G (Parts 1 and 2)

Use only *Daphnia magna* for this experiment. Once the *Daphnia* is trapped in the capillary tube, the heart beat will be easy to follow. Softened clay can be used to seal the end of the tube as an alternative to petroleum jelly. This method of restraining *Daphnia* is preferred for Q_{10} analysis because it is easy to change temperatures. You can, however, use the same method as that used for Part 2. Simply place the slide on top of a closed Petri dish of hot water or ice. Heat or cool the slide to the desired temperature and quickly transfer it to the microscope for observation.

VI.   ORDERING INFORMATION

human blood smear, Wright's stain (prepared slide)—Carolina Biological, # H1155
sickle cell anemia in crisis (prepared slide)—Carolina Biological, # PH1015
infectious mononucleosis (prepared slide)—Carolina Biological, # PH1085
frog blood smear (prepared slide)—Carolina Biological, # H1060
sheep heart—Carolina Biological, # P2140C; Ward's, # 69W7201
test tubes—Fisher, # 14-957A (10 X 75 mm), or #07-781D (6 X 50 mm)
cork (size # 1)—Fisher, # 07-781D

artery, cat (cross section, prepared slide)—Carolina Biological, # H1700
vein, cat (cross section, prepared slide)—Carolina Biological, # H1745
atherosclerosis, human (prepared slide)—Carolina Biological, # PH810
goldfish, live (small)—local pet store
microscope slides (75 X 25 mm)—Carolina Biological, # 63-2000; Fisher, # 12-544-1
coverslips (22 X 22)—Carolina Biological, # 63-3015; Fisher, # 12-542B
sphygmomanometer (blood pressure kit)—Carolina Biological, # 69-1030
stethoscope—Carolina Biological, # 69-1644
Daphnia magna—Wards, # 87W5210 (pure culture)
acetylcholine (1:10,000)—Carolina Biological, # 84-1611
epinephrine (adrenalin, 1:10,000)—Carolina Biological, # 84-2091
dissecting kit (with probe)—Carolina Biological, # 62-1136
scalpel—Carolina Biological, # 62-6031
scissors—Carolina Biological, # 62-2505
probe—Carolina Biological, # 62-7400
vinyl gloves—Fisher, # 11-388-61 (small); # 11-388-62 (medium); # 11-388-60 (large)

LABORATORY 28   The Physiology of Respiration and Immunity

I.   FOREWORD

This laboratory is designed to explore the functions of blood as a carrier of oxygen and its central role in the immune response. Exercises C and D build on Laboratory 27, Exercises A and B. Students will also explore the nature of the antigen-antibody response using the precipitin ring test.

II.   TIME REQUIREMENTS

Exercise A (Part 1)—30 minutes
Exercise A (Part 2)—45 minutes
Exercise B—20 minutes
Exercise C—20 minutes
Let's Investigate—20 minutes
Exercise D—30 minutes
Exercise E—30 minutes

III.   STUDENT MATERIALS AND EQUIPMENT

	Per Student	Per Pair (2)	Per Group (4)	Per Class (24)
Exercise A (Part 1)				
perch, preserved (1)		1		12
gill filaments (prepared slide)		1		12
scissors	1			24
probe	1			24
Exercise A (Part 2)				
sheep pluck (2)			1	6
air pump with hose				1
lung tissue, cat (cross section, prepared slide)		1		12
trachea, cat (cross section, prepared slide)		1		12
compound microscope	1			24
Exercise B				
cow's blood, tube (1 mL) (4)	1			24
2 mL pipette (to pipette blood)				1
conical centrifuge tube	1			24
0.9% saline, bottle (100 mL) (5)			1	6
clinical centrifuge				1
Pasteur pipette	1			24
rubber bulb	1			24

151

	Per Student	Per Pair (2)	Per Group (4)	Per Class (24)
Exercise B—continued				
test tube (10 X 75 mm), corked (#1)	1			24
activated yeast solution, bottle (50 mL) (**6**)			1	6
Petri dish	1			24
Exercise C				
balloon	1			24
ruler	1			24
Let's Investigate				
same materials as used for Exercise C				
Exercise D				
stethoscope		1		12
Exercise E				
microculture (Durham) tubes			5	30
rack for Durham tubes			1	6
Pasteur pipettes			4	24
rubber bulbs			1	6
antiserum, rabbit (vial) (**7**)				1
normal rabbit serum (vial) (**8**)				1
bovine serum albumin (0.05%, vial) (**9**)				1
PBS buffer (5 mL), bottle (**10**)			1	6
light (100 w bulb)			1	6

IV. PREPARATION OF MATERIALS AND SOLUTIONS

(**1**) perch—

Preserved specimens can be used. Any bony fish (teleost) is acceptable. If you have an enterprising student who likes to fish, fresh material can also be used. Fish heads, free from the grocery, can be frozen and stored until use.

(**2**) sheep pluck—

Preserved specimens can be used or fresh specimens can be obtained from the local abattoir. Use gloves to handle fresh specimens and wash hands afterwards. *Ascaris* may be present.

(**3**) trachea, cat (cross section)—

Two slides are necessary to observe both lung epithelium surrounding alveoli and the cartilage rings of the trachea (see Ordering Information).

(**4**) cow's blood—

Obtain cow's blood from the local abattoir—ask for heparanized blood so that it will not clot. Centrifuge it at a very low setting (3-4) in a clinical centrifuge and remove the top layer of serum proteins. Have instructor pipette 1 mL of blood into each student's centrifuge tube.

(5) 0.9% saline—
Weigh out 9 g NaCl and add distilled water to make 1000 mL of solution. Bottles of 100 mL will be sufficient for groups of four students. Attach a test tube to the bottle to hold a 5 mL pipette. Label pipette "NaCl."

(6) activated yeast solution—
Add one packet of dried yeast to 100 mL of warm 0.9% saline (do not use distilled water).

(7) rabbit antiserum—
Use Sigma Immunochemicals (B-7276) against bovine serum albumin (anti-BSA), containing at least 50 to 100 µg antibody protein per milliliter. You will add 2 mL deionized water to the contents of one vial. Rotate until dissolved. Follow accompanying instructions carefully. Make fresh before laboratory and keep refrigerated. One vial will provide enough material for 6 groups.

(8) normal rabbit serum—
Use Sigma Immunochemicals (R-9133), available in 5 mL amounts (enough for 12 groups). Store at –20° C (avoid frost-free freezers).

(9) bovine serum albumin (0.05%)—
Use Sigma Immunochemicals (A 9647), Fraction V powder, 96-99% albumin, available in 5 g amounts. Dilute 0.05 g to 100 mL with PBS buffer (see **(10)**).

(10) PBS buffer—
Phosphate buffered saline can be mixed by following the recipe given below:

$$0.23 \text{ g} \quad NaH_2PO_4 \text{ (anhydrous) (1.9 mM)}$$
$$1.15 \text{ g} \quad Na_2HPO_4 \text{ (anhydrous) (8.1 mM)}$$
$$9.00 \text{ g} \quad NaCl \text{ (154 mM)}$$

Add distilled water to 900 mL.
Adjust to pH 7.2 to 7.4, using 1 M NaOH or 1 M HCl
Add distilled water to 1 liter.

V.   PREPARATION SUGGESTIONS

Exercise A (Part 1)

This exercise can be done by each student or you can place a fresh or preserved fish on demonstration. Fish heads can be obtained free from the local grocery store and can be frozen until you are ready for this laboratory. If this is done, each student can have his or her own material and learning will be improved beyond what occurs with demonstration material. Unpreserved (fresh or frozen) material is more pliable and easier to use if it is available.

Exercise A (Part 2)

The sheep pluck can be obtained as a preserved specimen (see Ordering Information) or can be obtained from the local abattoir. If you use fresh material, make sure students wear gloves. You do not necessarily need an air compressor—a simple foot pump like those used to inflate rafts or swimming floats will work fine. Lung inflation is more obvious in fresh material than in fixed material and students may gain a better appreciation for the delicacy of lung structure using fresh organs.

Exercise B

For this experiment, obtain blood from the abattoir. Make sure that cows are free of *Brucilosis*. Use dry yeast in packets obtained in the grocery store. When adding yeast suspension to the blood, be sure that you can still see the reddish color (approximately 5 parts of blood to 1 part of yeast). Add less yeast and more blood if the mixture becomes opaque or colorless. The more yeast you add, the faster the reaction will take place. If you use larger tubes than those recommended (e.g. 10 mL), increase the amount of blood you start with to 2-3 mL and wash with 10 mL saline. After the final rinse, suspend cells in 8 mL of saline and yeast suspension. Don't forget to balance centrifuge tubes in the centrifuge. Directions call for 1 tuber per person (or pair). This should be balanced with another student's tube.

Exercise C

Make sure that students follow directions carefully. Most students want to completely empty their lungs and forcibly exhale. Have one student hold the ruler with an end on the table and the rest of the ruler sticking upward. Use a piece of paper or cardboard on top of the balloon to be sure that he or she is measuring the place where the diameter is maximum (this is very much like measuring someone's height by placing a book on the top of the head).

Let's Investigate

Combine this investigation with Exercise C. Students will find that smokers have a reduced lung capacity. You might also have students investigate whether there are differences in the lung capacities of males and females.

Exercise D

This exercise supplements Exercises E and F in Laboratory 27. Students should relate respiratory rates to pulse and heartbeat rates. BioBytes *Alien* is an excellent computer simulation that helps tie all aspects of cardio-pulmonary physiology together. Use *Alien* to extend Laboratories 27 and 28.

Exercise E

This exercise is designed so that the antibody is always on the bottom of the tube and antigen on the top (except when buffer is substituted for one or the other. Make sure that students understand the following relationships:

Ab = antiserum (antibody) = rabbit antiserum
(sensitized against bovine serum albumin—contains antibodies against the antigen BSA)
N = normal rabbit serum
(does not contain antibodies against BSA)
Ag = bovine serum albumin (BSA), the antigen

154

Only tube 5 will form a ring since it contains the antigen (BSA) and the antibodies against this antigen contained in Ab (rabbit antiserum). Use a light behind the tubes to make the ring easier to see.

In tubes 1, 3, 4, and 5, the bottom layer is already heavier. You will experience some mixing in tube 2. If you wish to increase the density of the bottom layer, you can mix each with a few grains of sucrose. Mix by tapping gently against your finger before adding the materials for the upper layer.

The Durham tubes are small. They will fit in the bottom part of a test tube rack, but be sure to put a paper towel under them on the rack so they do not fall through.

VI. ORDERING INFORMATION

perch, preserved—Carolina Biological, # P1410A

fish gills, filaments (prepared slide)—Carolina Biological, # Z3116

sheep pluck—Carolina Biological, # P 2150C

lung tissue, cat (cross section, prepared slide)—Carolina Biological, # H2460

trachea, cat (cross section, prepared slide)—Carolina Biological, # H2430 and H2435

test tubes—Fisher, # 14-957A (10 X 75 mm) or # 07-781D (6 X 50 mm)

corks (size #1)—Fisher, # 07-781D

conical centrifuge tubes—Carolina Biological, # 73-2014

pipette, 5 mL—Fisher, # 13-678-31H

pipette, 1 mL—Fisher, # 13-678-31E

Pasteur pipette—Carolina Biological, # 73-6060; Fisher, # 13-678-20C

rubber bulb—Fisher, # 14-065B

stethoscope—Carolina Biological, # 69-1638 or 69-1659; Fisher, # 14-409-110

micro culture tubes (6 X 50 mm)—Fisher, # 14-958A

tube rack—Fisher, # 14-754-15

rabbit antiserum—Sigma Immunochemicals, # B-7276

normal rabbit serum—Sigma Immunochemicals, # R-9133

bovine serum albumin (BSA)—Sigma Immunochemicals, # A-9647

LABORATORY 29   The Digestive, Excretory, and Reproductive Systems

I. FOREWORD

This laboratory is designed to examine the anatomy and physiology of the digestive and excretory systems. The chemistry of digestion is explored using amylase, pepsin, and lipase. The kidney is studied at the macroscopic and microscopic levels with reference to filtration functions. The reproductive structures are introduced as a part of the urogenital system, setting the foundation for further study in Laboratory 31, Animal Development.

II. TIME REQUIREMENTS

Exercise A (Part 1)—45 minutes
Exercise A (Part 2)—15 minutes
Exercise B (Part 1)—15 minutes
Let's Investigate—15 minutes
Exercise B (Part 2)—20 minutes and overnight incubation
Exercise B (Part 3)—20 minutes and overnight incubation
Exercise C (Part 1)—20 minutes
Exercise C (Part 2)—20 minutes
Exercise C (Part 3)—5 minutes

III. STUDENT MATERIALS AND EQUIPMENT

	Per Student	Per Pair (2)	Per Group (4)	Per Class (24)
Exercise A (Part 1)				
salivary glands, human (prepared slide)		1		12
pancreas, human (prepared slide)		1		12
liver, human (prepared slide)		1		12
small intestine (duodenum), human (prepared slide)		1		12
compound microscope	1			24
Exercise A (Part 2)				
glass or paper cup	1			24
stethoscope		1		12
Exercise B (Parts 1, 2, and 3)				
starch solution (1%), bottle (1)			1	6
amylase solution (2%), bottle (2)			1	6
Lugol's solution (I_2KI), dropping bottle (3)			1	6
porcelain spotting plate		1		12
Benedict's solution, bottle (4)			1	6

	Per Student	Per Pair (2)	Per Group (4)	Per Class (24)

Exercise B—continued

	Per Student	Per Pair (2)	Per Group (4)	Per Class (24)
maltose solution (1%), bottle (5)			1	6
TesTape			1	5
pepsin solution (5%) (6)			1	6
albumin solution (7)			1	6
2 N HCl (8)			1	6
photographic film (9)		2		24
biuret reagent (10)			1	6
ninhydrin reagent (11)			1	6
oil-emulsion agar plates (12)		2		24
copper sulfate (CuSO₄) solution (13)			1	6
lipase solution (14)			1	6
pipettes, 5 mL	4			96
Pasteur pipettes	6			144

Let's Investigate

same materials as used for Exercise B

Exercise C (Part 1)

	Per Student	Per Pair (2)	Per Group (4)	Per Class (24)
sheep or beef kidney (15)		1		12
scalpel		1		12
scissors		1		12
probe		1		12

Exercise C (Part 2)

	Per Student	Per Pair (2)	Per Group (4)	Per Class (24)
kidney tissue, monkey (prepared slide)	1			24

Exercise C (Part 3)

written laboratory materials

IV. PREPARATION OF MATERIALS AND SOLUTIONS

(1) starch solution (1%)—
   Bring 900 mL of distilled water to a boil. Mix 10 g of soluble potato starch in 100 mL distilled water and slowly pour this mixture into the 900 mL of boiling water. Heat the entire solution to a second boil, mix, and remove from the heat. Allow the solution to cool (cover with aluminum foil while cooling). Some starch may settle out of solution. Prepare fresh for each day.

(2) amylase solution (2%)—
   Dissolve 2 g of alpha amylase (fungal; breaks glucose into maltose) in enough distilled water to make 100 mL solution. Test this solution by adding 2 drops of amylase to 2 drops of starch. Then add 2 drops of Lugol's solution. If the solution immediately turns yellowish-gold, dilute amylase 1:10 (10 mL amylase to 90 mL distilled water). Repeat

test. Amylase strength varies (in units of activity) when purchased. You should obtain a brownish-red color with this test. As the time of incubation increases, a gold color will develop, indicating that starch has been catabolized to maltose.

(3) Lugol's solution (I_2KI)—

Dissolve 10 g potassium iodide in 100 mL distilled water and add 5 g of iodine. Store in a dark bottle.

(4) Benedict's solution—

Order prepared solution (see Ordering Information).

(5) maltose solution—

Dissolve 10 g of maltose in enough distilled water to make 1 liter of solution.

(6) pepsin (5%)—

Dissolve 50 g of pepsin in enough distilled water to make 1 liter of solution.

(7) albumin (1%)—

Dissolve 1 g powdered albumin in enough distilled water to make 100 mL of solution.

(8) 2N HCl—

Purchase already prepared (see Ordering Information).

(9) photographic film—

Remove black and white film from case and develop. Alternatively, use undeveloped film. Make sure you can identify the emulsion side on the developed film.

(10) biuret reagent—

Order prepared solution. Approximately 500 mL per class of 24.

(11) ninhydrin—

Dissolve 0.2 g of ninhydrin in 100 mL of 95% ethanol. Avoid breathing poisonous fumes.

(12) oil emulsion agar plates—

To 5 mL olive oil, add a pinch of bile salts (sodium taurocholate) and shake vigorously. Allow to stand for 10-15 minutes while you prepare agar.

Bring 100 mL of 2% agar (2 g Bacto-agar dissolved in distilled water to make 100 mL) to a boil.

Prepare 100 mL of a 5% soluble starch solution (5 g starch dissolved in distilled water to make 100 mL).

Combine the agar and starch. Shake the oil and combine it with the agar/starch mixture. Stir the mixture well and pour into Petri dishes, forming a thin layer.

(13) copper sulfate ($CuSO_4$)—

Prepare 100 mL saturated CuSO4. Add CuSO4 to 100 mL distilled water until no more will dissolve (approximately 65 g).

(14) lipase (5%)—

Dissolve 50 g lipase in enough distilled water to make 1 liter of solution.

(15) beef or sheep kidney—

Order preserved material (see Ordering Information) or obtain from local abattoir. Use gloves to handle fresh material.

V.   PREPARATION SUGGESTIONS

Exercise A (Part 1)

Students should examine prepared slides of organs responsible for production of enzymes and secretions used in the process of digestion, as well as a cross section of the intestine. Discuss the role of microvilli as part of the intestinal lining.

Exercise A (Part 2)

You will need a good stethoscope for this exercise. Make sure to use paper or plastic cups for drinking so that students do not share materials.

Exercise B (Part 1)

Salivary amylase (α amylase) is responsible for the breakdown of starch into a mixture of dextrins and maltose. It works on α(1-4) linkages between glucose units of amylose, but not the α(1,6) linkages of amylopectin. Recall that starch is composed of both amylose and amylopectin. Further digestion of dextrins and maltose residues occurs in the intestine. The enzyme maltase is responsible for breaking down maltose to make glucose molecules.

Make sure that you test your α amylase solution before you start (see Preparation of Materials and Solutions (2)). You should see a progressive change in color from black (α amylase + starch gives black rather than blue color when it reacts with Lugol's solution) to brownish-red to gold. This indicates a breakdown of starch into dextrins and finally into maltose. When you add 1% maltose, you will find that α amylase does not break this down further. The TesTape will NOT indicate that glucose is present. You may wish to add 2 mL of 5% maltase to the solution and retest with TesTape to verify the presence of glucose after maltase breaks down maltose.

Let's Investigate

This investigation asks students to think about where amylase and pepsin work. Students should realize that amylase does not work in the stomach but pepsin does. They should make appropriate hypotheses. Why isn't starch digested to dextrins in the stomach? Why couldn't pepsin work in the mouth? Students will be able to investigate the pH requirements for these enzymes. They can design experiments and collect qualitative results.

Exercise B (Part 2)

To test for the action of pepsin, you will use the Biuret test and the ninhydrin test, both described in Laboratory 5, Organic Molecules. Pepsin works in the stomach and has an optimum pH of 1.5 to 2.2. It is important that both your albumin and pepsin solutions should be at pH 7 before beginning this part of the experiment. The addition of 2N HCl to tube P_1 will lower the pH so that digestion will occur. Pepsin, however, does not reduce proteins to amino acids. Further hydrolysis by trypsin, chymotrypsin, and carboxypeptidase in the intestine continues to break down proteins. Tests with Biuret reagent will indicate the continual presence of proteins (remember, pepsin is itself a protein). Ninhydrin will turn purple in the presence of amino acids. More amino acids should be present in tubes containing pepsin at a low pH.

This experiment can also be done by treating a piece of exposed film with pepsin. Tape a piece of film to the bottom of a disposable Petri dish. Make sure that the dull side (emulsion side) is upward. Place a drop of each of the 4 solutions on the film. Wait overnight and wash the film, rubbing with your finger. A clear spot should result from the contents of tube 1. Note: you can substitute this procedure for the albumin procedure instead of doing both. In this case, you do not need the albumin in the 4 tubes—you just need pepsin, HCl, or water.

Exercise B (Part 3)

Make sure that you do not heat dishes to more than 30° C because the oil will run out of the agar. It is best to just leave this experiment incubating overnight. After treatment of your plates with copper sulfate ($CuSO_4$), you will need to pour off the $CuSO_4$ and rinse with water. Do this gently and be careful not to let the agar slip out of the plate (agar containing oil is very soft).

You might want to talk about saponification and the process of soap-making as students complete this exercise. The process of breaking the ester bonds between glycerol and the fatty acids produces free fatty acids. This can be done by using heat and a strong alkali such as NaOH. The fatty acids will react with Na^+ to form soaps. The soaps aggregate of form micelles with their hydrophobic fatty acid parts on the inside of the cluster of molecules and their hydrophilic Na+ ends on the outside. Cu^{2+} interacts with fatty acids in the same way.

Exercise C (Parts 1 and 2)

You can use a fresh or preserved kidney for this exercise. Make sure that students wear gloves if fresh material is used. Students should be able to identify anatomically the region of the kidney to be studied histologically. Have students trace the pathway for the flow of excretory wastes through the kidney.

Exercise C (Part 3)

The reproductive system will be studied in Laboratory 31. You should, however, make sure that students understand the relationship between the excretory system and the reproductive system. Explain how the ducts of the anterior kidney are "taken over" by the gonad and the old opisthonephric duct becomes the vas deferens while a new duct, the ureter, forms to drain the kidney of organisms with metanephric kidneys (reptiles, birds, and mammals)

VI.   ORDERING INFORMATION

salivary glands, sublingual gland, human (prepared slide)—Carolina Biological, # H8845
pancreas, human (prepared slide)—Carolina Biological, # H8122
liver, human (prepared slide)—Carolina Biological, # H8145
small intestine, duodenum, human (prepared slide)—Carolina Biological, # H8000 or H8010
stethoscope—Carolina Biological, #
starch, soluble potato—Carolina Biological, # 89-2530
amylase (alpha amylase, fungal)—Carolina Biological, # 20-2350

Lugol's solution (I2KI)—Carolina Biological, # 87-2793 (100 mL) or # 87-2795 (500 mL)
spotting plates—Carolina Biological, # 70-0600; Fisher, # 13-745
maltose—Carolina Biological, # 70-0600; Fisher, # M75-100
maltase—Sigma Chemical Company, # M3145
TesTape—Carolina Biological, # 89-3840
pepsin—Carolina Biological, # 87-9378
albumin—Carolina Biological, # 84-2250
2 N HCl—Fisher, # SA431-500
biuret reagent—Carolina Biological, # 84-8211 (120 mL)
ninhydrin (powder)—Carolina Biological, # 87-7460
lipase—Sigma Chemical Company, # L-1754
copper sulfate ($CuSO_4$)—Carolina Biological, # 85-6550; Fisher, # C 495-500

LABORATORY 30   The Nervous System

I.   FOREWORD

This laboratory is designed to explore aspects of our senses. Relationships to the activity of the nervous system are stressed whenever possible.

II.   TIME REQUIREMENTS

Exercise A—10 minutes
Exercise B—30 minutes
Let's Investigate—20 minutes
Let's Investigate—20 minutes
Exercise C—30 minutes
Exercise D (Parts 1 and 2)—15 minutes
Exercise E—15 minutes
Exercise F—15 minutes
Exercise G—10 minutes
Exercise H—10 minutes
Exercise I—30 minutes

III.   STUDENT MATERIALS AND EQUIPMENT

	Per Student	Per Pair (2)	Per Group (4)	Per Class (24)
Exercise A				
neuron, cow (prepared slide)				1
compound microscope				1
Exercise B				
unknown solution A, bottle (1)			1	6
unknown solution B, bottle (2)			1	6
unknown solution C, bottle (3)			1	6
unknown solution D, bottle (4)			1	6
unknown solution E, bottle (5)			1	6
cotton swabs	3			72
paper cups	1			24
Let's Investigate				
PTC taste paper (small pieces)	1			24
thiourea taste paper (small pieces)	1			24
sodium benzoate taste paper (small pieces)	1			24
control taste paper (small pieces)	1			24

	Per Student	Per Pair (2)	Per Group (4)	Per Class (24)

Let's Investigate

Life Savers—pieces in Petri dish (1 piece of each flavor: strawberry, tangerine, butterscotch, peppermint)	1			24

Exercise C

	Per Student	Per Pair (2)	Per Group (4)	Per Class (24)
sheep eye (preserved)	1			24
dissecting pan (with wax)	1			24
single edge razor blade	1			24
disposable gloves (pairs)	1			24

Exercise D (Part 1)

colored objects (balls, boxes, cardboard cut-outs)				12

Exercise E

	Per Student	Per Pair (2)	Per Group (4)	Per Class (24)
metric ruler (30 cm)		1		12
protractor		1		12

Exercise F

500 mL beaker			3	18

Exercise G

8 inch piece of string	1			24

Exercise H

rotating stool				4

Exercise I

sheep brain (preserved)		1		12

IV. PREPARATION OF MATERIALS AND SOLUTIONS

(1) solution A—10% NaCl
  Weigh 100 g NaCl. Add distilled water to 1 liter and mix.

(2) solution B—water
  Use 1 liter of distilled (or tap) water.

(3) solution C—10% sucrose
  Weigh 100 g sucrose. Add distilled water to 1 liter and mix.

(4) solution D—quinine
  Dissolve 1 capsule of quinine into each 1 liter of "almost" boiling distilled water.

(5) solution E—5% acetic acid
  Add 50 mL of glacial acetic acid slowly to 90 mL of distilled water.

V.   PREPARATION SUGGESTIONS

Exercise B

Give students five small paper cups (bathroom cup size) and have them label the cups A-E. Then, pour a small amount of the corresponding solution into each cup. Discard all cups when through. This might appear wasteful, but it is more sanitary since students may forget and dip a used cotton swab into one of the bottles of solution.

Let's Investigate

Cut tasting strips into squares to economize.

Let's Investigate

Break Life Savers into thirds (otherwise you will go broke on Life Savers).

Exercise D

Use single color objects with distinctly different shapes.

Exercise I

Sheep brains can be used from year to year. We find that there is less wear and tear on the brains if we remove them from their containers and place them on dissecting trays, ready to use by students. Cover the brains with wet paper towels so they do not dry out (put them back with preservative overnight).

VI.   ORDERING INFORMATION

neuron, cow (prepared slide)—Carolina Biological, # H1660
taste paper:
    PTC—Carolina Biological, # 17-4010
    sodium benzoate—Carolina Biological, # 17-4020
    thiourea—Carolina Biological, # 17-4030
    control—Carolina Biological, # 17-4000
sheep eye (preserved)—Carolina Biological, # P2130D
sheep brain (preserved)—Carolina Biological, # P2150F
quinine sulfate capsules—available at local pharmacies; Carolina Biological, # 88-6050

LABORATORY 31   Animal Development

I.   FOREWORD

This laboratory is designed to introduce students to the fundamentals of early developmental processes. While slides and preserved materials are used as a basis for the laboratory, the instructor should try to enhance the learning experience by using living organisms: sea urchin, frog, and chick, if possible. The feasibility of doing this will vary with location and time of year. Supplemental film loops and films might be used as an alternative, as suggested.

The BioBytes computer simulation, CYCLE, provides an excellent supplement for studying the role of hormones in gametogenesis and maintenance of the human embryo.

II.   TIME REQUIREMENTS

Exercise A (Parts 1 and 2)—30 minutes
Exercise B—10 minutes
Exercise C—30 minutes
Exercise D—30 minutes
Exercise E—30 minutes
Exercise F—15 minutes
Exercise G—15 minutes
Exercise H—30 minutes (or longer; optional experimental preparation, 8-15 days)

III.   STUDENT MATERIALS AND EQUIPMENT

	Per Student	Per Pair (2)	Per Group (4)	Per Class (24)
Exercise A				
testis, rat (prepared slide)			1	12
ovary, cat (prepared slide)			1	12
spermatozoa, human (prepared slide)			1	12
compound microscope	1			24
Exercise B				
Ascaris sperm entry (prepared slide)				1
compound microscope				1
Exercise C				
starfish development (prepared slide)			1	12
fertilized eggs, frog (preserved)				1
two-cell stage, frog (preserved)				1
early cleavage, frog (prepared slide)			1	12
depression slides				2

165

	Per Student	Per Pair (2)	Per Group (4)	Per Class (24)

Exercise C—continued

	Per Student	Per Pair (2)	Per Group (4)	Per Class (24)
compound microscope	1			24
dissecting microscope	1			24

Exercise D

	Per Student	Per Pair (2)	Per Group (4)	Per Class (24)
starfish development (prepared slide) (from Exercise C)		1		12
blastula, frog; sagittal section (prepared slide)		1		12
compound microscope	1			24

Exercise E

	Per Student	Per Pair (2)	Per Group (4)	Per Class (24)
starfish development (prepared slide) (from Exercise C)		1		12
dorsal lip, early gastrula, frog (preserved, per 12)				1
lateral lip, mid-gastrula, frog (preserved, per 12)				1
yolk plug, late gastrula, frog (preserved, per 12)				1
yolk plug, frog; sagittal section (prepared slide)		1		12
depression slide				2
compound microscope	1			24
dissecting microscope				2

Exercise F

	Per Student	Per Pair (2)	Per Group (4)	Per Class (24)
late neurula, frog; cross section (prepared slide)		1		12
neural groove, frog (preserved, per 12)				1
neural tube, frog (preserved, per 12)				1
tail bud, frog (preserved, per 12)				1
external gills, frog (preserved, per 12)				1
depression slide				2
compound microscope	1			24
dissecting microscope				2

Exercise G

	Per Student	Per Pair (2)	Per Group (4)	Per Class (24)
chick, 16 hour; whole mount (prepared slide)		1		12
chick, 33 hour; whole mount (prepared slide)				1
chick, 48 hour; whole mount (prepared slide)				1
chick, 72 hour; plastic mount				1
compound microscope	1			24
dissecting microscope				2

Exercise H

	Per Student	Per Pair (2)	Per Group (4)	Per Class (24)
chicken egg, incubated 96 hours		1		12
chicken egg, incubated 5-6 days		1		12
chick Ringer's solution (bottle) (1)			1	6
finger bowl	1			24
forceps	1			24

166

	Per Student	Per Pair (2)	Per Group (4)	Per Class (24)
Exercise H—continued				
dissecting microscope	1			24
Exercise I (optional)				
chicken egg, incubated 72 hours	2			48
Styrofoam cups	3			72
scissors	1			24
plastic wrap (new box)				1
betadine (**2**)			1	6
70% ethanol, bottle (**3**)			1	6
paper towels (small stack)		1		12
ultra-violet light (sterilizing)				1
250 mL beaker (sterile)		1		12
sterile Pasteur pipette (package of 12)				1
sterile Petri dishes (100 X 15 mm)	3			72
glass top incubator (38°C) (**4**)				1

IV. PREPARATION OF MATERIALS AND SOLUTIONS

(**1**) chick Ringer's solution—
Mix 7.2 g NaCl, 0.23 g CaCl·2H$_2$O, and 0.37 g KCl. Add distilled water to make 1000 mL.

(**2**) betadine—
This is a disinfectant solution that can be purchased from your local pharmacy.

(**3**) 70% ethanol—
Mix 700 mL of 95% ethanol with 250 mL of distilled water.

(**4**) how to construct a glass top incubator—
If you do not have an incubator, directions for making a small incubator are included in 4-H Manual 99, Revised July, 1984, *Embryology*, available from the Cooperative Extension Service, Communications Bulletin Room, Room 83, P&AS Building, Clemson University, Clemson, SC 29634 (803-656-3261; FAX 803-656-0742).

V. PREPARATION SUGGESTIONS

Exercise A

This exercise is designed to make students return to their previous study of meiosis (Laboratory 18). A discussion of Graffian follicle and corpus luteum development in relation to hormone levels (FSH, LH, estrogen, and progesterone) can also be enhanced by this visual demonstration of what occurs in the ovary. The Bio-Bytes computer simulation, CYCLE, provides an excellent student-interactive supplement to this discussion.

Exercise B

Recall that *Ascaris* eggs are ovulated prior to any maturation (meiotic) divisions. The spermatozoan enters the egg and triggers the meiotic process. Students will observe meiotic figures—these are the female chromosomes. The large dark dot inside the egg is the sperm which will remain in the egg cytoplasm until all of the meiotic divisions are complete. At that time, the sperm and egg chromosomal material will be mixed (amphimixis).

Exercises C-F

Two organisms, the starfish and frog have been chosen to study the process of development. The starfish (and sea urchin) gastrulate by a simple pushing inward (invagination) of the cells on one side of the blastula while in the frog, complicated epibolic and embolic movements allow cells to migrate across the surface of the blastula and to invaginate to the inside of the area of the blastopore. Try to help students see how these two processes manage to move some cells from the outside of the hollow blastula to the inside where they will contribute to the formation of internal organs.

You may wish to use live sea urchins to study echinoderm development. If so, substitute *Arabacia* slides for *Asterias*—the explanation for all developmental stages is the same except that the sea urchin larva is a pluteus rather than a bipinnaria.

Live sea urchins are available from several marine laboratories or may be collected if you have easy access to the coast. Urchins can be held in marine aquaria in a well-air conditioned room. *Arbacia* and *Lytechinus* urchins prefer temperatures of 18-23° C, while *Stronglyocentrotus* urchins do better at colder temperatures of 10° C. Urchins (usually *Lytechinus*) are available from Carolina Biological Supply Company. A sea urchin embryology kit is also available from the same vendor (see Ordering Information).

Sea water can be made from synthetic mixes (for example, Instant Ocean), or can be purchased in 5 gallon buckets of water collected at the coast (see Ordering Information). If you live near the coast, take several carboys to the beach and fill them with sea water (make sure that the carboys have never been washed out with soap—preferably they have never had materials other than distilled or sea water in them). Depending on the source of your urchins, you may need to adjust salinity. Test salinity in the shipping bags when the urchins arrive and compare to that in your tank. Specific gravity should be adjusted to 1.025. Be sure to use only calcium carbonate marine gravel in your holding tank. Set up the aquarium at least two weeks in advance.

Depending on the time of year, the species you must work with will be different and eggs will be different colors. If ordered from a biological supply house, be sure to tell the person you contact that you will be using the urchins to study embryology. Most suppliers ship their animals by air freight or express mail. Try to procure urchins as quickly as possible once they have reached their final destination. Equilibrate the temperature by floating the bags of urchins in your aquarium. Urchins should be fed after arrival if they are to be kept for more than a week. Use small pieces of frozen shrimp (uncooked) or kelp (fresh or dried). Feed sparingly—do not foul your tank.

Be sure that all glassware is clean. It is best to use glassware that has not been exposed to soap or any toxic chemical. Avoid overcrowding embryos and overheating them on the microscope stage. While students wait for the first cleavage to occur, have them remove their depression slides from the microscope stage. Be sure to have students check for evaporation during their wait. If the sea water is evaporating, introduce fresh sea water beneath the coverslip using a Pasteur pipette.

When injecting sea urchins with 0.5 M KCl, use only 0.1 to 1 mL. Inject this using a tuberculin syringe with a 26 or 30 gauge needle attached. Injections should be made in the soft tissue on the oral surface. Shake the urchin gently after injecting. Some urchins do not respond to KCl injection, but most respond to electrical stimulation as suggested in the student laboratory directions.

If you are using *Arbacia punctulata* or *Stronglyocentrotus purpuratus*, eggs can be kept for several hours in the refrigerator or in an ice bath. Likewise, semen, if collected "dry," can be stored on ice for several hours.

Once urchins have stopped shedding their gametes, return them to a DIFFERENT aquarium. If placed back into the aquarium from which they were taken, they may trigger other animals in the aquarium to spawn.

After students have prepared their slides, you may wish to fertilize the remaining eggs. Change the sea water (the eggs will have settled to the bottom of the beaker) and add several drops of dry sperm. Swirl to mix the eggs and sperm. After 10-15 minutes, when the eggs have again settled, pour off the sea water and add fresh sea water. Allow the eggs to settle and change the water a second time. Eggs develop best if stirred slowly with a magnetic stirring bar on a stir plate. They should be maintained at 20-25° C. If you teach multiple sections on consecutive days, have students take samples from beakers and try to identify stages of development by comparing with prepared slides. (See Ordering Information.)

For studying frog embryos, use depression slides. Place preserved frog embryos on demonstration. Check periodically to make sure that the embryos remain covered with preservative and do not dry out.

Depending on the season of the year, live frogs should be used if possible. Note that your use of these organisms requires the approval of your institution's animal care and use committee (IACUC)—be sure to submit your protocol in advance. Females can be artificially induced to ovulate (most easily from April through December) by injecting pituitaries from male or other female frogs. This provides sufficient LH to cause ovulation. Fresh pituitaries are best for use in this procedure. Pith chilled frogs (see Preparation Suggestions in the directions for Laboratory 25), destroying only the spinal cord. Cut the head off from the corner of the mouth, slanting posteriorly as far as possible (behind the eyes and through the tympanic membrane area). On the ventral side of the head (the roof of the mouth or palate), make two incisions directed anteriorly from the foramen magnum (the posterior opening of the cranial cavity leading to the spinal cord) and slightly outward from the midline of the skull. Lift up the flap of bone produced and the pituitary will be found, usually in the piece of bone removed. It is a small pink body 1-2 mm in size and often surrounded by white-shiny connective tissue (the dura mater). Place each pituitary in a small vial with about 1 mL of frog Ringer's solution. Collect the pituitary glands from about three females or six to eight males (depending on size). Inject all of the pituitaries collected (in Ringer's) into the abdominal cavity of a large female. Ovulation will occur in one to three days. Grasp the female firmly and push posteriorly on the abdomen using firm but gentle pressure. Once egg laying begins, maintain a gentle pressure to assist in the process.

Gonadotropin can also be supplied using pituitary extract (Carolina Biological Supply Company, pituitary kit, # L 1494K), but we have found that it is not as effective as fresh pituitaries in inducing ovulation.

Development is a process and students should be able to view it as such.

If live materials are not available, the following films are excellent:

echinoderm development—Richard A. Cloney, Kalmia Science Series 4011, 4012, 4013, and 4014. Kalmia Company, Inc., Department B6, 21 West Circle, Concord, Massachusetts 01742

frog development—Eugene Bell, Kalmia Science Series 4001, 4002 (address above). also in movie form—*Development of the Leopard Frog.*

Exercise G

Have students place chick embryos in a large plastic container. Dispose of this waste after Stress that gastrulation movements in the chick are like those in the frog, but on a flat surface. Show students how you can take the two ends of the chick blastodisc after gastrulation is complete and bring them together to form a cylinder that looks exactly like the cross section of a frog gastrula.

Exercise H

Use of live chicken embryos may require approval of your institution's animal care ans use committee (IACUC). Be sure to submit a protocol in advance.

Have students place chick embryos in a large plastic container. Dispose of this waste after the laboratory period.

The allantois will be most easily seen in 96 hour embryos, but the other membranes are more noticeable in older embryos. At this stage, the allantois is fairly extensive and is fused to the chorion and cannot be distinguished.

Exercise H (optional)

We are most grateful that Dr. Cynthia Fisher, Vassar College, introduced us to her "chick-in-a-cup" laboratory.

Each student should prepare several cups in case an egg breaks during the process. One or more ultraviolet lights can be placed in a cabinet for sterilizing the cups. Each student will become very interested in whether his or her own embryo "makes it." Development will not continue after about day 19 since it appears that some of the calcium (or other constituents) in the egg shell is necessary during the later stages of development. If too many students are involved in your laboratories, set up a series for demonstration purposes (give this to several students as a special project if you wish).

VI.   ORDERING INFORMATION

testis, rat; cross section (prepared slide)—Carolina Biological, # H4159
ovary, cat; Graffian follicles (prepared slide)—Carolina Biological, # H3785
spermatozoa, human (prepared slide)—Carolina Biological, # 8790
Ascaris, sperm entry (prepared slide)—Carolina Biological, # E325
sea urchin development (prepared slide)—Carolina Biological, # E465

170

sea urchin embryology kit—Carolina Biological, # 16-2505
sea water, artificial (5 gal. carboy)—Carolina Biological, # 16-3393
sea water, Gulf Coast, collected (5 gal. carboy)—Carolina Biological, # 16-3390
sea urchin larvae (prepared slide)—Carolina Biological, # E467
sea urchins (live)—Carolina Biological, # 16-2500[*]
Instant Ocean—local marine aquarium store or Aquarium Systems, Inc.[**]
marine gravel (10 lb)—Carolina Biological, # 16-3240
starfish development (prepared slide)—Carolina Biological, # E582
fertilized egg, frog (preserved, per 12)—Carolina Biological, # P1430AF
two cell cleavage, frog (preserved, per 12)—Carolina Biological, # P1530BF
early cleavage, frog (sagittal section, prepared slide)—Carolina Biological, E1630
blastula, frog (sagittal section, prepared slide—Carolina Biological, # E1650
dorsal lip, early gastrula, frog (preserved, per 12)—Carolina Biological, # P1530KF
lateral lip, mid-gastrula, frog (preserved, per 12)—Carolina Biological, # P1530MF
yolk plug, late gastrula, frog (preserved, per 12)—Carolina Biological, # P1530NF
yolk plug, frog; sagittal section (prepared slide)—Carolina Biological, # F1670
late neural tube, frog; cross section (prepared slide)—Carolina Biological, # E1691
neural groove, frog (preserved, per 12)—Carolina Biological, # P1530QF
neural tube, frog (preserved, per 12)—Carolina Biological, # P1530RF
tail bud, frog (preserved, per 12)—Carolina Biological, # P1530SF
external gills, frog (preserved, per 12)—Carolina Biological, # P1530UF
chick, 16 hour (prepared slide)—Carolina Biological, # E2020
chick, 33 hour (prepared slide)—Carolina Biological, # E2080
chick, 48 hour (prepared slide)—Carolina Biological, # E2120
chick, 72 hour (prepared slide)—Carolina Biological, # E2200
Styrofoam cups—local grocery store
Betadine—local pharmacy
ultraviolet germicidal bulb—Carolina Biological, # 70-3470

---

[*] Suppliers of live sea urchins: Gulf Specimen Company, PO Box 237, Panacea, FL 32346 (*Arabacia punctulata*); Pacific Bio-Marine Laboratories, Inc., Box 536, Venice, CA 90291 (*Lytechinus pictus* and *Stronglyocentrotus purpuratus*).
[**] Supplier of Instant Ocean: Aquarium Systems, Inc., 33208 Lakeland Blvd., East Lake, OH 44094.

LABORATORY 32   Plant Anatomy—
Roots, Stems, and Leaves

I.   FOREWORD

This laboratory is designed to introduce students to leaf, stem, and root anatomy. Students work individually but slides can be shared among pairs or groups to cut down on cost. Exercise B can also be split into several shorter activities if desired. Students can make their own thin sections of a variety of materials and can use their knowledge to identify monocot and dicot structures as well as cell types. Students find this to be much more fun than using prepared slides.

II.   TIME REQUIREMENTS

Exercise A—45 minutes
Let's Investigate—15 minutes (2-3 hour incubation)
Exercise B (Part 1)—45 minutes
Exercise B (Part 2)—60 minutes

Let's Investigate—open ended—30 minutes or more
Exercise B (Part 3)—20 minutes

III.   STUDENT MATERIALS AND EQUIPMENT

	Per Student	Per Pair (2)	Per Group (4)	Per Class (24)
Exercise A				
lettuce (head)				1
celery (stalk)				1
pear				1
microscope slides, box (75 X 25 mm)			1	6
coverslips, box (22 X 22 mm)			1	6
compound microscope	1			24
Let's Investigate				
celery	1			24
colored water, bottle (1000 mL)				1
beaker, 250 mL	1			24
Exercise B (Parts 1 and 2)				
Ranunculus (buttercup, dicot) root (prepared slide)		1		12
Zea mays (corn, monocot) root (prepared slide)	1			24
Salix (willow) branch root (prepared slide)		1		12
Mendicago sativa (alfalfa, dicot) stem (prepared slide)		1		12

172

	Per Student	Per Pair (2)	Per Group (4)	Per Class (24)
Exercise B (Parts 1 and 2)—continued				
Zea mays (monocot) stem (prepared slide)		1		12
Coleus plant (live)				2
single edge razor blade	1			24
50% ethanol, bottle **(1)**			1	6
toluidine blue O stain, dropping bottle **(2)**			1	6
distilled water, bottle			1	6
glycerine, bottle			1	6
Petri dishes (100 mm)	2			48
compound microscope	1			24
Let's Investigate				
locally collected flora (student collected)	1			24
same materials as used for Exercise B, Part 2C				
Exercise B (Part 3)				
Ligustrum (privet, dicot) leaf (prepared slide)			1	12
Zea mays (monocot) leaf (prepared slide)			1	12
compound microscope	1			24

IV.   PREPARATION OF MATERIALS AND SOLUTIONS

(1) 50% ethanol—
   Add 450 mL distilled water to 500 mL 95% ethanol and mix.

(2) toluidine blue O stain—
   Mix phosphate buffer as follows:

   (A) 4.24 g Na_2HPO_4. Add distilled water to 200 mL.
   (B) 4.13 g NaH_2PO_4. Add distilled water to 200 mL.

   Mix 51 mL (**A**) to 49 mL (**B**), pH 6.8, and add 0.05 g toluidine blue O. Mix 1:1 with distilled water for use. Do not use toluidine blue O that has been commercially prepared unless it is specified as "buffered." Toluidine blue O mixed in distilled water will only produce blue color when used to stain plant tissue instead of the metachromatic staining effect produced by buffered stain.

V.   PREPARATION SUGGESTIONS

Exercise A

Make sure that plant tissue sections are thin. Have instructor-prepared slides available for this tissue in the event that student slices are not acceptable. You can make your own preparations. Mount with glycerin and seal with colorless nail polish or paraffin. A tin can of paraffin or candle wax can be used. Melt it until a small pool of liquid wax is present. Bend a dissecting needle so that 1 inch of the needle is at a right angle to the handle. Submerge the needle in the wax and lay the needle along the side of the cover slip.

Let's Investigate

If you use a single piece of celery for the class, set this experiment up 24 hours ahead. Use red food coloring for the dye. The celery leaves will turn red. If individual students perform their own experiments, make sure that they cut their sections from the bottom of the stalk after soaking the celery for at least one hour. Enough colored liquid will have moved up the xylem by this time to produce good sections.

Exercise B (Parts 1 and 2)

Students should be encouraged to continually refer to Table 32B-1 as they try to summarize the monocot and dicot comparisons of root, stem, and leaf anatomy.

Slides of monocot and dicot roots and stems other than those specifically used in this exercise can be substituted if on hand, but students should be warned that the diagrams might not be an exact match (but major cell types and regions can still be identified by comparison). *Smilax* or greenbriar (a monocot) root is often used instead of the *Zea mays* or corn root. Likewise, *Helianthus* or sunflower (a dicot) stem is often used in place of the *Mendicago sativa* or alfafa root.

Toluidine blue O staining of living plant tissues is fun for students and results are usually colorful. Other plants can be used in addition to *Coleus*. Make sure that plants have herbaceous stems. Newly germinated sunflowers, beans, tomatoes, or Philodendron, Zebrina, and spider plants provide excellent material.

Let's Investigate

It is effective to have students collect weeds from the roadside and to make toluidine blue stained sections of the stems or roots of the plants to try to discern whether the plants are monocots or dicots. This gives students a chance to apply what they have learned about plant anatomy in a "living unknowns" laboratory.

Exercise B (Part 3)

A cross section of a pine needle can be used to provide an interesting comparison with angiosperm leaves.

VI.   ORDERING INFORMATION

Ranunculus (buttercup, dicot) root (prepared slide)—Carolina Biological, # B520
Zea mays (corn, monocot) root (prepared slide)—Carolina Biological, # 97-8050
Salix branch root (prepared slide)—Triarch, #1312-C
Mendicago sativa (alfafa, dicot) stem (prepared slide)—Carolina Biological, # 97-8220
Zea mays (monocot) stem (prepared slide)—Carolina Biological, # B571
toluidine blue O—Carolina Biological, # 89-6638
glycerine—Carolina Biological, # 86-5560
Ligustrum (dicot) leaf (prepared slide)—Carolina Biological, # B598D
Zea mays (monocot) leaf (prepared slide)—Carolina Biological, # B630
pine leaf, cross section (prepared slide)—Carolina Biological, # B478A

LABORATORY 33   Angiosperm Development— Fruit, Seeds, Meristems, and Secondary Growth

I. FOREWORD

This laboratory is an extension of Laboratory 21 in which we studied vascular plants. Formation of fruits and development of the seedling are emphasized. Both primary growth and secondary growth are considered. The laboratory exercises can easily be done singly and could be combined with Laboratory 35 which examines the effects of hormones on plant development.

II. TIME REQUIREMENTS

Exercise A—60 minutes
Exercise B (Part 1)—20 minutes
Exercise B (Part 2)—20 minutes
Exercise C—20 minutes
Exercise D (Part 1)—30 minutes
Exercise D (Part 2)—20 minute setup,10 day experiment
Exercise E (Part 1)—15 minutes
Exercise E (Part 2)—15 minutes
Exercise F—20 minutes

III. STUDENT MATERIALS AND EQUIPMENT

	Per Student	Per Pair (2)	Per Group (4)	Per Class (24)
Exercise A				
assorted fruits (1)				1
Exercise B (Parts 1 and 2)				
Phaseolus vulgaris (lima bean) seeds (2)	1			24
Zea mays (sweet or field corn) seeds (3)	1			24
Exercise C				
peanuts. bag	1			24
Exercise D (Parts 1 and 2)				
germinated lima bean seedling (4)		1		12
germinated pea seedling (5)		1		12
germinated sweet or field corn seedling (6)		1		12
Lugol's solution, dropping bottle			1	6
plastic cup	1			24

	Per Student	Per Pair (2)	Per Group (4)	Per Class (24)
Exercise D (Parts 1 and 2)—(continued)				
blotter paper **(7)**	1			24
soaked seeds (pea, bean, corn) **(8)**	2			48
Petri dish half (100 mm)	1			24
Exercise E (Parts 1 and 2)				
Coleus plant (live)			1	6
Coleus stem tip (prepared slide)	1			24
cabbage			1	6
brussel sprout	1			24
germinated radish or rye seed **(9)**	1			24
compound microscope	1			24
Exercise F				
Tilia, basswood (prepared slide)	1			24
tree, cross section (prepared slide) **(10)**	1			24
compound microscope	1			24

IV.   PREPARATION OF MATERIALS AND SOLUTIONS

(1) assorted fruits—

An assortment of simple fruits, cut in half and wrapped in plastic wrap should be provided on a demonstration table. Types of fruits may differ according to locality and time of year. Some suggestions include

peach (drupe)	squash or pumpkin (pepo)	nectarine (drupe)
cherry (drupe)	coconut (drupe)	plum (drupe)
apple (pome)	cucumber (pepo)	grapefruit (hesperidium)
pear (pome)	banana (berry)	orange (hesperidium)
avocado (drupe)	peanut (legume)	pea (legume)
tomato (berry)	milkweed (follicle)	bean (legume)
grape (berry)	sunflower (achene)	corn (grain)
pepper (berry)	maple (samara)	olive (drupe)
acorn (nut)		

(2) *Phaseolus vulgaris* (lima bean), seeds—

Soak *Phaseolus vulgaris* (garden or lima bean) seeds overnight in tap water. If they are soaked longer, place them in a refrigerator to retard mold growth. *Vicia faba*, the broad bean, is also excellent for dissection and can be substituted for lima beans. Due to their size, *Vicia faba* beans need to be soaked longer—at least 24 hours.

(3) *Zea mays* (sweet or field corn), seeds—

Soak *Zea mays* seeds overnight in tap water to make dissection easier. Either sweet or field corn can be used.

176

(4) (5) and (6) germinated seeds—

Seeds of lima bean, pea, and corn need to be germinated approximately 6 days before use. Small cups of soil (with holes punched in the bottom) or wooden flats can be used. Plant seeds approximately 1/4 inch below the soil surface. Alternatively, seeds can be germinated by laying them on wet paper towels which are then covered with more wet paper towels and rolled up and covered with aluminum foil. Older plants, 8 to 12 days, should also be planted for comparison. If this lab is prepared during the winter and the room is cold, place seeds in a warm incubator (about room temperature—21 to 22° C).

(7) blotter paper—

Blotter paper, purchased from a local stationery or office supply store, works best for this. Cut blotter paper to the proper size to fit closely around the inside of the plastic cup. Alternatively, have students supply straight-sided jars and cut their own. Wet paper towels can also be used if blotter paper is not available. The plastic cup is covered with the top or bottom half of a Petri dish.

(8) soaked seeds (pea, bean, corn)—

Soak pea, bean, or corn seeds overnight in tap water.

(9) germinated radish or rye seed—

Germinate radish seeds for 2 days by wrapping them in wet paper towels. These can be made into rolls by laying the seeds on wet paper towels, covering them with a second layer of wet paper towels, and then rolling the towels up. Cover the roll with aluminum foil. Alternatively, for small batches, simply fold a wet paper towel around some seeds and place this in a Petri dish. Place a rubber band around the Petri dish.

To germinate rye seeds, simply float them on a Petri dish of tap water. Allow 2 days for germination before use.

Place seeds in a warm incubator (21-22° C) if the room is cold.

(10) tree, cross section (prepared slide)—

Cross sections of tree trunks can be obtained from pine, cedar, oak, or other hardwood. Be sure to label the display so that a distinction is made between gymnosperms and angiosperms.

V. PREPARATION SUGGESTIONS

Exercise A

Check with the produce manager of your local grocery store. Fruit that has been bruised during shipment or fruit that has not been sold quickly enough is usually free for the asking. Make a collection of dry fruits and pods. These can be kept from year to year.

Exercise B (Parts 1 and 2)

Vicia faba (broad bean), if available, is excellent for these dissections. Make sure that beans have been soaked overnight so that they are easy to dissect. Broad beans will take up a great deal of water, so use a fairly large container for soaking.

Exercise C

Peanuts have been chosen since most students are familiar with these fruits. Dissection is easier if fresh peanuts are "roasted" at 275° F for approximately 40 minutes.

Exercise D (Parts 1 and 2)

If a large aquarium is available, place approximately 6 inches of soil in it. Plant seeds (previously soaked overnight) against the glass so that students can observe the process of germination. These can be planted on different days to give stages of 4 days through 12 days and can be turned in different directions to show that position will not affect the direction of epicotyl and hypocotyl growth. Alternatively, use a battery jar or a large glass jar lined with a cylinder of blotter paper. You can turn the jar upside down if desired—the blotter paper will provide enough moisture for the seeds.

Exercise E

Onion root tip slides (used for mitosis in Laboratory 12) may be used as a supplement for this exercise.

Exercise F

A cross section through the trunk of a palm tree provides an excellent comparison with a monocot whose trunk is made primarily of fibers formed during primary rather than secondary growth.

VI.   ORDERING INFORMATION

Phaseolus vulgaris (bush lima bean) seed—Carolina Biological, # 15-8330
Zea mays seeds:
>   sweet corn—Carolina Biological, # 15-9283
>   field corn—Carolina Biological, # 15-9243
pea (Little Marvel) seed—Carolina Biological, # 15-8883
Lugol's solution—Carolina Biological, # 87-2793
radish seed—Carolina Biological, # 15-9000
rye seed—Carolina Biological, # 15-9313
Coleus stem tip (prepared slide)—Carolina Biological, # B563
Tilia (basswood—three year stem, prepared slide)—Carolina Biological # B591A

LABORATORY 34   Water Movement and Mineral Nutrition in Plants

I.   FOREWORD

This laboratory is designed to introduce students to the ways in which plants take up and lose water. The importance of water and minerals to the plant is also emphasized. The BioBytes SEEDLING computer simulation provides an excellent supplement for this laboratory.

II.   TIME REQUIREMENTS

Exercise A—30 minutes
Exercise B (Part 1)—10 minutes
Exercise B (Part 2)—75 minutes
Exercise C—10 minutes
Exercise D—10 minutes
Exercise E—30 minutes (demonstration) or 45 minutes (experiment)
Let's Investigate—independent student set up

III.   STUDENT MATERIALS AND EQUIPMENT

	Per Student	Per Pair (2)	Per Group (4)	Per Class (24)
Exercise A				
Zebrina (wandering Jew), green plant				1
forceps	1			24
tap water, dropping bottle		1		12
microscope slides, box (75 X 25 mm)			1	6
coverslips, box (22 X 22 mm)			1	6
compound microscope	1			24
20% sucrose, dropping bottle (**1**)			1	6
Exercise B (Part 1)				
125 mL Erlenmeyer flask				3
Coleus shoots (**2**)				2
600 mL beaker				3
petroleum jelly, jar				3
Exercise B (Part 2)				
Wheaton bottle potometer (**3**)		1		12
1 mL in 1/100 pipette		1		12
2-hole rubber stopper (size 8 1/2)		1		12
fan				3
flood light (150 w)				3

	Per Student	Per Pair (2)	Per Group (4)	Per Class (24)
plastic bag				3

| | Per Student | Per Pair (2) | Per Group (4) | Per Class (24) |

Exercise B (Part 2)—continued

	Per Student	Per Pair (2)	Per Group (4)	Per Class (24)
petroleum jelly, jar				3
plant mister				3

Exercise C

	Per Student	Per Pair (2)	Per Group (4)	Per Class (24)
young barley seedlings, pot (4)				1
1000 mL beaker			1	6

Exercise D

	Per Student	Per Pair (2)	Per Group (4)	Per Class (24)
carnation (live)				1
two test tubes, taped together (5)				1
food coloring (red, green and blue—1 each)				1
Coplin jar				1
celery stalk with leaves				1
150 mL beaker				1
microscope slides, box (75 X 25 mm)	1			24
dissecting microscope				1

Exercise E

	Per Student	Per Pair (2)	Per Group (4)	Per Class (24)
quart Mason jars with 3 holes in lid (6)				8
sunflower plants grown in mineral deficient solutions (7)				16

Let's Investigate

	Per Student	Per Pair (2)	Per Group (4)	Per Class (24)
aquarium			1	
aerator			1	
Styrofoam board, 1 inch thick (8)			1	
Rap-id-gro hydroponics solution (10 gallons)			1	
peat pellets			10	
seeds—lettuce, spinach, kale, tomato, sunflower			20	

IV.   PREPARATION OF MATERIALS AND SOLUTIONS

(1)   20% sucrose, dropping bottle—
Weigh 20 g sucrose. Add distilled water to make 100 mL. Dispense in 6 dropping bottles.

(2)   *Coleus* shoots—
Cover the leaves on one *Coleus* shoot with petroleum jelly. Leave one uncovered. Place plants in 125 mL flasks filled with water. Place these and a flask of water (without a *Coleus* shoot) under the three 600 mL beakers. Leave for 1-2 hours before use if room is warm or use a flood lamp. Three or four hours is better if possible.

(3) Wheaton bottle potometer—

Place a pipette (1 mL in 1/100) tip down in one hole of a rubber stopper (# 8). Place a stalk of an appropriate plant (we use red tip, *Photinia*, in the southeast) into the other hole. The stem should be tight enough to fit very snugly. The bark may be stripped off as you insert the stem. If you wish, you can grow *Impatiens* plants up through the hole in the stopper. Cut off the roots for use in the potometer. You may need to try several types of plants prior to the laboratory in order to decide on a local genus that will work well.

(4) young barley seedlings, pot—

Sprinkle 25-30 barley seedlings on the surface of soil in a 6 inch Styrofoam pot. Cover with soil so that the seeds are 1/4 inch below the soil. Plant seeds approximately one week before use. Invert a 1000 mL beaker over the pot of seeds a few hours before use (water seedlings before placing them under the beaker).

(5) two test tubes, taped together—

Tape two test tubes together. Put green food coloring in one and red food coloring in the other. Use concentrated food coloring and fill the tubes up to the top. With a razor blade, split the stem of a carnation lengthwise and place one-half in each of the two different colors of dye.

Use blue or red food coloring for celery.

(6) and **(7)** sunflower plants grown in mineral deficient solutions—

Materials:

quart Mason jars—drill or punch 3 holes 2-3 cm apart in the central disk portion of a Mason jar lid

Solutions:

Prepare the following solutions by dissolving the indicated amount of each chemical into 500 mL of distilled water and add additional distilled water to make one liter.

Solution:	g/liter of solution:
1 M Ca(NO)$_3$)$_2$	236.15
1 M KNO$_3$	101.11
1 M MgSO$_4$	246.48
1 M KH$_2$PO$_4$	136.09
EDTA	32.90
1 M NaHO$_3$	84.99
1 M MgCl$_2$	203.31
1 M Na$_2$SO$_4$	142.04
1 M NaH$_2$PO$_4$	137.99
1 M CaCl$_2$	147.02
1 M KCl	74.56

Micronutrient Solutions:

Dissolve the indicated amounts of the combination of chemicals given below in 500 mL of distilled water and then add additional distilled water to make one liter.

Chemical:	Amount:
boric acid	2.86 g
manganese chloride, MnCl$_2$·4H$_2$O	1.81 g
zinc chloride, ZnCl$_2$	0.11 g

cupric chloride, $CuCl_2 \cdot 2H_2O$	0.05 g
sodium molybdate, $Na_2MoO_4 \cdot 2H_2O$	0.025 g

Germinate sunflower seeds in wet sterile sand or in a wet paper towel roll (lay seeds on several damp paper towels, cover with additional damp paper towels, and roll up). Cover with aluminum foil. Allow 2-3 weeks for growth.

Prepare Mason jars of solutions. If contamination occurred during previous use, wash and rinse jars with distilled water, re-rinse with dilute HCl, and autoclave. It is best to do each solution in duplicate or triplicate. You will need 16 or 24 Mason jars. Fill your jar two-thirds full with distilled water. Add the stock solutions given above to each Mason jar according to the chart on the next page. Add distilled water to fill the jar to about 1 inch from the top. Note that Fe is also given in this chart, but was not included in the six chemicals to be studied. You may add it if you desire.

Select three healthy, uniformly sized plant seedlings from those available. Rinse roots with distilled water. Wrap cotton around the stem (the cotton should not be wrapped so tightly that there is no room for stem expansion). Insert 1 seedling into each of the three holes in the lid of the Mason jar. Make sure that the cotton does not hang down and touch the solution. Cover the glass part of the jar with aluminum foil and label the jar. If a greenhouse is available, put the plants in the greenhouse (or leave them on a sunny window sill).

If preparing this exercise for demonstration, one set should be prepared 6 weeks prior to the laboratory and a second set should be prepared 3 weeks prior to the laboratory to demonstrate effects which are obvious quickly as opposed to those that take longer to appear. If only one set is made, look at the plants 4-5 weeks after setting them up.

CHART. Stocks for Preparing Mineral Nutrient Solutions

Stock Solution	Complete mL	Ca mL	S mL	Mg mL	K mL	N mL	P mL	Fe mL
1M Ca(NO$_3$)$_2$	5	0	5	5	5	0	5	5
1M KNO$_3$	5	5	5	5	0	0	5	5
1M MgSO$_4$	2	2	0	0	2	2	2	2
1 M KH2PO$_4$	1	1	1	1	0	1	0	1
FeNaEDTA	1	1	1	1	1	1	1	0
micronutrients	1	1	1	1	1	1	1	1
1 M NaNO$_3$	0	5	0	0	5	0	0	0
1 M MgCl$_2$	0	0	2	0	0	0	0	0
1 M Na$_2$SO$_4$	0	0	0	2	0	0	0	0
1 M NaH$_2$PO$_4$	0	0	0	0	1	0	0	0
1 M CaCl$_2$	0	0	0	0	0	5	0	0
1 M KCl	0	0	0	0	0	5	0	0

A Plant Mineral Requirement Kit is available from Carolina Biological Supply Company. It contains enough chemicals to prepare 10 liters each of 8 different nutrient solutions—potassium, calcium, nitrogen, phosphorous, magnesium, sulfur, and iron deficient media, as well as complete medium (see Ordering Information).

(8) Styrofoam board—

If jars are used instead of an aquarium (as shown in the laboratory manual), cut Styrofoam to fit the jar opening. If Mason jars are used, peat pellets can be broken in half for smaller width.

(9) Rap-id-gro hydroponics solution—

Use 5 g Rap-id-gro or Miracle-gro to 1 gallon of water. Let water sit overnight to get rid of chlorine before adding Rap-id-gro mix.

V.   PREPARATION SUGGESTIONS

Exercise A

Other types of plants can be used for this exercise, including *Bryophyllumor*, *Kalanchoe*, or other types of *Zebrina* (wandering Jew). Some types of privet can also be used. If these plants are not available, the structural features of the epidermis on other types can be studied by using cellulose acetate film.

Exercise B

If you wish to have data from the transpiration experiment (Part 2) expressed in the most accurate way, students can strip all leaves from the plant after taking transpiration readings. Trace around all leaves on 20 lb mimeograph paper. Cut out the leaf tracings and weigh them as an estimate of the leaf surface area of the plant. Mimeograph paper weighs 0.0077 g/cm^2. By dividing the total weight of the paper tracings by 0.0077 and multiplying by 2 (for both surfaces), you will determine the total leaf area. Each student should express average rate for the two conditions tested (room and experimental) as mL water translocated/hour/cm^2 of leaf surface. Make sure that you use a 100 w flood lamp for this experiment.

Note—it is important to remind students to calculate surface area for both surfaces, no matter which paper-tracing method is used.

Alternatively, the instructor can determine the weight of 1 cm^2 of leaf tissue from the type of plant used for the experiment. Use a razor blade to cut 10 squares, each 1 cm^2. Determine the mass and divide by 10. If students simply find the mass of all leaves stripped from their plants and divide by the mass of 1 cm^2, this will give the total surface area in cm^2.

Exercises C and D

See directions in Preparation of Materials and Solutions.

Exercise E

Plant mineral nutrition can be set up by the instructor as a demonstration or students can begin the experiment 6 weeks before this Laboratory and check the results each week by making measurements of shoot and root growth, and recording the appearance of the leaves. If used as a demonstration, have two sets of plants available for student observation in the laboratory—one set at 6 weeks of treatment and another set with 3 weeks of treatment. Remember to germinate sunflower seeds 3 weeks before beginning nutrient treatment. Data can then be summarized, graphed, and discussed as a part of Laboratory 34 if desired. Simply have each student or pair of students follow the directions under note (**6**). Provide the bottles of nutrient solutions, each with a pipette (labeled and held in a test tube attached to the matching bottle)—avoiding mixing of solutions is important. Give each student (or pair) a Mason jar and provide a flat of sunflower seeds grown in sand. Make sure students label their jars. We take them to the greenhouse and bring them back to the lab for study during each of the following 6 weeks. Cotton and aluminum foil must also be provided. If you desire to use only two plants per jar, then plug the third hole with cotton.

Let's Investigate

Students can try many different types of experiments with hydroponics. Exercise E can be combined with this exercise for an excellent independent student investigation since Exercise E is carried out hydroponically using specific nutrient solutions. Students can test for removal or supplements of various macronutrients or micronutrients as in Exercise E, or can ask more general questions about light, temperature, or other chemical additives (phosphates, excess fertilizers) using the Rap-id-gro technique. It will take 5 weeks to carry out this experiment, but students usually enjoy the experience. Have students read about hydroponics. Collaborative work and journal-keeping can be used during this experiment.

VI.   ORDERING INFORMATION

Wheaton bottle, collecting (16 oz) 500 mL Wheaton # 214209:
    Van Waters and Rogers Scientific, # 16175-160
    American Scientific, #B7545-250
two hole rubber stopper (# 8), Fisher # 14-140K; Carolina Biological, # 71-2472
boric acid (H_3BO_3)—Fisher, # A74-500; Carolina Biological, # 84-8440
manganese chloride ($MnCl_2 \cdot 4H_2O$)—Fisher, # M87-100; Carolina Biological, # 87-3860
zinc chloride ($ZnCl_2$)—Fisher, # Z33-500; Carolina Biological, # 89-9518
sodium molybdate ($Na_2MoO_4 \cdot 2H_2O$)—Fisher, # S336-500, or Carolina Biological, # 88-9810
cupric chloride ($CuCl_2 \cdot 2H_2O$)—Fisher, # C455-500; Carolina Biological, # 85-6440
ethylenediamine tetraacetic acid (EDTA)—Fisher, #E-478-500; Carolina Biological, # 86-1790
calcium nitrate ($Ca(NO_3)_2$)—Fisher, # C108-3; Carolina Biological, # 85-2208
potassium nitrate (KNO_3)—Fisher, #P263-500; Carolina Biological, # 88-3940
Rap-id-gro fertilizaer—local hardware store or greenhouse facility; Carolina Biological, # 15-9763
peat pellets—local hardware store or greenhouse facility
Mineral Requirements Set—Carolina Biological, # 20-7922

LABORATORY 35   Plant Responses to Stimuli

I.   FOREWORD

This laboratory is designed to introduce students to the effects of various plant hormones on development and growth. Several of the experiments in Exercise A can be set up by students at the end of the previous week's laboratory and the results can be considered during the laboratory itself. Other experiments, included in Exercise B, can be set up during the laboratory period and the results can be analyzed during the following week.

II.   TIME REQUIREMENTS

Exercise A (Parts 1 and 2)—30 minutes set up, 30 minutes interpretation, second week
Exercise A (Part 3)—20 minutes set up, 30 minutes interpretation, second week
Exercise B (Parts 1, 2, 3, and 4)—60 minutes
Exercise C—40 minutes
Let's Investigate—30 minutes setup, one week experiment
Exercise D—20 minutes

III.   STUDENT MATERIALS AND EQUIPMENT

	Per Student	Per Pair (2)	Per Group (4)	Per Class (24)
Exercise A (Part 1)				
sunflowers, pot (1)			1	6
forceps or razor blade			1	6
lanolin paste, jar			1	6
lanolin paste, jar, containing 5000 ppm IAA (2)			1	6
plant markers, tags			1	6
toothpicks			2	12
metric ruler (30 cm)			1	6
Exercise A (Part 2)				
Coleus plant			1	6
single edged razor blade			1	6
reinforcement rings			3	18
lanolin paste, jar—as in Part 1			1	6
lanolin paste, jar, containing 5000 ppm IAA—as in part 1 (2)				1
Exercise A (Part 3)				
dwarf pea plants, pot (3)			2	12
metric ruler (30 cm)			1	6
GA$_3$ solution, dropping bottle (4)			1	6
control solution, dropping bottle (5)			1	6

	Per Student	Per Pair (2)	Per Group (4)	Per Class (24)

Exercise A (Part 3)—continued

	Per Student	Per Pair (2)	Per Group (4)	Per Class (24)
plant markers, tags			2	12

Exercise B (Part 1)

	Per Student	Per Pair (2)	Per Group (4)	Per Class (24)
chicken gizzard plant (**6**)				2

Exercise B (Part 2)

	Per Student	Per Pair (2)	Per Group (4)	Per Class (24)
corn seeds (**7**)	3			72
Petri dish (100 mm)	1			24
paper towels, stack	1			24
masking tape, roll			1	6
black pencil	1			24
forceps	1			24

Exercise B (Part 3)

	Per Student	Per Pair (2)	Per Group (4)	Per Class (24)
bush beans (germinated) (**8**)	4			96
Petri dish (100 mm)	1			24
single edged razor blade	1			24
paper towels, stack	1			24

Exercise B (Part 4)

	Per Student	Per Pair (2)	Per Group (4)	Per Class (24)
wheat seedlings, pot (**9**)				1
tomato plant, pot (**10**)				1
150 w flood lamp				1

Exercise C

	Per Student	Per Pair (2)	Per Group (4)	Per Class (24)
Great Lakes lettuce seeds (germinated in continuous darkness) (**11**)				50
Grand Rapids lettuce seeds (germinated in continuous darkness) (**11**)				50
Great Lakes lettuce seeds (germinated in light) (**11**)				50
Grand Rapids lettuce seeds (germinated in light) (**11**)				50

Let's Investigate

	Per Student	Per Pair (2)	Per Group (4)	Per Class (24)
Grand Rapids lettuce seeds (germinated in 30 minutes of red light) (**12**)				50
Grand Rapids lettuce seeds (germinated in 30 minutes of far-red light) (**12**)				50
Grand Rapids lettuce seeds (germinated in 30 minutes of blue light) (**12**)				50
Grand Rapids lettuce seeds (germinated in 30 minutes of green light) (**12**)				50

Exercise D

	Per Student	Per Pair (2)	Per Group (4)	Per Class (24)
petunia or morning glory plants (**13**)				2
spinach or radish plants (**13**)				2
kidney bean plants (**13**)				2

IV. PREPARATION OF MATERIALS AND SOLUTIONS

(1) sunflowers, pot—
Plant sunflower seeds (5 or 6 to a pot) approximately 1/4 inch below the soil in a 6 inch Styrofoam pot. Plant four weeks before use. The number of seeds you plant depends on the viability of the seeds you are using. It is usually best to plant more than you will need.

(2) lanolin paste, 5000 ppm IAA—
Order prepared.

(3) dwarf pea plants, pot—
Plant peas about 12 days before lab. Place in moist soil, four to a pot.

(4) GA_3 solution—
Gather together the following materials:
> triethanolamine
> Tween-20
> gibberellic acid

Procedure:
> Part A: Dissolve 0.1 g gibberellic acid in 4 mL of triethanolamine and dilute up to 100 mL with distilled water.
> Part B: Mix 10 mL of Part A solution with 90 mL of distilled water. Add 2 drops of Tween-20 as a wetting agent.

(5) control solution—
Mix 2 drops of Tween-20 into 100 mL of distilled water.

(6) chicken gizzard plant—
Place plants in the dark (a dark cabinet will do). Allow one to remain vertical and place the other on its side. You may also wish to place a plant on a ring stand upside down (cover the soil with gauze so it will not fall out). Do this 2-3 days prior to the laboratory.

(7) corn seeds—
Soak overnight in tap water.

(8) bush beans (germinated)—
Soak bush bean seeds overnight in tap water. Lay beans flat on several layers of moist paper towels. Cover seeds with another layer of paper towels. Roll the towels up and wrap in aluminum foil. Allow two days for germination. If done during the winter season and the room is cold, place the seed roll into a warm oven or incubator (21-23° C).

(9) wheat seedlings—
Sprinkle 25-30 seeds in a pot. Cover with a sprinkling of soil so that seeds are about 1/4 inch below the surface. Plant seeds approximately one week before use. Put light on one side after they have germinated so that the seedlings bend toward the light.

(10) tomato plant—

Obtain a 6-8 inch tomato plant from a local greenhouse or store if in season. Otherwise, plant seed and allow 2 weeks for growth. Place the pot sideways on a ring stand and suspend a light from above, attached to the ring stand. Avoid using too large of a bulb or you will kill the plant.

(11) Great Lakes and Grand Rapids germinated lettuce seeds—

Place 50 Grand Rapids seeds on each of two Petri dishes containing dampened filter paper. Place 50 Great Lakes seeds on each of two similarly prepared Petri dishes. Label each dish. Place one dish of each lettuce variety in the light and the other two plates in the dark for 48 hours prior to the laboratory.

(12) germinated Grand Rapids seeds for Let's Investigate—

Seeds for this investigation must be treated properly. Since these are light induced, the seeds must first be given some time in the dark to imbibe the water necessary for germination.

Place filter paper in each of 8 Petri dishes and dampen with 8 mL of distilled water. In a darkened room, scatter 25 lettuce seeds (soaked overnight) in each dish. Place all dishes in the dark for 12 hours for imbibition to occur. After 12 hours remove the dishes to be light treated, put them in shoe boxes with the appropriate color filter, and place them under the appropriate light source for at least 30 minutes. Seeds receiving fluorescent light should be placed 30 cm from a 40 watt fluorescent tube. Place the seeds receiving incandescent light 50 cm from a 150 w incandescent lamp. After exposure, return the dishes to the dark cabinet. Keep the dark control in the dark at all times.

Use Great Lakes (light insensitive) and Grand Rapids (light sensitive) seeds in the following dishes:

Dish 1 Dark Control—Great Lakes variety
Dish 2 Dark Control—Grand Rapids variety
 (wrap both dishes in aluminum foil and keep in the dark)
Dish 3 Light Control—Great Lakes variety
Dish 4 Light Control—Grand Rapids variety
 (expose both dishes in fluorescent light, cover with clear polyethylene)

Use only Grand Rapids variety (light sensitive) in the following dishes:

Dish 5 Blue Light (390-590 nm)—expose to fluorescent light,
 3 layers of dark blue cellophane
Dish 6 Green Light (480-630 nm)—expose to fluorescent light,
 3 layers of dark green cellophane
Dish 7 Red Light (580-630 nm)—expose to fluorescent light,
 2 layers of dark red cellophane
Dish 8 Far-red Light (670 nm)—expose to incandescent light,
 3 layers of dark blue and 2 layers of dark red cellophane

Observe the seeds in each treatment 24 hours after exposure and determine the % germination in each dish. Which light treatment was most effective? How do the two varieties differ in their response to light?

(13) petunia, morning glory, spinach, kidney bean, or radish plants—

Expose one plant of each type to 8 hours of light and 16 hours of dark (8L:16D) and the other to 16 hours of light and 8 hours of dark (16L:8D). This is best done in a growth chamber under controlled temperature (approximately 22° C). Start plants from seeds. It will take approximately 35 days (6-8 weeks) for flowering. Spinach and radishes are long day plants. Petunias and morning glories are short day plants. Kidney beans are day neutral. Do about 6-8 weeks before use.

V. PREPARATION SUGGESTIONS

Exercise A

The hormone experiments in Exercises A take 2 weeks to complete. The set up is simple and can be done during the previous week. Results can then be analyzed during this laboratory period.

Exercise B

Tropism experiments with seeds can be set up during this laboratory and analyzed at the beginning of the following week's laboratory period. Phototropism experiments should be set up two weeks prior to this laboratory.

Exercise C

This experiment must be set up by the preparators two days before the laboratory. Results from this experiment provide the foundation for students to understand the Let's Investigate activity that follows.

Of interest in this study of light-induced germination is the fact that gibberellic acid (GA_3) can also induce germination in light-sensitive seeds that are kept in the dark. Dissolve 100 mg of gibberellic acid in 1000 mL distilled water and use this to soak the filter paper for the germination chambers (Petri dishes). Place 20 seeds in each of two dishes lined with water-soaked filter paper and 20 seeds in each of two dishes with GA_3-soaked paper. Keep one water and one GA_3 dish in the dark and the other two in low light. Keep moist. Determine the per cent germination after one week.

Let's Investigate

Twelve hours before the laboratory, prepare Grand Rapids seeds and place all seeds in the dark on wet filter paper to imbibe water for germination. Since Grand Rapids seeds are light-induced, no germination will have occurred before students are ready to use the seeds. Turn out the lights and work in a room that is as dark as possible. Have students place seeds in appropriate colored-light chambers. These can be made from shoe boxes with colored cellophane filters inserted into a window in the top of the box (almost the same size as the box lid). Glue the appropriate "filters" in place. An optional exercise demonstrates how gibberellic acid substitutes for light and can induce germination in light sensitive seeds.

Exercise D

This can best be done in a growth chamber. Plants should be started from seeds (or from very small plants) and will need approximately 6-8 weeks on the correct light regime. Follow preparation directions (**13**) for choice of plants.

indole-3-acetic acid paste (5000 ppm)—Carolina Biological, # 20-7602

control lanolin paste—Carolina Biological, # 20-7850

gibberellic acid—Carolina Biological, # 20-7565

triethanolamine (reagent)—Carolina Biological, # 89-6850

Tween 20—Fisher, # BP337-500

dark red, green, and blue cellophane—Fisher, Life Science catalog # S52570

sunflower seeds—Carolina Biological, # 15-9063

dwarf pea seeds (Little Marvel)—Carolina Biological, # 15-8883

corn seeds—Carolina Biological, # 15-9243

bush bean seeds—Carolina Biological, # 15-8330

Great Lakes lettuce seeds—Carolina Biological, # 15-8686

Grand Rapids lettuce seeds—Carolina Biological, # 15-8680

wheat seeds—Carolina Biological, # 15-9395

petunia seeds—local seed store

morning glory seeds—Carolina Biological, # 15-8780

spinach seeds—local seed store

radish seeds—Carolina Biological, # 15-9000

kidney bean seeds—Carolina Biological, # 15-8420

LABORATORY 36   Communities and Ecosystems

I.   FOREWORD

This laboratory examines several properties of interacting organisms and their environments, beginning with a repetition of Gause's classic competition experiments in *Paramecium* (this exercise also illustrates the nature of population growth in monocultures). Invertebrate organisms in leaf litter communities are sampled to show the diversity of organisms in different samples taken from areas with different environmental conditions. Finally, some features of climate that affect biomes are examined.

II.   TIME REQUIREMENTS

Exercise A—30 minutes
Exercise B—60 minutes
Exercise C—30 minutes

III.   STUDENT MATERIALS AND EQUIPMENT

	Per Student	Per Pair (2)	Per Group (4)	Per Class (24)
Exercise A				
Paramecium caudatum, P. aurelia, and *P. caudatum-P. aurelia* cultures (1)				9
microscope slides, box (75 X 25 mm)			1	6
0.01 mL (10 µL) pipette	1			24
compound microscope	1			24
Exercise B				
organisms from leaf litter (2)				1
figure of representative organisms (included)	1			24
dissecting microscope	1			24
small Petri dishes			1	12
Exercise C				
weather data (included)	1			24
world map				1
graph paper	1			24

IV.   PREPARATION OF MATERIALS AND SOLUTIONS

(1)   *Paramecium* cultures—
      Gather together the following materials:
           Paramecium caudatum (live culture)
           Paramecium aurelia (live culture)

2000 mL Erlenmeyer flask
9 sterile Erlenmeyer flasks
10 sterile cotton plugs (cheesecloth covered)
two 2 mL sterile pipettes
timothy hay

Procedure:

Order 1 culture for a class of 30 students each of *Paramecium caudatum* and *P. aurelia* for delivery 3 weeks before the laboratory, a second set of cultures (one of each species) for delivery 2 weeks before the laboratory, and a third set of cultures (one of each species) for delivery 1 week before the laboratory. These sets of cultures will be sufficient for multiple laboratory sections, but should be ordered fresh to start each population flask.

On the day before each culture set is to arrive (i.e., 3 weeks and a day before the lab, 2 weeks and a day before the lab, and 1 week and a day before the lab), prepare a hay solution as follows: add 1000 mL of pond water and a handful of timothy hay to a 2000 mL Erlenmeyer flask and bring the mixture to a boil. Boil slowly (avoid boiling over) for 10 minutes and plug with a sterile, cheesecloth wrapped, cotton plug. Remove from the burner or hot plate and cool at room temperature overnight. Pour 100 mL of supernatant (filter through 4 layers of sterile cheesecloth if necessary) into each of three 250 mL sterile Erlenmeyer flasks and stopper each with a sterile, cheesecloth wrapped, cotton plug.

Label one flask "A." Stir a *Paramecium aurelia* culture with a sterile 2 mL pipette to suspend the organisms evenly in the stock jar (being careful to dislodge any organisms adhering to the sides). Use the pipette to transfer 4 mL of medium (containing about 400 organisms) to the flask and replace the sterile plug. Label a second flask "C." Aseptically, transfer 2 mL of *P. aurelia* culture to this flask (containing about 200 organisms) and stopper. Stir the *P. caudatum* culture with a second sterile 2 mL pipette and add 1.6 mL of medium (also containing about 200 organisms) to the same flask and stopper. Label a third flask "B." Aseptically, transfer 3.2 mL (about 400 organisms) to this flask and replace the sterile stopper. Add the age (3 weeks, 2 weeks, or 1 week) to the label on each flask and hold them at room temperature out of direct sunlight until the laboratory period. Note that this process needs to be repeated three times to supply a total of 9 cultures for each laboratory: 6 control flasks (3 of each species) and 3 experimental flasks. These cultures can be used by several successive laboratories over 2 days or so, if cultures are not spilled or badly contaminated.

There is the potential for large sampling errors in this experiment, but barring problems from contamination, population growth and competition should both be demonstrated. Remember to use aseptic technique when preparing the cultures and when sampling from the cultures if you will be using them for more than one laboratory period.

Alternatives:

Other methods exist for the preparation of the culture medium used in this experiment. One involves the use of protozoan pellets (Carolina Biological Supply Company) and sterile pond water. A second method involves boiling grains of wheat (50 g) in 500 mL of water to make a stock medium which is then diluted using 10 mL stock to 100 mL of sterile pond water. Try to minimize contamination in whatever method is used—we want students to see how the two species of paramecia interact, not bacteria or other microorganisms!

(2) leaf litter—
Gather together the following materials:
litter samples
plastic bags
shelf for extraction apparatus
100 w light bulbs
plastic funnels (150 mm top diameter, 28 mm stem diameter)
250 mL Erlenmeyer flasks
70% ethanol
Procedure:
Prepare an extraction rack for collecting soil invertebrates. A wooden rack should be built with three shelves to hold the apparatus: the lowest shelf will hold 250 mL Erlenmeyer flasks directly below the small opening of funnels protruding through holes drilled in the middle shelf. The top shelf holds 100 w light bulbs used to provide light and gentle heat to drive organisms from the soil. Construct the rack to hold 3-10 "collectors" depending on the numbers of samples needed. The tip of each funnel should be slightly below the top of each flask so organisms extracted fall into the flask. Light bulbs should be about 6 inches (15 cm) above the tops of each of the funnels.

Several days before this laboratory, collect samples of leaf litter taken from shaded areas that are relatively moist. Place them in plastic bags. [Samples should include decomposing leaf litter down into the upper soil layer at least 1 cm deep. Each sample should be approximately 500 mL in volume.] Try to collect samples from contrasting habitats—deciduous woodland, coniferous forest, riparian habitat, etc. Label your samples. Students could make these collections if you wish to expose them to different habitats and the sampling process.

Place a small piece of screen wire in the bottom of each funnel to keep nonliving portions of your sample from falling into the flasks below. Use a different funnel for each sample. After the funnels with samples are in place, carefully place a 250 mL Erlenmeyer funnel with 50 mL of 70% ethanol below each. [Mix 700 mL of 95% ethanol with 250 mL of distilled water to make 70% alcohol.] Turn on the bulb over each funnel (be sure that nothing flammable can come in contact with a bulb and that the wiring is safe). Leave the apparatus overnight (longer if the soil is especially wet).

Carefully remove each flask (do not bump the funnels—the dry litter will contaminate samples easily). Stopper and label each flask for use in the laboratory.
Provide small dishes for pairs of students to share samples while they study them under the dissecting microscope. Samples can be used in several laboratories if students are careful to return all organisms to the proper flask at the end of the laboratory.

If time permits, some students might find it especially interesting to examine fresh samples and see some of the organisms live. Carefully remove intact samples of leaf litter about 2-3 cm deep and wrap in plastic and aluminum foil to keep them moist. Allow students to work on these samples with dissecting needles under high magnification on a dissecting microscope.

V. PREPARATION SUGGESTIONS

See notes in section IV above.

Exercise B

The Shannon-Weaver index for small samples has a large variance, so caution students not to attach importance to minimal differences in indices. On the whole we would expect mature forests to be more diverse than early succession stages and deciduous woodlands should be more diverse than coniferous areas—particularly monoculture plantations. Riparian habitats could be intermediate, depending on the sites sampled.

A simple key to microarthropods and drawings of representative soil invertebrates are included on p. 210-211 at the end of the Preparator's Guide.

Exercise C

Weather data for several cities are tabulated on p. 213 at the end of the Preparator's Guide. Make copies for the students to use. This part of the laboratory could be done at home if there is not time in the laboratory period to complete the exercise. Use a textbook map of biomes to display in class or refer students to the map if the exercise is to be done at home.

VI. ORDERING INFORMATION

Paramecium caudatum (live culture)—Carolina Biological, # L2A
Paramecium aurelia (live culture)— Carolina Biological, # L2B
protozoan pellets—Carolina Biological, # L50P
sterile spring water—Carolina Biological, # L51X (1 liter)
100 mL microcapillary pipette—Fisher, # 21-4517
plastic funnel, polypropylene (OD: 150 mm top, 28 mm bottom)—Fisher, # 10-348D or
 # 73-4016 (6" polypropylene)

PREP GUIDE FOR LABORATORIES 34/D1 THROUGH 37/D4
Dissection of the Fetal Pig

I. FOREWORD

These related laboratories are designed to teach students some of the major landmarks of mammalian structure and introduce them to dissection techniques.

II. TIME REQUIREMENTS

2.5 to 3 hours for each laboratory

III. STUDENT MATERIALS AND EQUIPMENT

	Per Student	Per Pair (2)	Per Group (4)	Per Class (24)
<u>Laboratory 34/D1, Exercise A</u>				
materials contained in the manual				
<u>Laboratory 34/D1, Exercise B</u>				
dissecting kit (1)	1			24
pig embryo, double injected (2)	1			24
dissecting pan	1			24
plastic gloves (one pair/laboratory) (3)	4			96
<u>Laboratory 34/D1, Exercise C</u>				
cat skeleton			1	6
OR human skeleton (4)				1
<u>Laboratory 34/D1, Exercise D</u>				
dissecting pins (2 inch)	6			144
rubber bands or string	4			96
<u>Laboratory 35/D2, Exercises A-F</u>				
use materials for Laboratory 34/D1, Exercises B and D				
<u>Laboratory 36/D3, Exercises A-D</u>				
use materials for Laboratory 36/D3, Exercises B and D				
<u>Laboratory 37/D4, Exercises A-D</u>				
use materials for Laboratory 34/D1, Exercises B and C				
sheep brain (optional) (5)			1	6

IV. PREPARATION OF MATERIALS AND SOLUTIONS

(1) **Dissecting Kits.** It is desirable to have students buy their own dissecting kits (dissecting tools disappear!). Each kit should include a good pair of surgical scissors, a probe and seeker, and two dissecting needles. A one-piece scalpel or cartilage knife should be used for dissecting cartilage and bone. Be sure that the scalpel is not used to section tissues—encourage students to use fingers and probes to separate organs from surrounding tissues without cutting. Have instructors show students how to expose a difficult structure so that all aspects of the organ can be seen.

(2) Preserved Fetal Pigs. Pig embryos are available with several preservatives, in different sizes, and with differing combinations of injections. We recommend the largest specimens available, preserved in formalin, with both veins and arteries injected.

(3) Plastic Gloves. Disposable gloves should be available in small, medium, and large sizes. Students with sensitivity to preservatives should be encouraged to wear gloves while handling specimens.

(4) Skeletons. If either a human skeleton or a cat skeleton is available, they would be useful in Exercise C of Laboratory 34/D1. If disarticulated vertebrae are available (from a dead deer, dog, or other animal), place them on the demonstration bench and let students sort them into piles representing different regions of the spinal column.

(5) Sheep Brain. Neural tissues in the fetal pig are very soft and difficult to dissect. Whole and hemisected sheep's brains may be shown on demonstration if they are available.

V. PREPARATION SUGGESTIONS

All Laboratories

Each student should retain his or her own pig from laboratory to laboratory. Waterproof labels with names can be tied around a leg. If pigs are stored together, keep a separate bucket for each laboratory. It is preferable to place each pig in a plastic bag, wrapped in moistened paper towels, and sealed with a wire tie. Each pig can then be placed in a separate shoe box (have each student bring his or her own to class) with name and section number on the end of each box. Store these boxes on shelves or on top of cabinets from week to week.

As dissection proceeds, bits and pieces of tissues will be discarded. Maintain a trash can with a plastic bag for these tissues. Be sure that students clean out sinks in which dissecting pans are washed, placing all residue in the trash can. Empty this can after each day of laboratories.

Provide added demonstration materials as available. Various bones, bone fragments, vertebrae, limbs, skulls, etc., may be displayed for examination. A fresh cow or pig heart may be ordered from your butcher and used to demonstrate some of the internal structures, including valves, found in the heart. If there is a spare embalmed male cat left over from the anatomy lab, borrow it to show the adult male genital structures. Feel free to supplement exercises as desired.

VI. ORDERING INFORMATION

pig embryo, double injected—Carolina Biological, # P-1897F

disposable gloves—Carolina Biological, # 70-6345, 70-6346, and 70-6347 (order small, medium, and large sizes)

dissecting trays—Carolina Biological, # 62-9004

dissecting pins (2 inch)—Carolina Biological, # 62-9122

dissecting kits—see Carolina Biological catalog (include # 62-2225 scissors, # 62-6152 scalpel, 2 # 62-7200 dissecting needles, and # 62-7400 probe and seeker if ordering individual items)

sheep brain (whole, with dura intact)—Carolina Biological, # P2100F (optional)

MEIOSIS IN *Sordaria*

The fungus, *Sordaria fimicola*, is often used to study the processes of gene segregation and crossing over during meiosis. This common fungus spends most of its life cycle in the haploid condition (Figure 1). Its body is composed of haploid (*n*) cells attached end-to-end to form hairlike filamentous hyphae that intertwine to form a mass (*mycelium*). When hyphal cells of two different mycelia come together, they fuse and their haploid nuclei combine to form a diploid (*2n*) zygote nucleus. The diploid nucleus immediately undergoes meiosis to form four nuclei, returning the organism to its haploid state. These haploid nuclei then divide mitotically to yield a total of eight haploid cells. These cells develop thick, resistant cell walls and are called **ascospores**. The ascospores are arranged in a linear array within a sac called an **ascus** (plural, asci). Many such asci grouped together line the inside of a fruiting body (**ascocarp**), formed from tightly fused hyphae. In *Sordaria* the ascocarp, called a **perithecium**, is flask-shaped with a small hole through which mature spores escape when the asci rupture.

Figure 1. Sordaria fimicola
 life cycle.

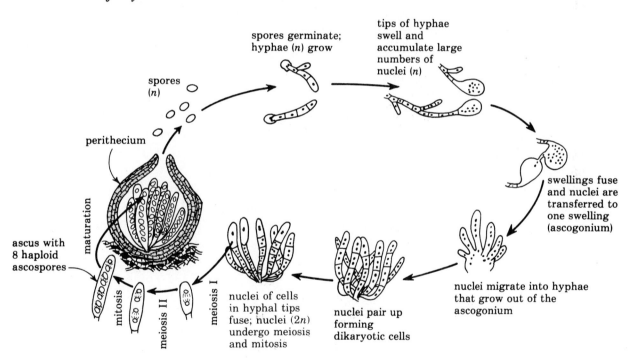

Ascospores of *Sordaria* are normally black (wild type of "+"). However, several different genes can be involved in determining sport color and each of these genes can have several allelic forms. Black spores can only be produced in both of two genes controlling color are wild type (g^+ and t^+). A mutation in one such gene can result in a gray mutant allele (*g*), whereas a mutation in a different gene can result in a tan mutant allele (*t*). Gray spores are produced if one wild type (*g*⁺) allele and one tan (*t*) mutant allele are present. If both tan and gray mutant alleles are present, the cumulative effect of both mutations is that the ascospores are colorless (Figure 2). Ascospores are haploid, so only one allele is present at each locus. As a result, the spore's phenotype (physical characteristic) is equivalent to its genotype—the expression of the allele cannot be "masked by a different (and perhaps dominant) allele at the same locus on the homologous chromosome. This equivalence is one of the major reasons that fungi such as *Sordaria* (an ascomycete) are used extensively in genetic research.

Figure 2. *Two different genes control ascospore color.*

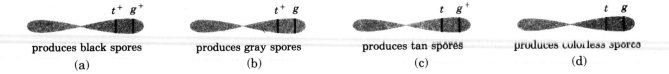

produces black spores	produces gray spores	produces tan spores	produces colorless spores
(a)	(b)	(c)	(d)

Procedure:
1. Obtain a *Sordaria* cross plate from the demonstration area in your laboratory.
2. Where the mycelia of two strains of *Sordaria* overlap and fuse, dark lines of time perithecia will be visible. Use a toothpick or spatula to gently scrape the surface of the agar to collect perithecia. (It is usually best to collect perithecia toward the outer rim of the dish.)
3. Place the perithecia in a drop of water on a slide. Cover with a coverslip and gently press on the coverslip (use a small cork) to rupture the perithecia. Be gentle so that the ascospores remain in the asci.
4. View the slide using the 10 × objective and locate a group of hybrid asci (recall that asci produced by fusion of two identical strains, both black or both tan, will result in ascospores that are all of the same color within an ascus—disregard these asci). Hybrid asci contain both black and tan ascospores within each ascus.
5. Count at least 50 asci and score them as either MI asci (4 + 4 arrangement), in which no crossing over occurred and alleles segregated in meiosis I, or MII asci (2 + 2 + 2 + 2 or 2 + 4 + 2) in which crossing over occurred and alleles segregated in meiosis II (refer to Figure 3 for details on ascospore patterns). Record your results in Table 1.

Table 1.

MI Number of 4:4 asci	MII Number of asci showing crossover	Total asci MI + MII	Percentage of asci showing crossover, divided by 2	Gene to centromere distance (map units)
○○○○●●●● ●●●●○○○○	○○●●○○●● ●●○○●●○○ ○○●●●●○○ ●●○○○○●●			

198

In this exercise, since you are studying only one gene, you will map its distance from the centromere by determining the frequency of crossover events involving that gene—crossovers that occur somewhere between the centromere and the gene and result in its recombination with the chromatid of a different chromosome.

Recall that the frequency of crossing over between two genes is largely controlled by the distance between genes (or between a gene and a centromere, as in this case); the probability of a crossover occurring between two particular genes on the same chromosome increases as the distance between those genes becomes larger. The frequency of crossing over is, therefore, generally used to describe distances between linked genes. A map unit is equal to a 1% frequency of crossovers. For instance, when there is a 30% frequency of crossing over between two genes, these genes are 30 map units apart.

6. Determine the frequency of crossing over (percentage of crossovers) by dividing the number of MII crossover asci by the total number of asci counted, and multiplying by 100:

$$\text{frequency of crossing over} = (\text{MII} / (\text{MI} + \text{MII})) \times 100$$

7. In *Sordaria*, since only 4 of the 8 ascospores in each ascus are the direct result of meiotic crossovers (the other 4 result from mitotic division), the relationship between frequency of crossing over and map distance is expressed as:

    number of map units =
          [(4 × number of recombinant (MII) asci) / (8 × total number of asci)] × 100
    or
    number of map units = (frequency of crossing over) / 2

8. Record the map distance of gene *t* or *t*⁺ from the centromere. _____ Record the map distance in Table 1. Published results indicate that the map distance of the tan spore color gene from the centromere in *Sordaria fimicola* is 26 map units. How closely do your data fit this measurement? _____

Figure 3. Sordaria *(a) Formation of hybrid MI non-crossover asci results from fusion of hyphae from two different color strains but no crossing over prior to meiosis I. (b) Formation of MII crossover asci occurs after fusion of hyphae from two different color strains and crossing over during meiosis I. Chromatids of the two chromosomes carrying the color genes recombine. Meiosis II, followed by mitosis, results in a 2 + 2 + 2 + 2 pattern or a 2 + 4 + 2 pattern of colored ascospores. The symbol "+" indicates the wild type allele.*

Formation of Non-crossover Asci

Meiosis I   Meiosis II   Mitosis

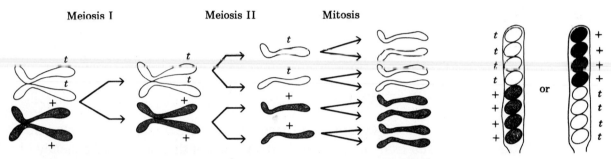

Two homologous chromosomes lining up at metaphase I of meiosis. The two chromatids of one chromosome each contain the allele for tan spore color (t) and the two chromatids of the other chromosome each contain the allele for wild type spore color (+).

The first meiotic division (MI) results in two cells each containing just one type of spore color allele (either tan or wild type.) Therefore, segregation of these alleles has occurred at the first meiotic division.

The second meiotic division (MII) results in four cells, each with the haploid number of chromosomes (1 n).

A mitotic division simply duplicates these cells resulting in 8 spores. They are arranged in the 4:4 pattern.

(a)

Formation of Crossover Asci

Meiosis I   Meiosis II   Mitosis

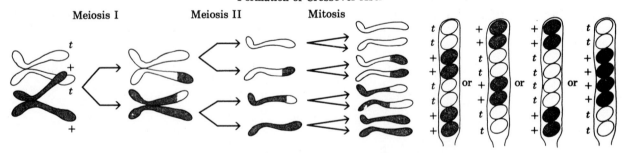

In this case, crossing over occurs in the region between the gene for spore color and centromere as the homologous chromosomes line up at metaphase I.

This time, MI results in two cells each containing both alleles (1 tan, 1 wild-type), therefore, the alleles for spore color have not yet segregated.

MII results in segregation of the two alleles for spore color.

The mitotic division results in 8 spores arranged in the 2:2:2:2 or 2:4:2 pattern.

(b)

200

metaphase spread, normal female

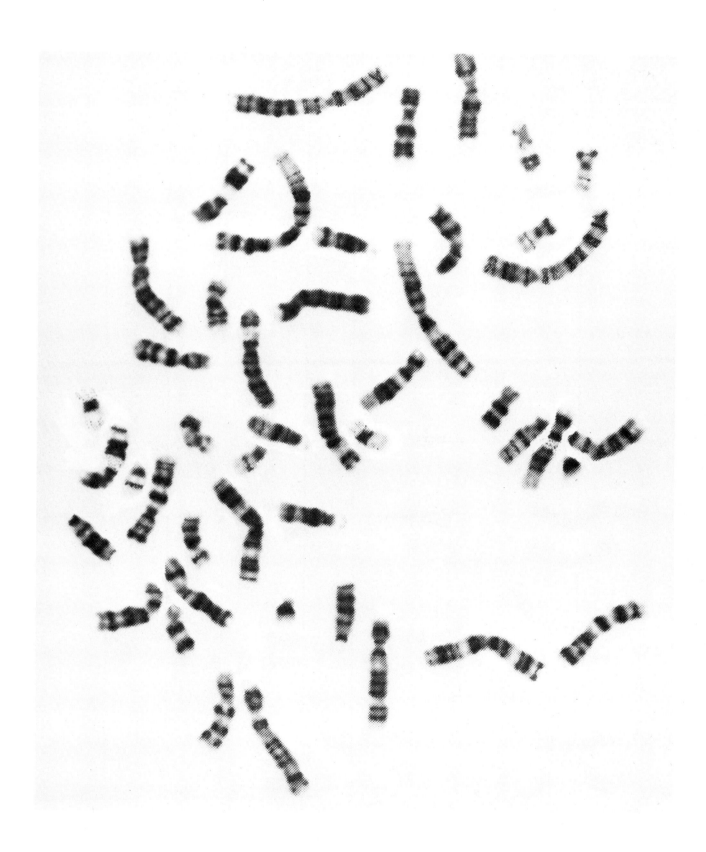

karyotype, normal female

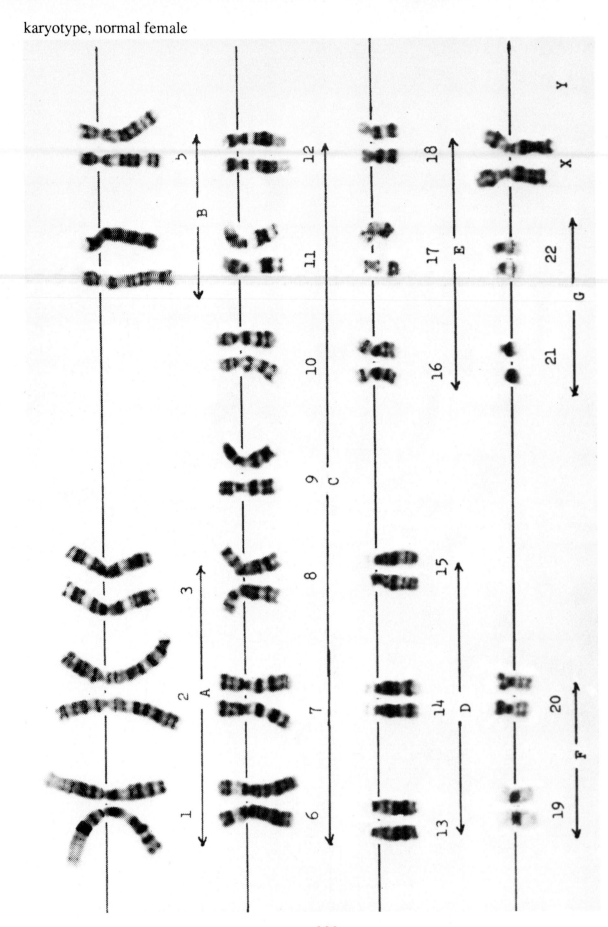

metaphase spread, Down's syndrome, male

karyotype, Down's syndrome, male

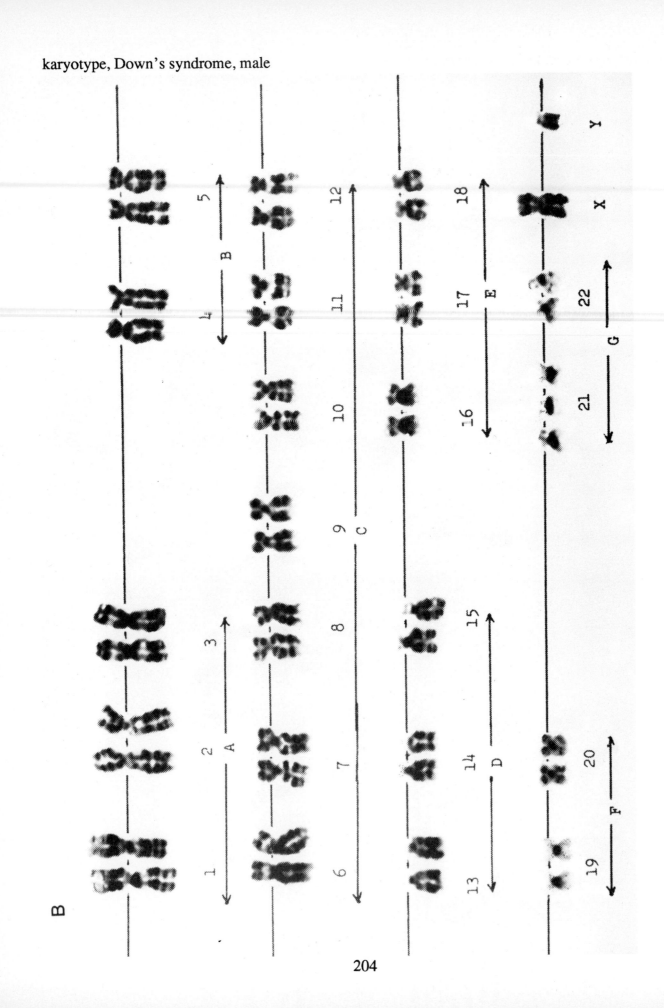

metaphase spread, Down's syndrome, female

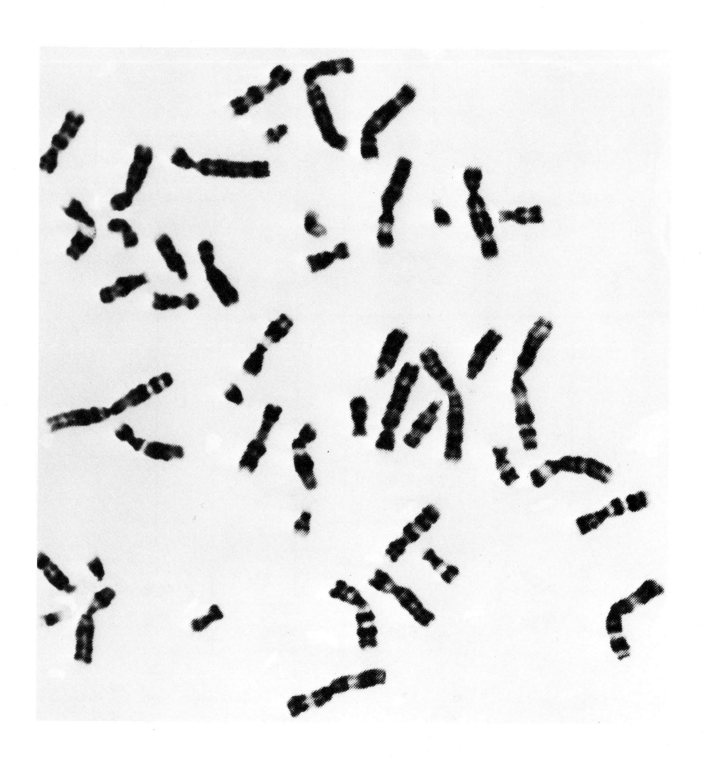

karyotope, Down's syndrome, female

metaphase spread, trisomy 18, male

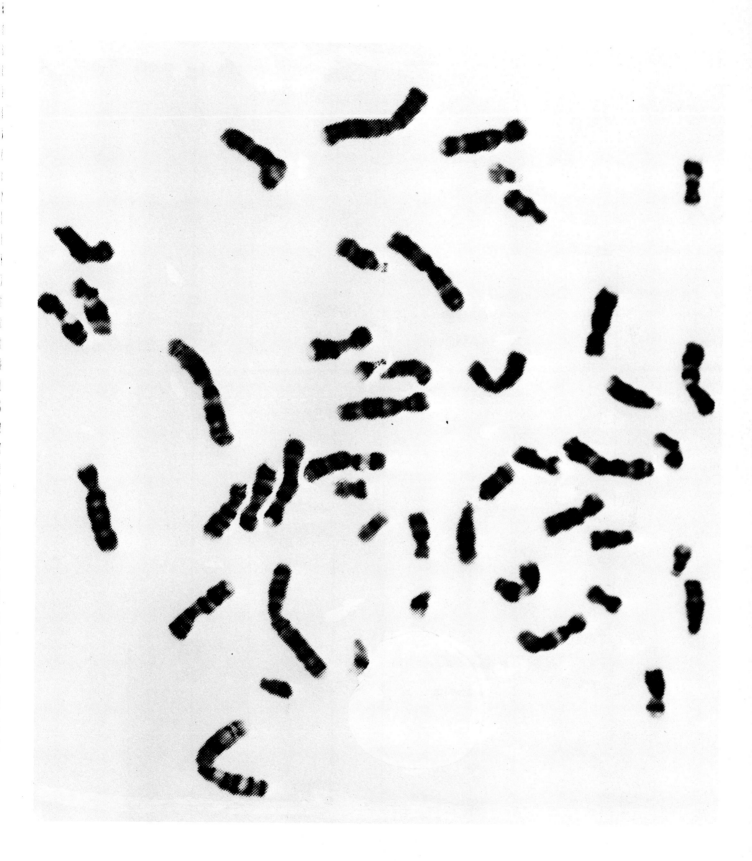

karyotype, trisomy 18, male

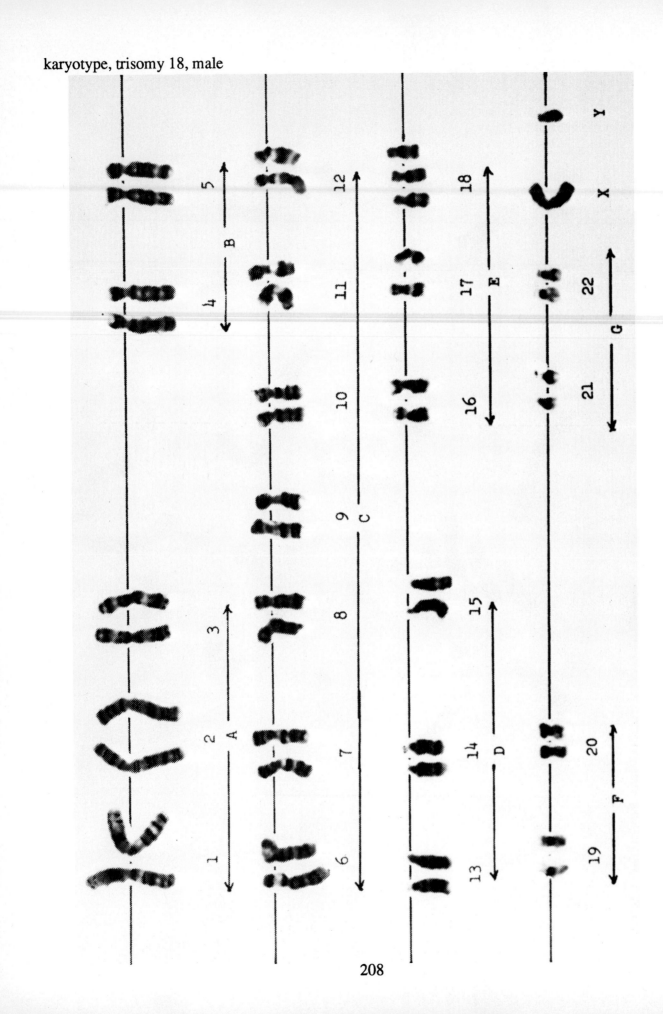

MUSCLES OF THE CHICKEN WING

Figure 1. Muscles of the right wing of the pigeon. Ventral view. The overlying pectoralis muscle has been removed on the right side.

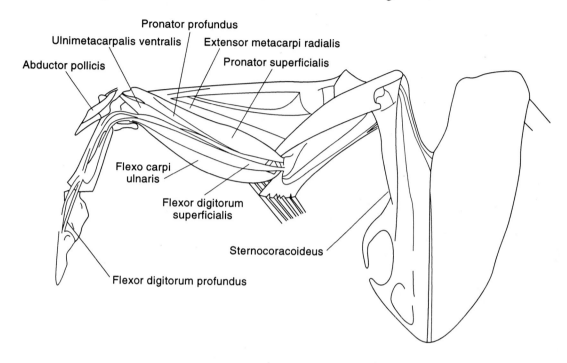

Pronator profundus

Ulnimetacarpalis ventralis

Extensor metacarpi radialis

Abductor pollicis

Pronator superficialis

Flexo carpi ulnaris

Flexor digitorum superficialis

Sternocoracoideus

Flexor digitorum profundus

Figure 2.   Muscles of the right wing of the pigeon, dorsal view.

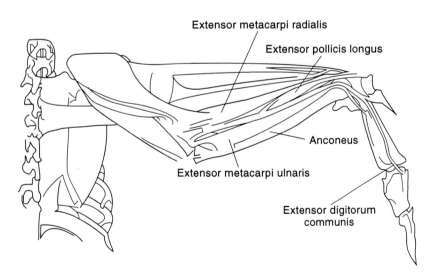

Extensor metacarpi radialis

Extensor pollicis longus

Anconeus

Extensor metacarpi ulnaris

Extensor digitorum communis

From Pettingill, O. S. Jr. 1970. *Ornithology in Laboratory and Field.* 4 th. ed. Burgess Publishing Company, Minneapolis. p. 73

KEY TO SOIL MICROARTHROPODS

1a Six legs, distinct head, segmented thorax and abdomen (**Class Insecta**)   2
1b More than six legs   5

   2a Antennae, eyes, and cerci absent, 9-12 abdominal segments   (**Order Protura**)
   2b Antennae present, cerci absent or present   3

3a Antennae with 10-12 segments; 2-3 cerci on tip of abdomen as filaments or pincers
          (**Order Thysanura**)
3b Antennae present, cerci absent   4

   4a Antennae with 4-8 segments, 6 abdominal segments, forked appendage ("spring") for
      leaping (usually on fourth abdominal segment)   (**Order Collembola**)
   4b Antennae with 5 segments, body cylindrical, claws absent on legs (**Order Thysanoptera**)

5a Head and thorax fused together, 8 legs (**Class Arachnida**)   6
5b More than 8 legs on body   8

   6a Abdomen distinctly segmented, first pair of leglike appendages (palpi) contain large
      pincerlike claws, 4 pairs of true legs   **Pseudoscorpions**
   6b Abdomen not segmented   7

7a Body smooth, without hairs or projections   ticks (**Order Acarina**)
7b Hair on body and legs   mites (**Order Acarina**)

   8a One pair of legs on each abdominal segment   (**Order Chilopoda**)
   8b Two pairs of legs on each abdominal segment   (**Order Diplopoda**)

See Borror, D. J. and R. E. White, 1970 (*A Field Guide to the Insects of America North of Mexico*. Houghton Mifflin Company, Boston. 404 p.) for a pictorial key to the orders of insects.

Soil Invertebrates

PHYLUM ARTHROPODA
Class Insecta

Order Protura
(proturans)

Order Thysanura
(silverfishes)

Order Collembola
(springtails)

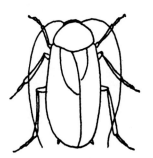

Order Thysanoptera
(thrips)

Order Coleoptera
(beetles)

Order Orthoptera
(roaches)

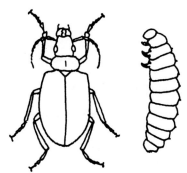

Order Hymenoptera
(ants)

Order Siphonaptera
(fleas)

Order Hemiptera
(true bugs)

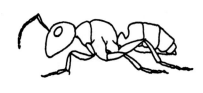

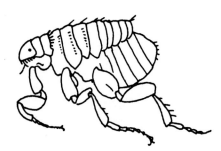

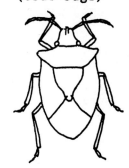

Order Diptera
(flies)

Order Psocoptera
(bark lice)

Order Isoptera
(termites)

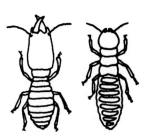

PHYLUM ARTHROPODA
Class Arachnida

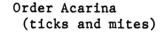

Order Araneae
(spiders)

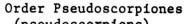

Order Acarina
(ticks and mites)

Order Pseudoscorpiones
(pseudoscorpions)

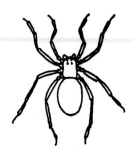

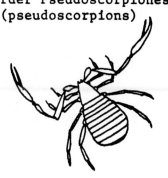

Order Opiliones
(daddy long-legs, harvestmen)

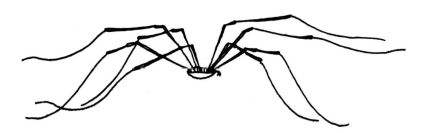

Class Crustacea
Order Isopoda
(sow bugs, pill bugs)

Class Diplopoda
(millipedes)

Class Chilopoda
(centipedes)

PHYLUM NEMATODA
(roundworms)

PHYLUM ANNELIDA
Class Oligochaeta
(earthworms)

PHYLUM MOLLUSCA
Class Gastropoda
(slugs, snails)

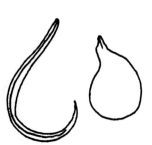

212

JohnNorton

CLIMATOLOGICAL DATA FROM DIFFERENT BIOMES

Sta	Var	Jan	Feb	Mar	Apr	May	Jun	Jul	Aug	Sep	Oct	Nov	Dec
1	T	0.3	0.6	2.4	6.8	17.2	19.9	22.7	22.8	14.9	11.8	7.9	0.5
	PT	8.5	11.8	11.7	5.8	4.7	11.6	11.1	19.2	12.9	8.8	4.5	7.4
2	T	26.8	25.4	24.6	19.4	13.3	11.8	11.6	11.4	13.9	19.3	23.3	25.8
	PT	0.5	3.3	4.0	0.8	2.8	1.4	0.3	3.1	1.4	0.0	2.3	2.3
3	T	5.4	5.4	13.6	18.6	19.4	25.2	26.5	26.3	21.6	17.0	9.7	4.3
	PT	2.0	0.5	6.3	14.5	10.8	5.8	3.1	3.6	8.0	7.4	1.0	2.6
4	T	8.4	11.3	12.7	12.3	16.4	19.5	22.4	23.5	22.4	17.3	13.3	11.8
	PT	3.2	2.3	5.4	8.7	2.3	4.7	2.1	0.6	3.8	8.4	0.0	2.0
5	T	24.4	29.0	32.5	30.0	28.2	26.3	24.9	24.9	25.3	26.0	24.5	23.8
	PT	0.0	0.0	0.0	4.1	13.6	11.1	23.6	45.0	18.5	2.6	0.0	0.0
6	T	25.9	26.6	27.1	27.1	27.5	27.2	26.9	27.4	26.8	26.8	25.9	25.7
	PT	29.0	9.3	18.8	14.6	17.5	19.7	16.7	13.0	18.5	14.3	35.7	67.0
7	T	-31.9	-33.0	-32.7	-20.5	-12.6	-0.7	1.0	-0.4	-1.3	-9.8	-19.1	-30.0
	PT	0.8	2.0	0.6	1.7	1.2	2.0	2.6	0.7	1.7	1.8	1.8	0.4
8	T	-24.8	-18.7	-21.4	-6.8	4.2	8.1	12.5	11.0	4.1	-2.1	-11.7	-19.9
	PT	4.0	3.7	4.8	1.9	7.0	16.4	17.2	21.6	11.4	8.0	4.7	3.2
9	T	26.2	26.6	26.4	26.6	27.2	25.1	24.8	24.4	25.8	26.0	26.0	26.4
	PT	0.8	27.5	15.0	14.2	29.0	8.7	30.8	15.3	4.2	6.5	1.1	6.5

Sta--station, see below for location
Var--variable: T = temperature in °C; PT = precipitation in cm
Jan, Feb,...Dec--months

Stations listed include:
1. Pittsburgh, PA, USA; latitude 40° 30' N, longitude 80° 13' W; temperate forest
2. Kalgoorlie, Australia; latitude 30° 46' S, longitude 121° 27' E; desert
3. Oklahoma City, OK, USA; latitude 35° 24' N, longitude 97° 36' W; temperate grassland
4. Barcelona, Spain; latitude 41° 24' N, longitude 2° 9' E; Mediterranean (chapparal)
5. Moundou, Chad; latitude 8° 37' N, longitude 16° 4' E; savannah
6. Singapore; latitude 1° 22' N, longitude 103° 55' E; tropical forest
7. Cape Cheljuskin, USSR; latitude 77° 43' N, longitude 104° 17' E; tundra
8. Nitchequon, Canada; latitude 53° 12' N, longitude 70° 54' W; taiga
9. Aracaju, Brazil; latitude 10° 55' S, longitude 37° 3' W; monsoon forest

Sources:

Gale Research. 1981. Weather of US Cities. Vol. 2. Gale Research, Detroit.
    and 1975 data.
National Climatic Center. 1978 and 1979. NOAA. Asheville.

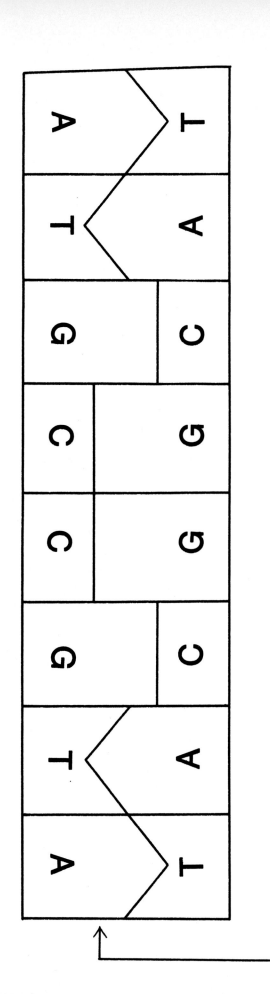

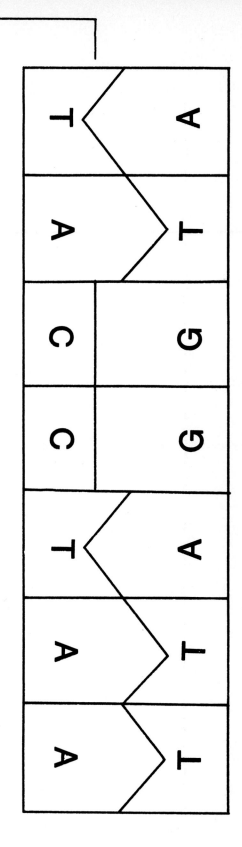

Attach the two ends as indicated

Copy onto white paper

1

G	G	G	G	G	G
G	G	G	G	G	G

C	C	C	C	C	C
∀	∀	∀	∀	∀	∀
T	T	T	T	T	T

∀	∀	∀			
U	U	U	C	C	C

Copy onto green paper and copy onto blue paper

U	U	U	U	U	U

2

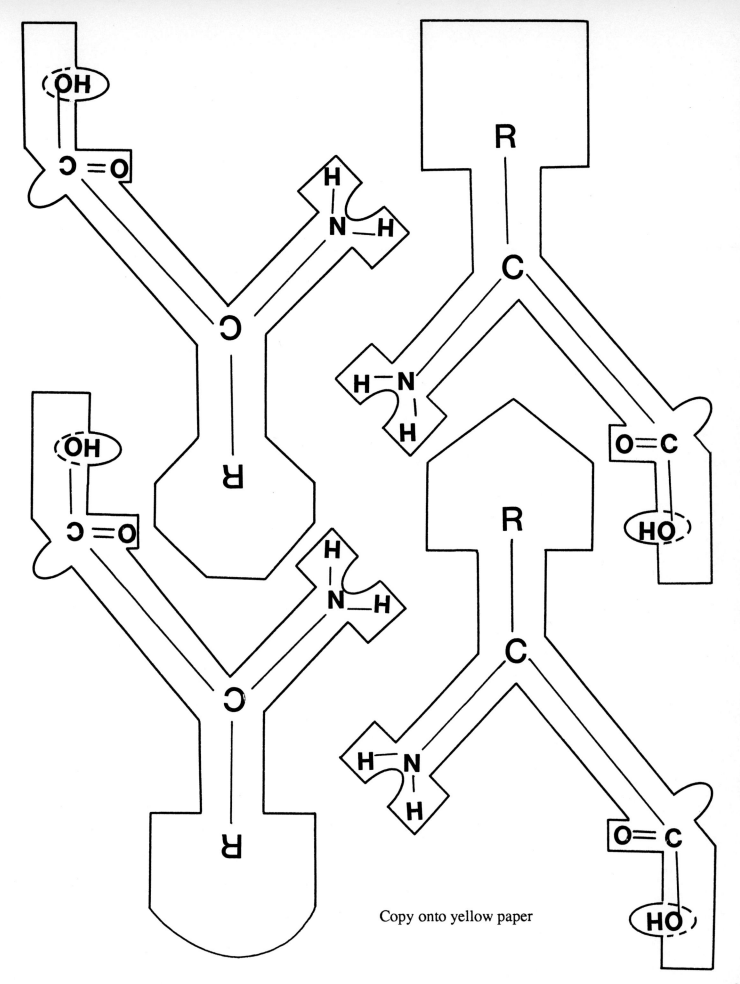

Copy onto yellow paper

3

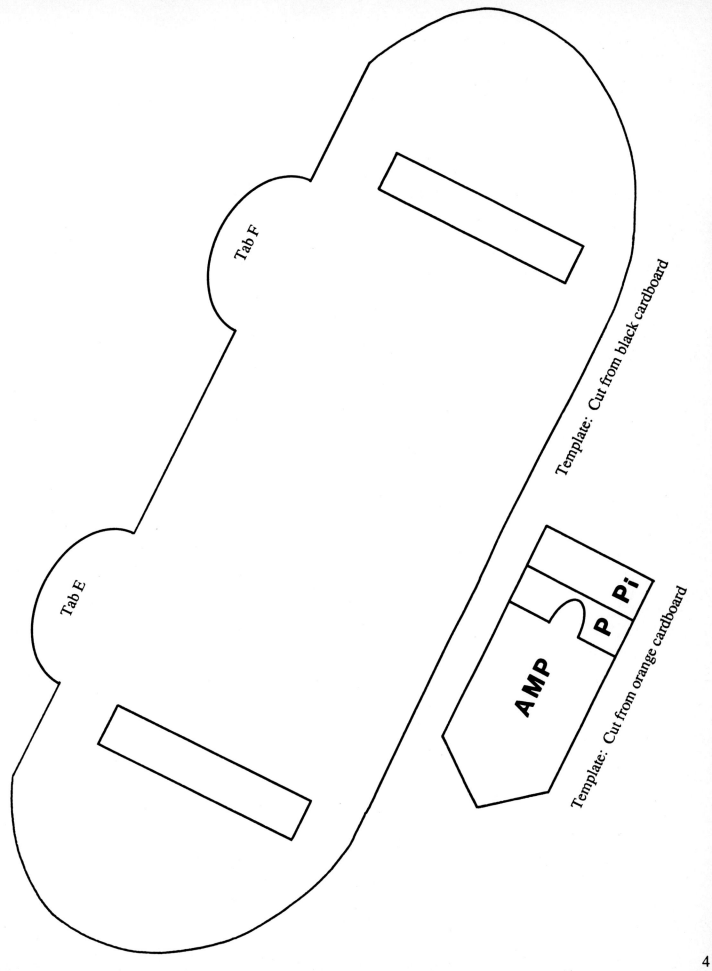

Tab F

Tab E

Template: Cut from black cardboard

AMP P Pi

Template: Cut from orange cardboard

4

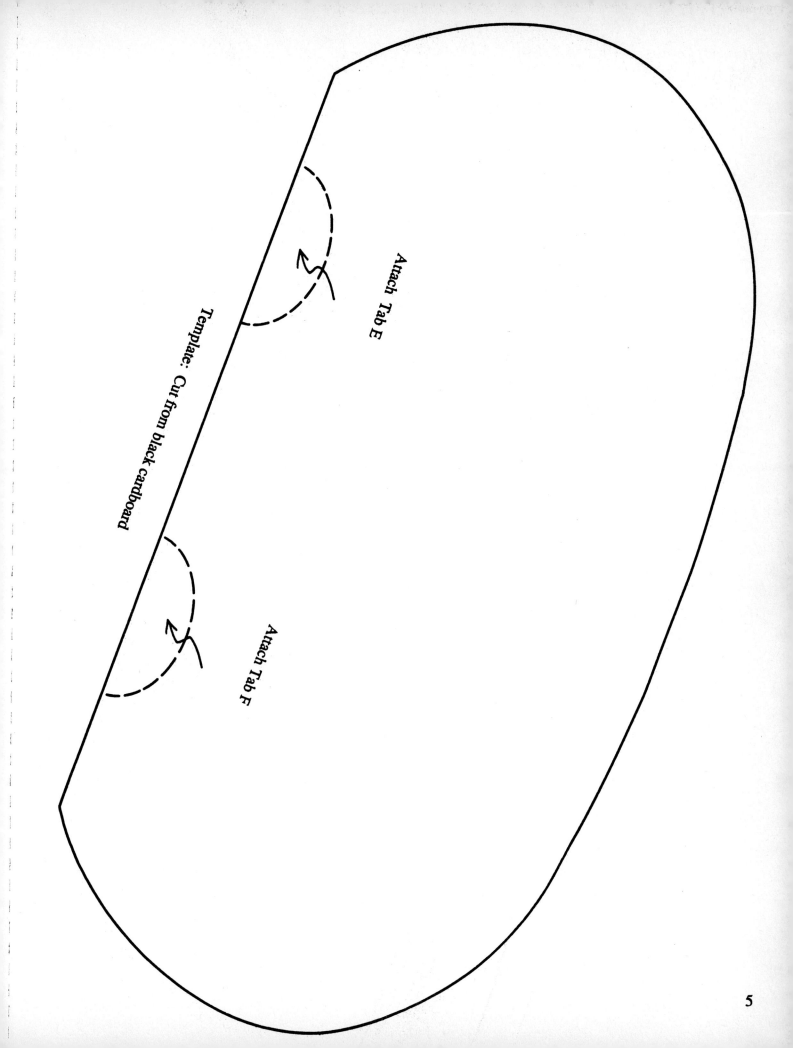

Attach Tab E

Attach Tab F

Template: Cut from black cardboard

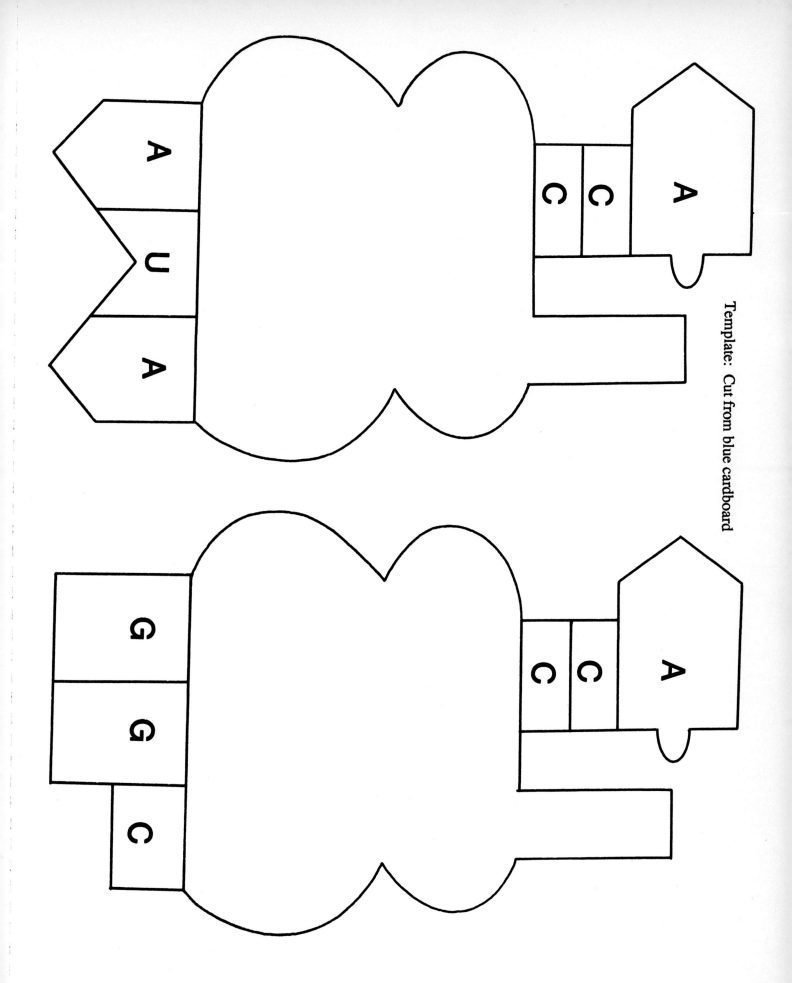

Template: Cut from blue cardboard

6

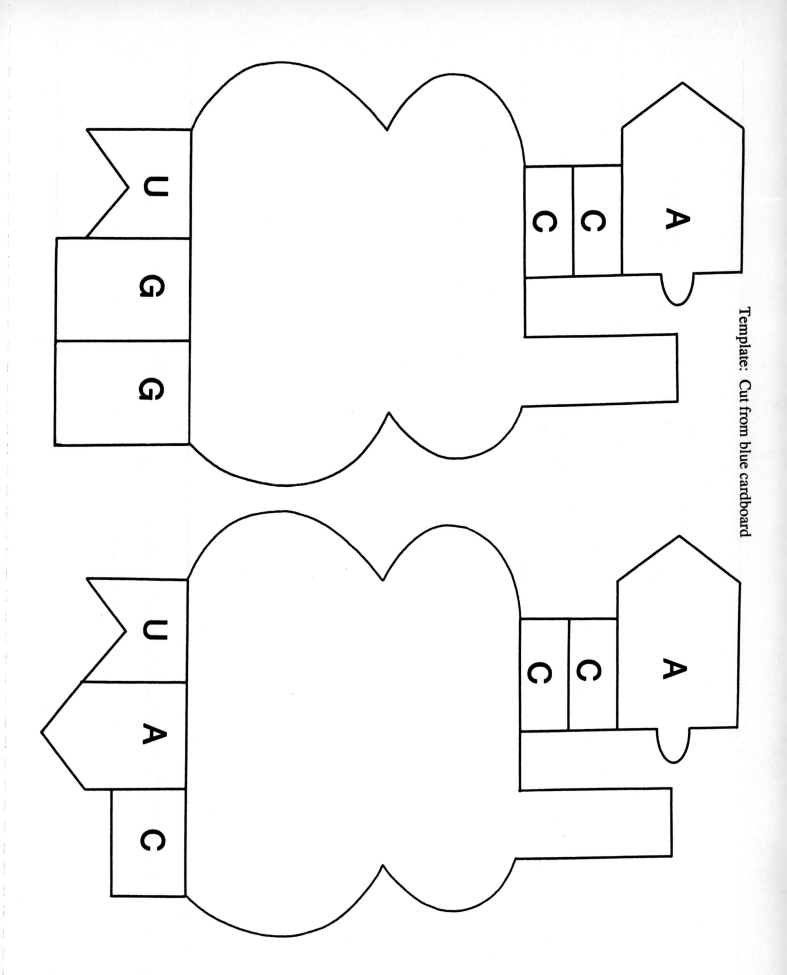

Template: Cut from blue cardboard

7

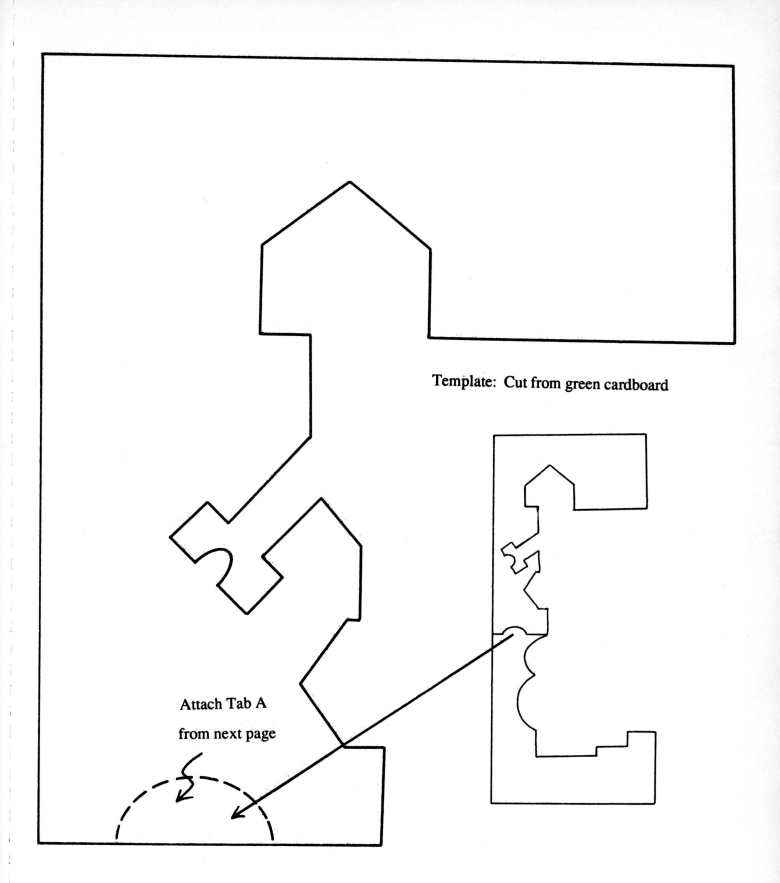

Template: Cut from green cardboard

Attach Tab A

from next page

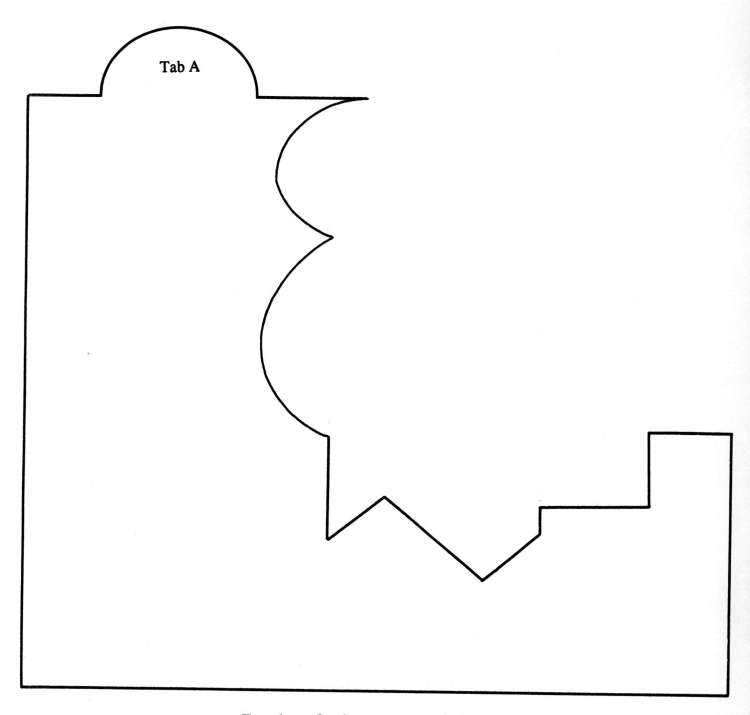

Tab A

Template: Cut from green cardboard

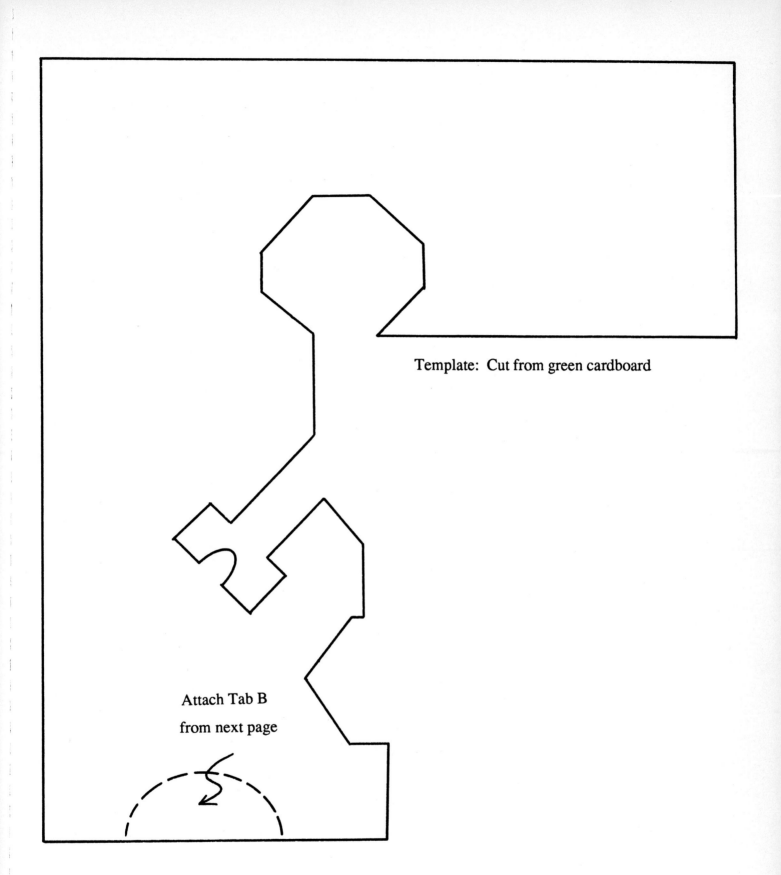

Template: Cut from green cardboard

Attach Tab B

from next page

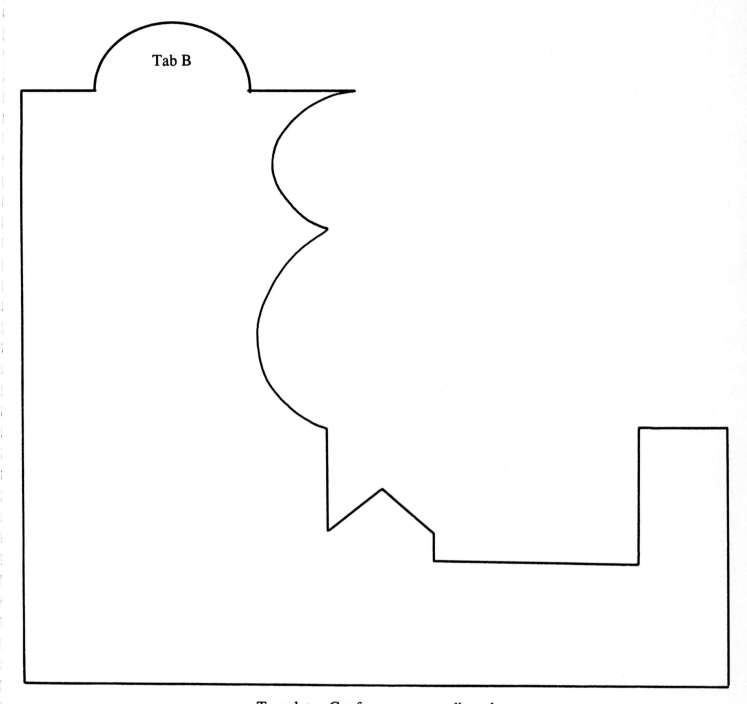

Template: Cut from green cardboard

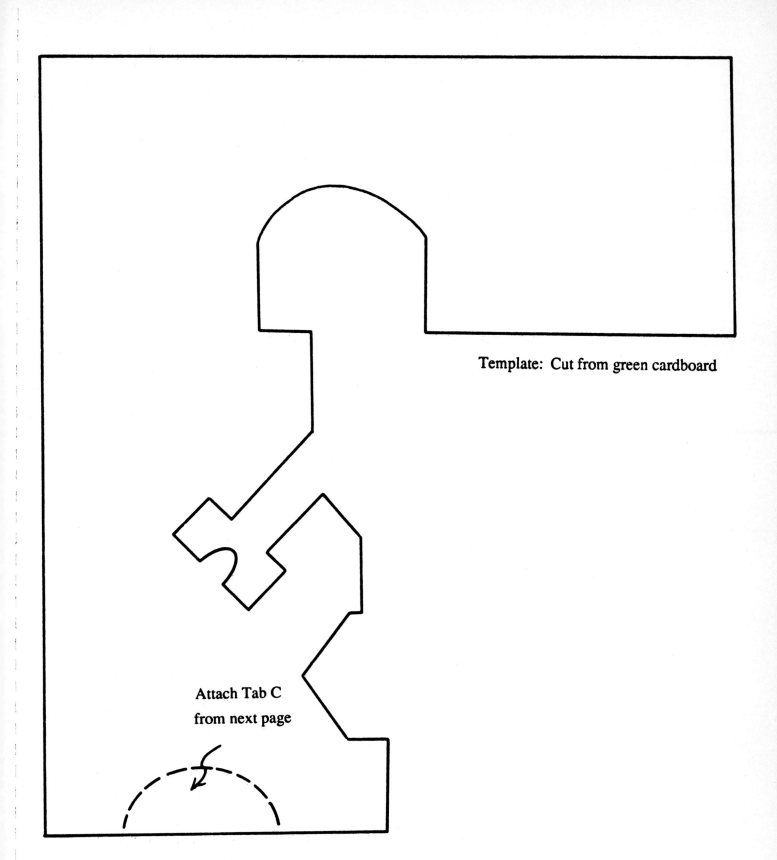

Template: Cut from green cardboard

Attach Tab C
from next page

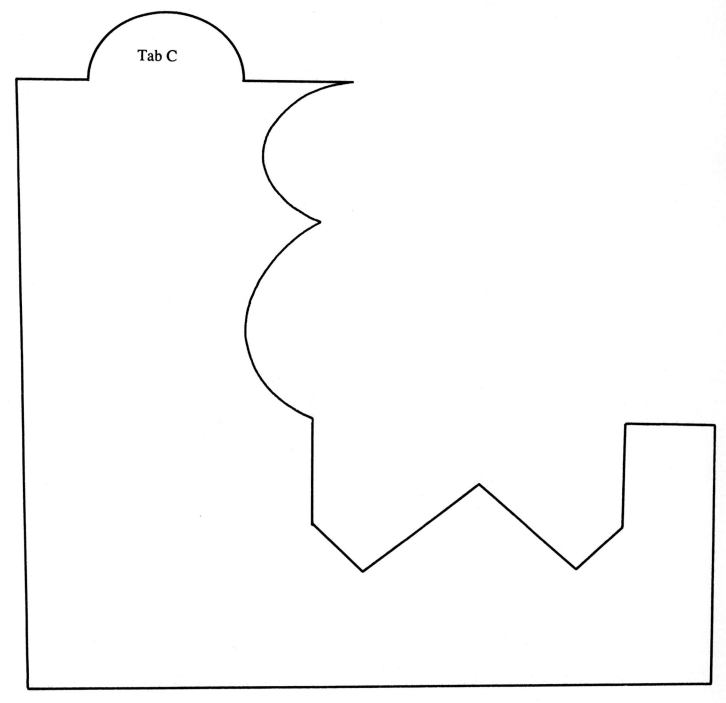

Tab C

Template: Cut from green cardboard

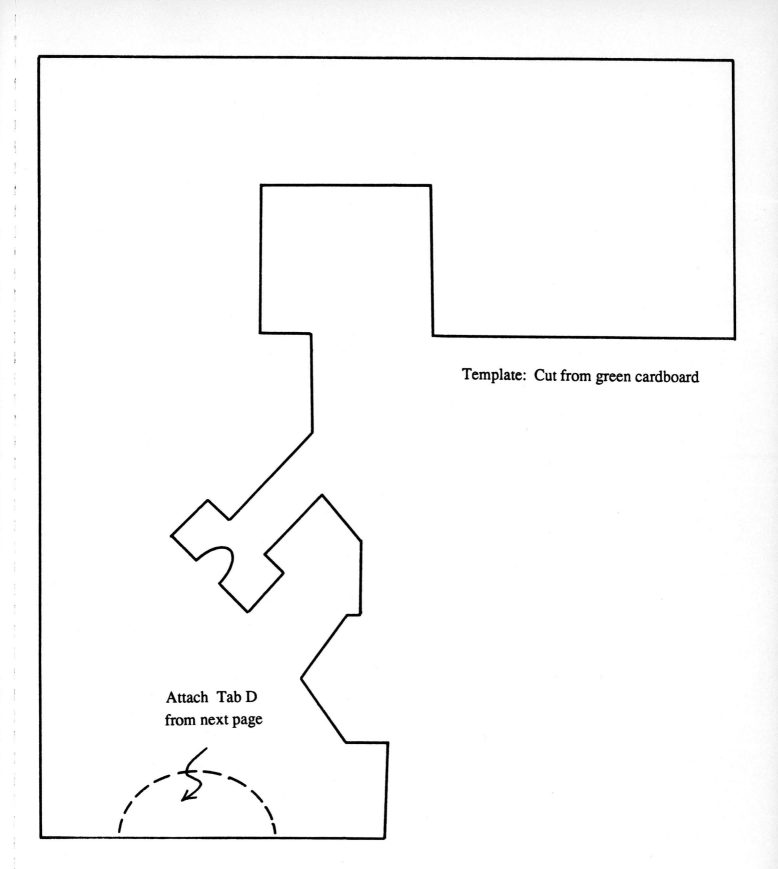

Template: Cut from green cardboard

Attach Tab D
from next page

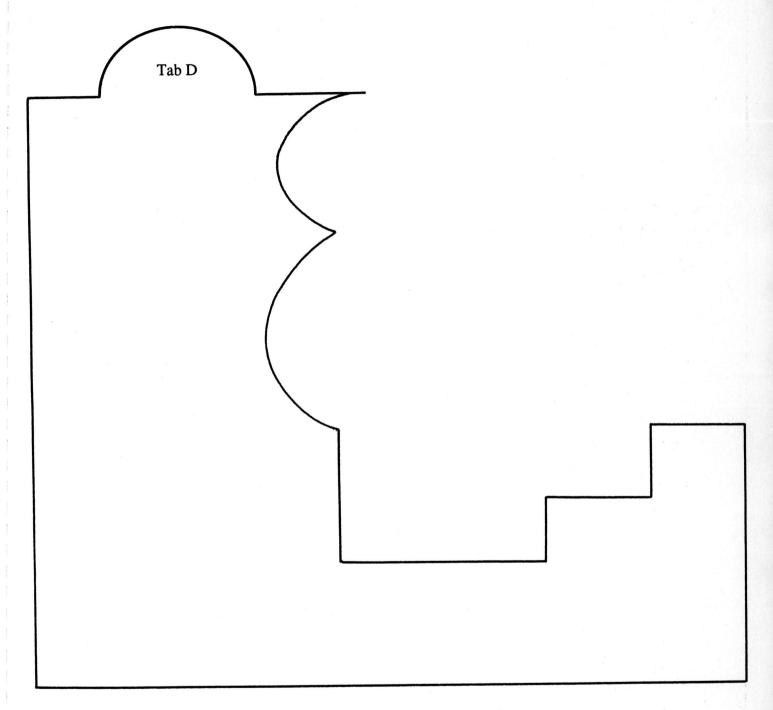

Template: Cut from green cardboard

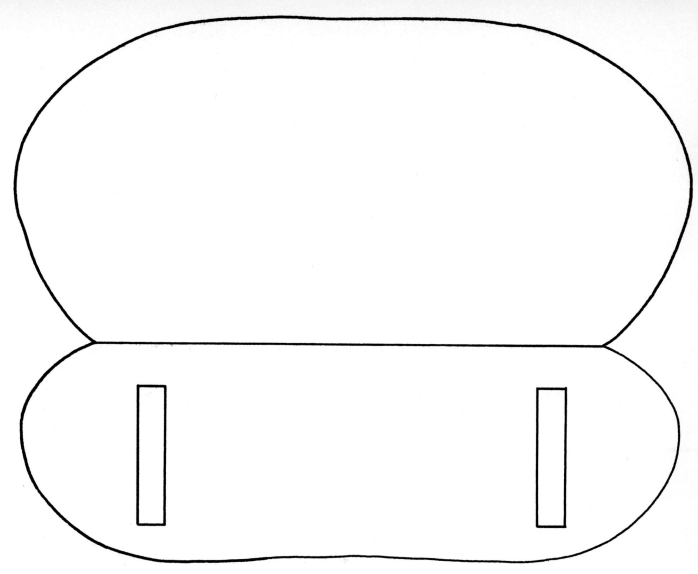

Transparency master: copy onto overhead transparency and cut out pieces

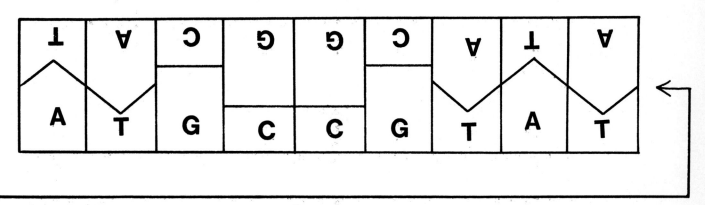

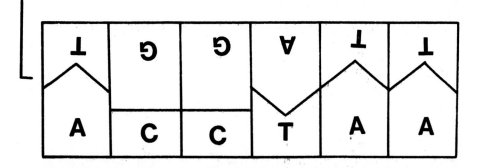

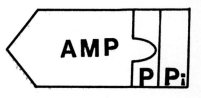

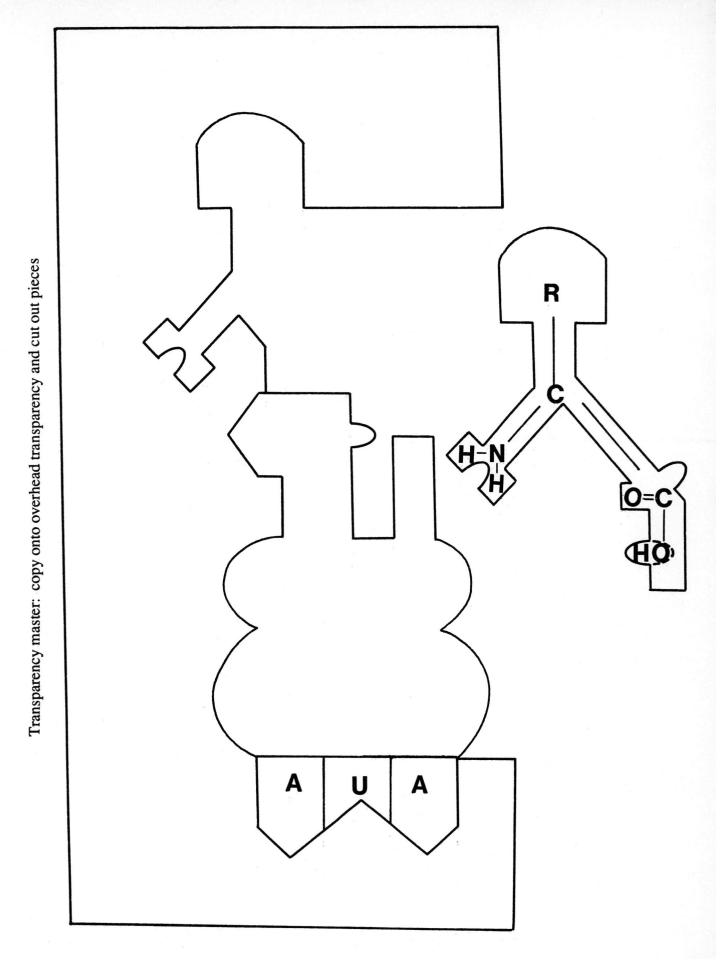

Transparency master: copy onto overhead transparency and cut out pieces

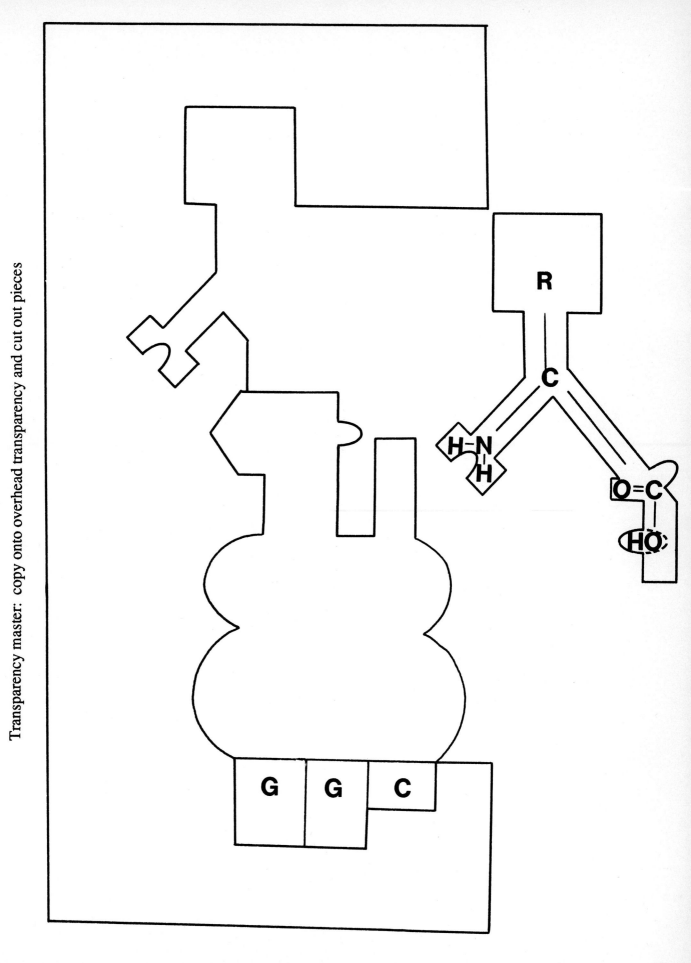

R

C

H—N

H

O=C

HO

U A C

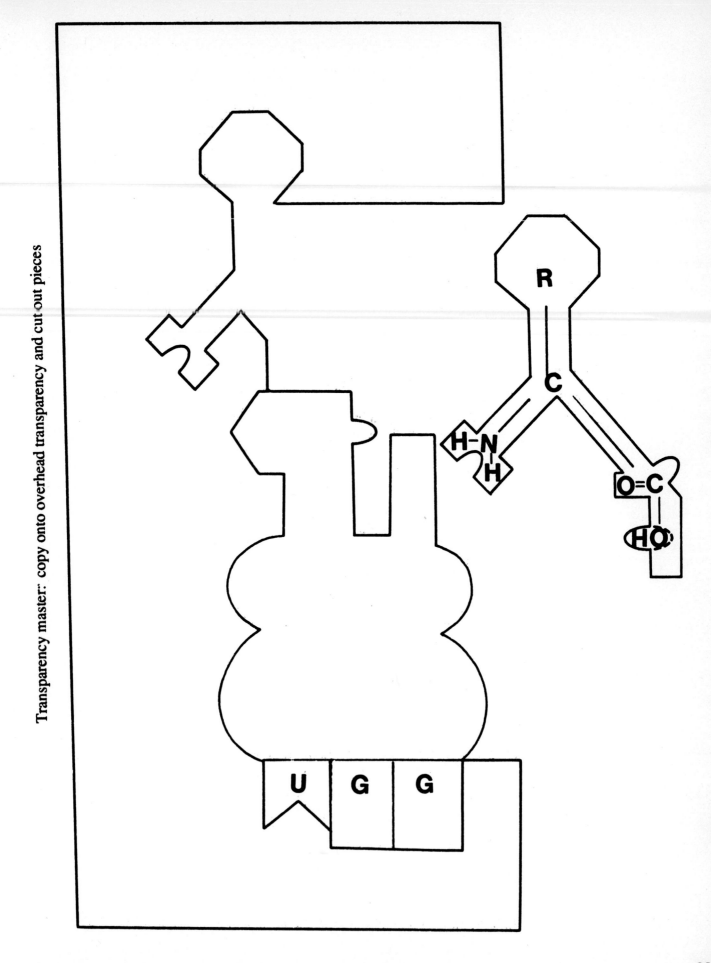

Transparency master: copy onto overhead transparency and cut out pieces

20